POLITICAL COMMUNICATION ETHICS

Communication, Media, and Politics

Series Editor: Robert E. Denton, Jr., Virginia Tech

This series features a range of work dealing with the role and function of communication in the realm of politics, broadly defined. Including general academic books and texts for use in graduate and advanced undergraduate courses, the series encompasses humanistic, critical, historical, and empirical studies in political communication in the United States. Primary subject areas include campaigns and elections, media, and political institutions. *Communication, Media, and Politics* books will be of interest to students, teachers, and scholars of political communication from the disciplines of communication, rhetorical studies, political science, journalism, and political sociology.

The 2004 Presidential Campaign: A Communication Perspective
Edited by Robert E. Denton, Jr.

Transforming Conflict: Communication and Ethnopolitical Conflict
Donald G. Ellis

Bush's War: Media Bias and Justifications for War in a Terrorist Age
Jim A. Kuypers

Center Stage: Media and the Performance of American Politics
Gary C. Woodward

Message Control: How News Is Made on the Campaign Trail
Elizabeth A. Skewes

Tag Teaming the Press: How Bill and Hillary Clinton Work Together to Handle the Media
James E. Mueller

The 2008 Presidential Campaign: A Communication Perspective
Edited by Robert E. Denton, Jr.

The 2012 Presidential Campaign: A Communication Perspective
Edited by Robert E. Denton, Jr.

Last Man Standing: Media, Framing, and the 2012 Republican Primaries
Danielle Sarver Coombs

Partisan Journalism: A History of Media Bias in the United States
Jim A. Kuypers

The American Political Scandal: Free Speech, Public Discourse, and Democracy
David R. Dewberry

Political Campaign Communication: Principles and Practices, Ninth Edition
Judith S. Trent, Robert V. Friedenberg, and Robert E. Denton, Jr.

Political Communication Ethics: Theory and Practice
Edited by Peter Loge

POLITICAL COMMUNICATION ETHICS

Theory and Practice

EDITED BY
PETER LOGE
The George Washington University

ROWMAN & LITTLEFIELD
Lanham · Boulder · New York · London

Executive Editor: Natalie Mandziuk
Editorial Assistant: Deni Remsberg
Higher Education Channel Manager: Jonathan Raeder

Credits and acknowledgments for material borrowed from other sources, and reproduced with permission, appear on the appropriate pages within the text.

Published by Rowman & Littlefield
An imprint of The Rowman & Littlefield Publishing Group, Inc.
4501 Forbes Boulevard, Suite 200, Lanham, Maryland 20706
www.rowman.com

6 Tinworth Street, London SE11 5AL, United Kingdom

British Library Cataloguing in Publication Information Available

Library of Congress Cataloging-in-Publication Data
Names: Loge, Peter, 1965– editor.
Title: Political communication ethics : theory and practice / edited by Peter Loge.
Other titles: Political communication ethics (Rowman and Littlefield, Inc.)
Description: Lanham, Maryland : Rowman & Littlefield, 2021. | Series: Communication, media, and politics | Includes bibliographical references and index.
Identifiers: LCCN 2020000869 (print) | LCCN 2020000870 (ebook) | ISBN 9781538129968 (cloth) | ISBN 9781538129975 (paperback) | ISBN 9781538129982 (epub)
Subjects: LCSH: Communication in politics—Moral and ethical aspects.
Classification: LCC JA85 .P646 2021 (print) | LCC JA85 (ebook) | DDC 172—dc23
LC record available at https://lccn.loc.gov/2020000869
LC ebook record available at https://lccn.loc.gov/2020000870

♾™ The paper used in this publication meets the minimum requirements of American National Standard for Information Sciences—Permanence of Paper for Printed Library Materials, ANSI/NISO Z39.48-1992.

Contents

Acknowledgments

E dited volumes are by definition written by a number of people. I owe everyone who contributed a chapter to this book a huge debt of gratitude. All of them were busy with academic and political projects, and all found the time to be part of this project.

In addition to the authors and the many others who have been a part of this book, I need to highlight a few names. First is Professor Robert Denton, who has been the voice of ethics in political communication for decades and whose support is the reason this book exists. I was able to take advantage of the opportunity Professor Denton created because of the support of my colleagues in the School of Media and Public Affairs (SMPA) at The George Washington University. All of my colleagues have encouraged my work on ethics in political communication, and all make ethics part of what they teach. Even here, there are several people I need to mention by name: Professor Steve Livingston brought me into SMPA as an adjunct many years ago and has been a friend and invaluable colleague; Professor Steve Roberts, who suggested I teach ethics in political communication; and SMPA's director Frank Sesno, who has supported the Project on Ethics in Political Communication every step of the way. I also owe a huge thanks to SMPA student Conor Kilgore for his invaluable help bringing the chapters together into a final manuscript and for providing honest feedback. Finally, I need to thank my students in SMPA, especially those in political communication ethics courses. Willingly or otherwise, these students serve as an informal brain trust and focus group for the Project on Ethics in Political Communication.

The greatest thanks go to my lovely young wife, Zoe, whose infinite patience is matched only by her unwavering support.

Peter Loge

Introduction

Peter Loge

> The world is still in want of clear-headed citizens, tempered by historical perspective, disciplined by rational thinking and moral compass, who speak well and write plainly.
>
> —Professor Lee Pelton, president of Emerson College[1]

Peter Wehner, former senior adviser to President Reagan and both Presidents Bush, wrote: "Democracy requires that we honor the culture of words."[2] Democracy is a political process that produces policy outcomes. It is also an outcome in itself; it is both a means and an end. Democracy is premised on communication; we talk through problems rather than beat each other up (at least that's the idea). If democracy is a way to choose policies, and policy choice happens through communication, we ought to take that communication seriously.

The authors in this volume do just that. They come at political communication from different angles within academia, from different types of political communication, and from a range of political perspectives. In the first half of the book academics weigh in on ethics in political communication, and in the second half of the book working political communication professionals offer their views on ethics in the field. All of the authors wrestle with the question of what ethical responsibility, if any, political communication professionals have and to whom or what they have that responsibility. Theirs are not the last or only thoughts on the topic by a long shot, but hopefully they are enough to get you thinking and to persuade you to honor our culture of words as well.

As you read these chapters and evaluate the authors' arguments, think about two other things. First, what counts as "political communication"? Most of us think this means things like speeches and campaigns, and several authors here address those topics. For example, Andrew Lautz looks at opposition research, and veteran Republican strategist Edward Brookover points out that campaigns have always been ethically questionable affairs. But most political communication is about issues, policies, or ideas rather than for candidates. What are the ethical obligations of those trying to stop torture (a question Elisa Massimino takes up)? The bipartisan team of Matthew L. Johnson and Israel S. Klein tackle the ethics of lobbying, a specialized form of political communication.

Second, what counts as ethically important or presents an ethical challenge? For example, Jennifer Lees-Marshment and Vincent Raynauld are two of the world's leading scholars on digital ethics, and Cheryl Contee and Rosalyn Lemieux are two leading digital practitioners. What these two sets of authors have to say is interesting, and so are what they consider to be ethical questions facing digital political communication. Similarly, consider both how and what leading rhetorical scholar David A. Frank and top Democratic speechwriter Rachel Wallace think the ethical issues facing speechwriting are, as well as how they address those issues. Veteran Democratic consultant Anson Kaye suggests that an overreliance on fact-checking raises its own set of ethical questions in the reality of modern campaigns.

Benjamin Voth, Mark L. McPhail, and Peter Loge offer their perspectives on the ethical foundations that should undergird all contemporary political communication, however it is defined. Former senior Obama official Kip F. Wainscott suggests what law has to offer, as well as the limits of relying on the law for ethical guidance when it comes to political communication.

The phrase "now more than ever" does not make a lot of sense. We read the phrase long after it was written, making it "then more than ever," with "then" being whenever it was the author first thought about using the cliché (or else things are always "now more than ever," meaning they are constantly going from bad to worse, and then from worse to worse). The temporal impossibility or depressing nature of "now more than ever" is not the only problem with the phrase when it comes to complaints about political rhetoric. By the time George Orwell wrote that "political writing is bad writing" and that political language "gives the appearance of solidity to pure wind" in 1946,[3] complaints about political rhetoric, spin, and consultants were already several thousand years old. The Roman orator Quintilian criticized "hack-advocates" and people who would rather be "eloquent than good."[4] He was echoing Plato, who chastised Protagoras for claiming to teach "the art of politics."[5] Professors Janet M. Atwill and Kenneth R. Chase point out that the ethics of political rhetoric was as least as much a concern of the ancients as it is today. As Alexander S. Duff points out, Machiavelli also had something to say on the matter. But as I write this in late 2019, there does seem to be some urgency to find ways to reunite the fields of ethics, rhetoric, and politics. As Edward Brookover puts it in his chapter, we must do better.

Notes

[1] "Acceptance Speech," September 8, 2010, https://www.emerson.edu/about-emerson/leadership/office-president/speeches-remarks/acceptance-speech.

[2] Peter Wehner, *The Death of Politics* (New York: HarperOne, 2019), 99.

[3] George Orwell, "Politics and the English Language," in *George Orwell: A Collection of Essays* (New York: Harcourt, 1981), 165, 171.

4 Marcus Fabius Quintilianus, *The Institutio Oratoria of Quintilian*, trans. H. E. Butler (New York: G. P. Putnam's Sons, 1922), 369, 373.
5 Plato, "Protagoras," in *Plato: Protagoras and Meno*, trans. W. K. C. Guthrie (London: Penguin, 1956), 50.

Bibliography

Orwell, George. "Politics and the English Language." In *George Orwell: A Collection of Essays*. New York: Harcourt, 1981.

Plato. "Protagoras." In *Plato: Protagoras and Meno*. Translated by W. K. C. Guthrie. London: Penguin, 1956.

Quintilianus, Marcus Fabius. *The Institutio Oratoria of Quintilian*. Translated by H. E. Butler. New York: G. P. Putnam's Sons, 1922.

Wehner, Peter. *The Death of Politics*. New York: HarperOne, 2019.

PART I
Political Communication Ethics in Theory

1

Ancient Democracy and Ethical Persuasion

Kenneth R. Chase

Life and death, freedom and enslavement, victory and defeat, love and loss, public acclaim and public humiliation—these are occasions handled with the finest of words or, perhaps more frequently, with the blunders of miscommunication. The promise of democracy is that we the people have the freedom and the responsibility to speak into life's twists and turns with whatever words we can muster, be they beautiful or flawed.

We owe this privilege to the ancient Greeks, who envisioned and enacted a remarkably successful democracy, one dependent on the power of human words. The Greeks knew well that this power could be used for good or for ill. In fact, depending on the listener's point of view, the same words often could be heard as both beneficial and destructive. Take, for example, a clever, though likely fictional, tale about the origins of strategic persuasion in ancient Greek democracy.

The story comes to us from the mid-fifth century BCE Greek colony of Syracuse on Sicily in the years shortly after the colony dramatically transformed from an autocracy (rule by one) to a democracy (rule by the people).[1] A young student named Tisias supposedly sought out a master teacher named Corax, who promised his students success in the art of persuasion. Eager to embrace the opportunities of the fledgling democracy, Tisias agreed to pay Corax for lessons on the condition that Tisias would, in fact, become persuasive. After completing the lessons, though, Tisias took Corax to court, claiming that the promise was unfulfilled. Arguing before the judge, Tisias and Corax showcased questionable verbal ploys. For some, these ploys promised the hope of the finest words and a new era of human self-governance. For others, though, these very same ploys exposed the bluster of trickery and deception. Before the judge, Corax claimed that if he won the verdict against Tisias, then of course he should be paid. Yet Corax also claimed that if he were to lose the verdict he still should get paid, since his promise of Tisias becoming persuasive would be proved through Tisias's victory. Tisias, for his part, offered a similar reversible logic. If he won the verdict, then he

7

should not pay, since he would have proved to the judge that Corax did not fulfill his promise. But if Tisias lost the verdict, he still should not pay, since clearly Corax's teaching had failed to equip him for persuasive success. The moral of the story? The judge tossed them both out of court for being ridiculous. The spark of brilliance that provided Corax and Tisias with the ability to argue for their own sides no matter the circumstances is also the spark of fear that humans will find a way to turn good ideas into destructive ones.

Learning strategies of persuasion, then, provides no guarantees that good legal decisions will be rendered. Nor will applying these same strategies to political debates guarantee wise political judgment prevails. But within the alternatives to democratic governance (such as autocracy or even oligarchy, rule by the few), those strategies of persuasion fare no better. If we want a political system that allows free expression, equality before the law, the just consideration of grievances, and opportunities for shared control of political decisions, then we live with the risks and rewards of verbal trickery. We also rightly seek guidance for the best uses of our communicative abilities, for sussing out the political discourses that foster democracy and those that threaten its very existence.

Fortunately the remarkable success of classical Athenian democracy provides ample resources for generating an ethic of political persuasion. For Athenian citizens, political communication was integral to the quality of their lives and the desirability of their governance. Therefore, we first must understand the particular democracy that developed in Athens and how it was sustained for two hundred years. Then we can identify the central role persuasion played within that democracy. Finally, we can take stock of classical persuasion and recommend specific practices of persuasion to advance contemporary democratic ideals.

Athenian Democracy

The Athenian democracy was unusual and remains to this day one of the great wonders in the history of Western political systems.[2] Democracy was formally instituted in Athens in 508 BCE and thrived, despite some serious setbacks, until Athens's devastating military defeat by Philip of Macedon in 338 BCE led to Macedonian rule in 322 BCE. Even after the formal demise of Athens's democratic governance in the late fourth century BCE, many of the democratic ideals and political instincts of Athenian citizens survived—and at times thrived—in the Hellenistic centuries prior to the ultimate domination of Greece by the Roman Empire.

Unlike the current democratic republic of the US Constitution, Athenian democracy for most of nearly two centuries placed decision-making authority directly in the hands of citizens without relying on elected representatives. Thus, for Athens's most consequential decisions in domestic and international affairs, six to eight thousand citizens would gather as an assembly and vote. Deliberation was carried by speakers (*rhētores*), who would stand in front of the gathering and persuade. Any citizen was eligible to speak, although, given the size and potential impact of the decision, the actual pool of able and willing speakers probably was much smaller. Decisions had to be determined by the end of the day, so deliberation likely was focused, intense, volatile, competitive, frustrating, and yet ultimately bound by citizenly cooperation.

This democratic mind-set extended to all matters of governance. Those charged with more frequent meetings, handling the business of government not requiring the Assembly's deliberation, were selected by lot, giving every citizen an equal chance of serving on the Council (which had five hundred members). For the day-to-day requirements of running the government—such as the collection and distribution of taxes and the management of laws and courts—multiple managerial boards were appointed consisting of ten citizens each, most of whom were selected by lot. Only the military generals were handpicked, based on expertise.

Juries were likewise selected by lot, and their decisions were definitive. Between two hundred and five hundred selected citizens would listen to plaintiffs and defendants speak without the assistance of attorneys. Jurors would hear both sides, including presentations of evidence and rebuttal speeches, then cast their votes without any collective deliberation. The votes were tabulated and the verdict rendered.

Did Democracy Work?

According to the best available historical evidence, democracy did work. During the two centuries of Athenian democracy, Athens experienced a notable increase in wealth (per capita and as a city-state), health (greater longevity/life span), and cultural products (education, literature, philosophy, athletics, theater, music, arts and crafts). By these measures, the overall quality of Athenian life exceeded that of any other ancient regime and, remarkably, the relative degree of human flourishing during these centuries was unparalled in the history of Greece until the dawn of the twentieth century.[3]

The historical record, however, clearly indicates that Athenian democracy was not self-generating, as if once the citizens had put democratic structures in place the machinations of governance would smoothly prevail regardless of external or internal challenges. The achievements of Athenian democracy occurred within regular debates about the best sort of government and through numerous military and political conflicts with democracy's opponents. Democratic reforms began in the sixth century BCE when Athenian oligarchs (wealthy land owners and tribal leaders) faced hostility from fellow-Greek laborers who increasingly found themselves indebted to the wealthy and unable to earn enough to repay those debts. In turn, the oligarchs faced increasing tensions with each other over land and opportunity. Threatened by civil war, they appointed Solon to mediate conflicts and institute some social reforms. Through numerous remarkable and decisive actions, such as canceling debts and lowering the financial bar for eligibility to hold political office, Solon shifted the direction of ancient Athens away from a severe class division among native-born Greeks, in which indebted workers functioned as slaves in service to their more privileged compatriots. Solon's reforms could only go so far, though, and it took a series of failed coups and military defeats before Cleisthenes, with the strong support of the lower-class Athenians, established citizenship for all males, regardless of wealth, subdivided Athenian lands into political regions ("demes"), and provided the foundation for successful military recruitment. In the first third of the fifth century the new Athenian military was able to withstand threats from the Persians, and this success generated additional democratic reforms and the formation of strategic military alliances with other Greek city-states, needed to allow Athenian economic and cultural growth. Not all military actions were successful; military losses led to brief interludes of oligarchic rule in 411–410 BCE and 404 BCE, but in each case democracy was restored, leading to improvements in law, taxation, and regional alliances, as well as numerous economic and cultural advances.

In sum, Athens was a highly progressive but never static democratic state. Democracy won the day for nearly two hundred years, and we benefit from that legacy. Of course we cannot reproduce the Athenian democracy, nor should we try. Athens was a city-state with a population estimated at 250,000 inhabiting an area smaller than Rhode Island, so it could scale direct democratic participation more effectively than a modern nation-state, with its larger populations, land mass, and global political interests. Furthermore, and importantly, the ancient world typically did not countenance the rights of women, children, and foreign-born residents, and slavery was accepted as an economic and military necessity. Indeed, in classical Athens, only free native-born adult males qualified as citizens, so although these men were rigorously and admirably egalitarian in their practice of citizen participation, they did not grant citizenship to any others.

Despite these substantive differences between the Athenian democracy and contemporary democracies, the Athenian experience remains an inspiration, test case, and analog for Western governments that find democratic ideals of equality, free expression, citizen responsibility, and political accountability as coordinates for a political system that maximizes self-fulfillment and social flourishing. Once we correct for those social biases and discriminations of the ancient world, we can look back to Athens as providing resources of thought and practice to assist our reflection on successful political practices.

Keys to Success

What did Athenians do to make democracy work? What was the genius for their flourishing? Probably the best current explanation for the successes of Athenian democracy comes from Josiah Ober, who applies contemporary social science research methods to a meticulous collection of all available information about the classical world.[4] Ober's overall analysis rests on a fundamental and sensible assumption about human social behavior—namely, that humans are cost-benefit creatures, seeking overall to reduce harms or hassles while increasing rewards.[5] So, for instance, an Athenian citizen faced with a decision about raising taxes will consider the effect of an increase on his own household finances and whatever extra work he might have to do to compensate for the reduced income, then evaluate the costs in relation to the presumed benefits that come from increased military pay or providing pay for jurors. In the latter, Athens would be strengthened overall—stronger at land and sea, and able to continue the current court system, which would increase the chances of receiving a fair verdict. As Ober explains, the citizen's decision balances personal and collective goods; the citizen recognizes that the long-term benefits of a stronger Athens may outweigh the small decrease in household income, and that his own interest in protecting himself and his family from enemies abroad and from unjust verdicts at home provides a net gain in overall well-being.[6] As Athens flourishes, so do its citizens. The trick in Athenian democracy, then, is for citizens to construct government processes and cultural practices that equally distribute costs and benefits. Citizens need social insitutions in place that promote cooperation while protecting personal interests. Jurors, for instance, need to be paid to ensure that service does not cut into their earnings, and it is in everyone's best interest to have jurors' interests protected while they are serving the state.

Thus, the key to Athens's success is for citizens to benefit individually from cooperative action. Ober identifies three overaching processes the Athenians used for integrating their interests into collaborative and mutually beneficial public actions:

- increasing the quantity of knowledge that citizens contribute to solving public problems (aggregation)
- enabling citizens to coordinate their knowledge in relation to shared vision and values (alignment)
- securing the trustworthiness and reliability of institutional structures so citizens can count on social rewards (codification)[7]

These processes constitute, in effect, a three-legged stool for a working democracy; without any one of these, the democracy becomes unstable and unlikely to provide the equilibrium between invidual interests and collective interests that makes decision making and government action in a democracy more desirable than in an oligarchy or a monarchy. To compensate for the inefficiencies of collective decision making (such as gathering an assembly of six thousand citizens to debate the issues), the quality of decisions must provide superior benefits. Thus, democracies must take advantage of a wide range of diverse views, representing the collected knowledge of people in all stages of life, in all occupations, and with varied experiences. Citizens must have opportunities to innovate in their thinking for knowledge to be expanded and variety enhanced. Also, citizens are expected to provide voice and to vote on the issues. But this aggregated knowledge needs to be understood and applied to public problems, which requires that citizens have some common experiences and an overall shared commitment to using such knowledge in collaborative decision making. Thus, Athens supported cultural festivals, athletic games, theaters, parades, and public rituals to align values and build cooperative vision. Finally, citizens need to know their interests are protected. Thus, if a citizen pays taxes faithfully, then the tax money must be used honestly according to collectively determined laws and projects. Athens therefore published and distributed laws (emphasizing fairness), established common currency, and provided citizens with opportunities for airing grievances and receiving equal treatment by the legal system.

The Athenian democracy therefore placed citizen equality at its core and built institutions to ensure that citizens shared knowledge, cooperative values, mutual accountability, and trustworthy economic and legal practices. As Ober explains, this version of democracy was far more than a simple practice of majority rule. Decisions were made not through party affiliations or by aggregating preferences and using these to sway a decision maker.[8] Rather, citizens had shared responsibility for the collective well-being of the state through direct participation in law, policy, and justice.

Persuasion and Democracy

If we find within classical Athens resources for our own democratic ideals, then we certainly also find there extraordinary resources for the ideals of our public persuasion. Athens was first and foremost a culture committed to, and shaped by, the capacity of citizens to speak with one another—to make appeals, hear disputes, give speeches, criticize decisions, and negotiate interests. Athenians understood themselves as, and took pride in their abilities as, persuaders. Democracy's proponents and opponents alike saw Athenians this way. Those who celebrated democracy promoted oratory not only in the Assembly and the law courts, but also in civic ceremonies and as a competitive feature of festivals. The development of rigorous educational programs was frequently linked to promises of prowess in public speaking. Those who disliked democracy often did so precisely because it placed too much power in the mouths of orators and speechwriters. The weakness of democracy, the critics claimed, is the weakness of decisions made through an utter dependence on merely persuading public opinion.

The history of Athenian democracy, then, is also a history of public persuasion. By the last third of the fifth century BCE, Athenians had actively cultivated their "rhetorical" imagination. Although rhetoric as art and theory had not yet been formalized (that would develop early in the fourth century BCE), the contributions of theater, the growth of philosophical inquiry, and the prominence of political oratory represent the foundational commitments to persuasion within the democratic citizenry. I review briefly here notable exemplars in each of these areas, with special attention to oratory, before consolidating the historical evidence into guidelines for ethical communication.

Theater

Through numerous productions, including both tragedy and comedy, playwrights wrestled with the ideals and flaws of Greek traditions, religions, families, and myths. Theater as public spectacle and civic ritual empowered citizens to reflect on personal and collective responsibilities. To take but one example, the great playwright Aeschylus (ca. 525–ca. 456 BCE) presented *The Oresteia*, his trilogy of tragedies, in Athens in 458. The third play, *The Eumenides*, concludes with what had to be for the many thousands of Athenians in attendance an exhilarating affirmation of persuasion and the institutions of deliberation as the much-needed solution to the problem of generational dysfunction and conflicting divine decrees.[9] Throughout the trilogy, Aeschylus presents the family of King Agammemnon—the leader of Greek armies in the ancient Trojan War—as crumbling through the weight of murderous plots, unfaithfulness, child sacrifice, and the competing designs of rival gods. In the third play, Agammemnon's son is on the run after killing his mother in revenge for her murder of his father. Athena, the goddess of Athens and daughter of Zeus, cannot resolve the dispute between the god Apollo, who sanctioned the murder, and the Furies, goddesses sworn to punish murderers. Through the assistance of Peitho (the goddess of persuasion), Athena forms a jury and inaugurates a legal case featuring prosecution and defense arguments. Although the jury splits, unable to decide the fate of young Orestes, Athena casts the deciding vote and orders the Furies to no longer torment citizens but to care for and protect them. Athenians, states Athena, are "upright men, a breed brought free from grief."[10] The Furies accept Athena's offer. Renamed in the play's title as the Eumenides (the "kindly ones"), they now seek the flourishing of the beloved Athenians.[11] Through this verdict, the responsibilities for the just governance of the city shift decisively toward human decision making. Athens's future depends on the dignity and capabilities of its citizens.

Philosophical Inquiry

For Athens to conduct justice through deliberation rather than divine oracle (or a king's commands), citizens had to accept their responsibility in determining verdicts and policies. While Aeschylus was crafting his award-winning trilogy, Sophists, such as Protagoras (ca. 490–420 BCE), were providing the philosophical insights that freed Athenians from the presumption of divine decrees and promoted persuasive discourse as the mechanism for making judgments.[12] Although we have only fragments of his sayings, and even the accounts of his life from others cannot always be trusted, the quantity of references, and the seriousness with which others engaged Protagoras's reported sayings, pins him as an educator and public intellectual of considerable influence. He is most famous, perhaps, for the "human-measure" fragment: "Of all things the measure is man, of things that are that they are, and of things that are not that they are not."[13] Placing humans at the center of knowledge elevates human responsibility and provokes human inquiry. Protagoras identified the human capacity for speech and reason as logos, the very means of citizen deliberation. Protagoras also is said to have been the first to claim that every issue has two sides, which opens every matter to debate. Protagoras and the Sophists (the professional intellectuals; *sophos* = clever, wise) secured the widespread appreciation of training in legal and political debate. Protagoras's contemporaries likewise promoted "probability" thinking, observing that any human decision involves unprovable assumptions and uniquely variable situations. Thus, any defendant in a court of law could find some reason that he would be innocent, and any prosecutor could find some reason for his guilt. Protagoras and the Sophists unleashed human deliberative potential.

Oratory

The most famous speech of the fifth century was delivered not by a Sophist but by Pericles (ca. 495–429 BCE), the military general who guided Athens through the early years of the Peloponnesian War. The genre of the funeral oration (*epitaphioi*) had developed decades earlier as a powerful tool for shaping the ideology of democracy.[14] Pericles's funeral oration, delivered after the initial losses in a battle with Sparta, was celebrated then as it is today as a pinnacle achievement of the genre.[15] Given the fears and mourning occasioned by the deaths of so many Athenians in battle, Pericles speaks to honor the dead and inspire the living. He does so by, first and foremost, delivering an eloquent affirmation of democratic ideals. He locates all Athenians—both dead and living—within the democratic distinctions of Athens, in contrast to the lesser governments of their enemies. "The constitution by which we live," Pericles proclaims, "is an example to others rather than an imitation of them. It is called democracy because power does not rest with the few, but with the many, and in law, as it touches individuals, all are equal. . . . Liberty marks both our public politics and the feelings which touch our daily life together."[16] Pericles's exposition of democratic commitments and the integration of values with Athenian pride and military determination both reflect and advance the passion for popular rule animating civic life.

By the early fourth century, then, the democratic ideology was mature and secure. For some, most notably Plato, this was not at all desirable. Plato's mentor Socrates (469–399 BCE) had battled intellectually with the Sophists and with Athenian democratic sensibilities. Socrates's gadfly reputation led to the accusation that he was corrupting the minds of the youth. In one of the most tragic failures of the Athenian legal process, Socrates was tried and condemned to death. Plato (ca. 429–347 BCE) faulted democracy, and in his masterwork, *Republic*, he proposed oligarchy as an ideal political system in which a selection of learned individuals (men and women) would govern through philosophical inquiry. The art of the persuasive orator, which he called *rhētorikē*, would be reserved for those philosopher-kings whose knowledge and wisdom would enable truth to reign and whose own persuasion of the masses would strip Protagoras-like debating of its value and power.[17] For Plato, the persuasion by the Sophists and whatever rhetorical training they promised to their students and clients were nothing more than flattery. Plato maintained that citizens aspiring to truly human flourishing must avoid any pseudo-arts that merely mimic what is truly good. Just as cosmetics and tasty foods are ways to flatter the body without truly doing it good, so are sophistry and rhetoric ways to flatter the human soul without truly advancing justice and wise policy.[18]

Plato's powerful criticism of sophistry and rhetoric lives to this day. Whenever we lament political rhetoric (as manipulative, evading, dissembling, spinning, and so forth) and yearn for political reality, we are channeling Plato. When we accuse a politician of being a sophist, we evidence the massive influence of Plato on Western views of persuasion. But within fourth-century BCE Athens, Plato's critique of democratic persuasion fell mostly on deaf ears. Even Socrates himself, in the decades prior to his execution in 399 BCE, was publicly ridiculed as an airy intellectual and an off-center crank. When Plato developed his critique of democracy, then, he was fighting an uphill battle; after all, the very educational and richly textured conversational opportunities provided to Socrates (for most of his life) and Plato depended fully on the diversity and equality of Athenian democracy.[19] Indeed, Plato's own most accomplished student, Aristotle (384–322 BCE), distanced himself from Plato's harsh criticism of democratic persuasion and reformulated *rhētorikē* as a worthy democratic art.

Although Plato's criticism of the abuse of persuasion still lurks in today's conversation about ethical communication, Aristotle provided our most rewarding account of persuasion's value and strategy. His *Rhetoric* affirmed the need for an art of persuasion in those areas of human decision making where it is not possible to have certain truths and unassailable knowledge. In Aristotle's analysis, democratic citizens are called upon to make three kinds of judgments: public policy, court verdicts, and the affirmation of civic value and civic blame.[20] It is the distinctive province of human persuasion to cultivate techniques of argumentation, emotional appeal, and influential character (logos, pathos, ethos) that effect all these occasions of collective decision making.[21]

However, for all their extraordinary contributions to Western philosophy and rhetoric, neither Plato nor Aristotle had as much impact on fourth-century Athenian citizenship as the educator and orator Isocrates (436–338 BCE). Having been directly influenced by both Socrates and the sophist Gorgias (ca. 483–375 BCE), Isocrates forged an educational program in persuasion that affirmed a Platonic-Aristotelian commitment to virtuous rhetoric with a sophistic celebration of oratorical eloquence.[22] Isocrates served as both critic and patron of democracy. He was quick to denounce the exploitative orations of demagogues, who took advantage of free speech to pander for selfish gain, yet he also celebrated in word and deed those very freedoms as providing the occasions for the wonder that is human persuasion. In his oft-quoted paean to the powers of human speech, which, like Protagoras, he identified as logos, Isocrates explains:

> But since we have the ability to persuade one another and to make clear to ourselves what we want, not only do we avoid living like animals, but have come together, built cities, made laws, and invented arts. Speech [*logos*] is responsible for nearly all our inventions. It legislated in matters of justice and injustice and beauty and baseness, and without these laws, we could not live with one another.[23]

The power of human persuasion not only reaches outward to fellow citizens but extends into one's own reasoning. We "make clear to ourselves what we want," Isocrates explains. We use the same practice of persuasive speech when speaking to others and "in our own deliberations."[24] Since political decision making requires candid advice and insightful analysis, then logos is crucial: "We regard as sound advisers those who debate with themselves most skillfully about public affairs."[25]

Isocrates was passionate about extending the virtues of logos throughout the citizenry. Although he is nearly forgotten in any contemporary pantheon of influential Greek intellectuals, his speeches and letters located persuasion at the heart of ethical society. Fittingly, the last couple decades of his life found him embroiled in political debate about the future of Athens and the supremacy of Greek ideals. Isocrates believed Athens's democracy was threatened by imperial forces abroad and a failing democratic will at home. Only Philip of Macedon, he thought, had the military power to organize a new coalition of Greek city-states that would defeat enemies and in turn stiffen the spines of citizenly public service. Yet as Isocrates quickly realized upon Athens's defeat, Philip proved to be not a friend but the lesser of its enemies. It was one of Isocrates's oratorical rivals, Demosthenes (ca. 385–322 BCE), with persuasive powers second to none in classical Greece, who had won the public debate and convinced Athens to resist Philip's military advance, which then led to Athens's crippling military defeat.[26] In the crucible of democratic deliberation and the freedoms provided for Isocrates and Demosthenes to debate the very future of democracy itself we find the ethical excellences of government by the people and the tragic reality that governments, regardless of their democratic, oligarchic, or monarchic constitutions, do not last forever.

Best Practices for Democratic Communication

As good citizens, the Athenian educators, orators, artists, and philosophers rarely agreed. Through their disagreements, though, they built a culture of human dignity and free expression that gave nearly unparalleled opportunities within the ancient world for self-determination, achievement, and overall social flourishing. They were neighbors whose skirmishes contributed to larger public goods and whose most destructive battles (for the most part) were limited to the fight against democracy's enemies.

Cutting across their diverse views of truth, knowledge, and the whole range of beliefs about social and political goods were enduring commitments to citizenly communication. Gorgias and Socrates clashed over the value of rhetoric; Plato and Isocrates penned very different comments on the contributions of philosophy; Protagoras and Aristotle constructed fundamentally different ideals for rational argumentation. In the midst of these differences, however, we find a shared awe at the powers of human communication, a respect for the potential harms and benefits of persons endowed with the gift of persuasion. Collectively, the Athenian citizens give us an ethic of political persuasion.

Ethics looks different to our eyes than it did to the ancients. Today when we raise the question of ethical political communication, we tend to identify rules of civility or principles of effective decision making or a point-by-point code of professional conduct. Our contemporary approach will equate ethics with, for example, truth-telling, factual accuracy, transparency, and personal accountability. The Athenians tended to interpret ethical persuasion according to qualities of human excellence. The right and best type of political persuasion, then, was that which fostered virtues, such as justice, self-control, courage, and wisdom.[27] Importantly, these virtues were not only for the individual citizen but were to be characteristic of the larger society. Thus, as both Plato and Isocrates insisted, shaping the souls of individuals through persuasion also shapes the soul of the city-state. The ideals of living well transfer to the ideals of the city, and the ideals of the city become the ideals of the citizen. Pericles captured the vital link between citizens, education, and character when he declared that "our whole city is an education for Greece, and every individual in it would, I think, be capable in more respects than any other of fitting himself for many parts with grace and ease."[28] Athens, he boasted, was a model for all other Greek cities, and its citizens were models for all other Greeks. Life in Athens was rich because the city allowed its citizens unparalleled opportunities to develop abilities and character, leading to fulfilled and flourishing lives.

In our contemporary era, however, a tight connection between self and society may strike us as anything but ethical. The Periclean picture of a shared civic identity and a patriotism of reinforced values can seem too restrictive for the individual creativity we crave. But this criticism misses the genius of the classical democracy and the ideals of human flourishing. The education of the "soul"—both individual and collective—enabled *both* differences and cooperation. One without the other is social breakdown. Individual differences without cooperation become anarchy, and cooperation without differences is a stifling comformity. When the equilibrium is lost, democracy's carefully cultivated structures of popular rule either morph into a politics of domination and control or quicken society's advance toward decline and dissolution.

Democracy holds together our desire for autonomy and creative freedom with ideals of citizenship, through which our shared social life becomes a source of growth and exploration. The genius of democracy, as we learn from the Greeks, is that popular rule requires a deep appreciation for the balance of self and others. Consider again Ober's three processes for successful Athenian democracy: aggregation, alignment, and codification. Athens constructed specific legal, economic, cultural, and political institutions (such as courts, the Assembly, the Council, theater, festivals, and coinage) to make sure that citizens were making the most of their collective knowledge, aligning that knowledge with shared values and common goals, and stabilizing their decisions so they could count on the shared benefits of making potentially self-sacrificing collective decisions. All of these social, economic, and political institutions, though, presume that citizens are capable of, and participating in, persuasive speech. Influencing one another is the fabric by which the tapestry of democracy is woven.

Thus, ethical political communication provides the daily practices of shared social life through which democracy happens. When we handle political business, we ought to communicate in ways consistent with the personal and social ideals that make democracy our best option for collective governance. Therefore, ethical political communicators support three overlapping principles, discussed in the following sections.

Number 1: Expanding Resources for Judgment

Political persuasion ought to foster the expansion of knowledge, perspectives, and voices.

Despite their significant differences, Athenian orators, educators, and philosophers consistently affirmed the importance of diverse viewpoints. Consider, for example, the Sophist Antiphon (ca. 480–411 BCE), who constructed fictional training exercises in courtroom oratory. Dated roughly 430 BCE, his three *Tetralogies* are three separate murder/manslaughter trials, each consisting of four speeches (*tetra* = four, *logoi* = speeches) alternating between prosecution and defense. That these cases are fiction allows Antiphon significant inventional latitude in this experiment in antilogy. Relying for the most part on existing Athenian homicide law and referencing plausible (although extreme) scenarios that citizens might face, Antiphon constructs his prosecution and defense speeches as if hard evidence does not exist.[29] In the second tetralogy, for instance, a boy was killed by an errant javelin throw during athletic training. Both sides admit the basic facts of the case: the boy who threw the javelin was authorized to do so, and the boy who died also was officially scheduled to be assisting on the field. Antiphon has the litigants reference testimony and some circumstantial evidence, but each testimony is readily contradicted by alternative explanations, and even the available evidence is mired in ambiguity and uncertainty. Is the boy who threw the javelin guilty of manslaughter, or did the deceased boy err by not paying sufficient attention to the training exercise? Did a coach distract the victim by calling his name? Did the boy throw the javelin with disregard for others in the target area?[30] By providing full speeches for each side, Antiphon expands the repertoire of argumentation for citizens who must litigate their own cases. His *Tetralogies* provide Athenians with examples and patterns that can be used for deliberating when the facts themselves are either hopelessly confused, are unavailable, or lead to contradictory conclusions. Antiphon expands the range of deliberative resources for wrestling through to a possible conclusion, providing citizens with the limits and possibilities of rhetorical maneuvering.[31]

As previously noted, Plato had no patience for a Sophist's rhetorical games, like Antiphon's exercizes in sheer legal maneuvering. Yet in his dialogues, Plato portrays Socrates as one who is "sick with the love of discourse," unable to resist conversations with others, through which souls are tested and refined by vigorous discourse.[32] Plato's philosophical method, as described and illustrated in one of his most famous dialogues, *Phaedrus*, requires the give and take of divergent views, for only through questions and challenges of dialectic was Socrates able to dig beneath the Sophists' mere opinions—and their showy orations—to extract the truths of justice, beauty, love, wisdom, and knowledge itself. Even though Plato rejected the endless conjecturing of sophistic persuasion, he portrayed his mentor Socrates as endlessly committed to multiple perspectives and a society constructed through the blessings of speech.

Number 2: Cultivating the Virtues of Self and Society

Political persuasion ought to promote the excellence of a human life by promoting the excellence of a society in which lives flourish.

Early in his teaching career, Isocrates published *Against the Sophists*, a pamphlet promoting his own educational program as superior to those of many popular rivals. For him, the Sophists were misguided educators who overpromised and underperformed. They made extraordinary claims about the value of their education yet provided students with nothing but the most basic speaking techniques. Isocrates made no such grandiose promises about his own program, but he did offer a grandiose vision. Namely, Isocrates believed his educational training in political speech would best assist students to become "fairminded," have "soundness of mind," and develop a "sense of justice."[33] We learn more about his specific educational method in a later speech, *Antidosis*, in which he defends and describes his view of logos and citizenship. Students can grow their sense of justice and their overall excellence of character by studying and performing political speeches.[34] For Isocrates, a political speech is not merely an appeal to a political base but an attempt to persuade those with whom one disagrees. To do so—to actually seek to persuade those who disagree—requires an ability to see mulitiple sides of issues, to weigh multiple viewpoints, and then to make a balanced appeal to one's opponents that assesses pros and cons. Thus, becoming persuasive—truly persuasive and not merely a political panderer—involves students in a journey of character formation in which judgments are formed with justice and a due respect for those they seek to influence. For Isocrates, the more a society is characterized by persuasion, the more that society will itself be a democracy of justice and overall virtue.

Although he was one of Isocrates's intellectual rivals, Aristotle was not a sophist by any reckoning. In Isocrates's eyes, Aristotle's educational program provided too little emphasis on the doing of persuasion and too much emphasis on the theories of persuasion. Regardless, they shared a deep commitment to human excellence as central to the democratic citizenry. For Aristotle, virtues such as justice, self-control, wisdom, and courage were cultivated not by persuasive speaking directly but only indirectly, as by-products of a democratic society in which citizens relied on persuasion to make judgments about costs and benefits. For Aristotle, the human is a "political animal" with "the gift of speech," which is a power "intended to set forth the expedient and the inexpedient, and therefore likewise the just and the unjust."[35] This power of speech can be used for good or for ill, so Aristotle emphasizes the need for good laws and healthy social relations through which citizens are formed into wise decision makers whose persuasion reflects ideals of character. As one of Aristotle's three techniques or modes of persuasion (mentioned previously), the ethos of the speaker is crucial. A persuader needs to be believable to the democratic audience; a credible persuader, Aristotle explains, is one who expresses good will toward the audience (wanting what is best for them), a practical wisdom of judgment on the issues (competently navigating the information and perspectives), and virtue (the overall excellence of character that commends the speaker to the audience as trustworthy).[36] Thus for Aristotle, as for Isocrates, political persuasion is the process through which the character qualities of democratic citizenship are publicly affirmed and socially cultivated.

Number 3: Sharpening Techniques for Citizen Deliberation

Political persuasion ought to skillfully enable citizens to make knowledgeable decisions.

In the Athenian Assembly, when thousands of citizens were required to make consequential decisions within a limited time and facing the distractions of an outdoor mass gathering (without voice amplification, of course), the orators needed to be engaging, focused, and insightful. From the mid-fifth century onward, the Sophists created a whole repertoire of speech strategies designed to increase the chances that a speech delivered would be a speech well heard. Gorgias, perhaps the most famous of the fifth-century sophistic orators, wowed audiences with his sophisticated use of prose rhythm to create a sort of poetic political style that has more in common with today's spoken-word poets than with US senators addressing the chamber.[37] For a mass audience, though, clever wordplay and a captivating style promote attention and memory. This creativity shows a serious commitment to the potential of persuasion. Democracy must foster and honor innovation and the courage to experiment with persuasive appeals.

Importantly, Gorgias also recognized that speech structure carries ideas to minds, enabling mass audiences to track argumentation and place evidence in context. In the *Encomium of Helen*, Gorgias's only surviving full speech, he builds a multipart explanation of why Helen, ancient Greece's most beautiful woman, was not responsible for causing the Trojan War.[38] Gorgias's topic here is playful, for no pressing Athenian business of the later fifth century BCE depended on public judgment about twelfth-century BCE mythologized history. Yet beyond showcasing his skills, Gorgias's oration had a public point to make. In defending Helen, Gorgias invents an argumentation process in which he lists and expounds upon a series of plausible explanations for Helen abandoning her Greek home to be with the prince of Troy.[39] Like Antiphon, then, Gorgias's oratory expands citizen imagination of what humans, armed with language, can accomplish when freed from political tyranny and given opportunity for persuasive artistry.

In addition to the stylistic virtuosity and innovative argumentation, Gorgias's *Encomium* employs a clear, overarching organizational pattern, which assists listeners in following his analysis and assessing its worth. His *prooemium* (introduction) stresses the ethical importance of honorific speeches praising the praiseworthy and blaming the blameworthy. The *narration* provides a brief biography of Helen emphasizing the glories of her divinely bestowed beauty. The *proposition* is the thesis, in which Gorgias rhythmically summarizes the overall claim of Helen's innocence: "For either by fate's will and gods' wishes and necessity's decrees she did what she did / or by force reduced or by words seduced or by love induced."[40] The *proof* is the bulk of the speech, in which Gorgias affirms the power of each possible explanation: fate, gods, necessity, force, seduction, love. He closes with a short *epilogue* (conclusion) that summarizes the thesis and celebrates his own oratorical achievement.

Gorgias's accomplishment in the art of oratory may not impress us today, for the lessons learned from the democratic Greeks about oratorical structure and reasoning have become today's settled conventions for public speaking. Yet we should not take such conventions for granted. When Aristotle lectured on rhetoric nearly a century after Gorgias made his first impression on Athenian audiences, Aristotle recognized that technical skill in the power of persuasion was essential for guiding citizens into wise decisions. Organizational patterns and systematic reasoning were indispensable. The art of rhetoric, according to Aristotle, prepares us to "argue persuasively on either side of a question . . . not that we may actually do both (for one should not persuade what is debased) but in order that it may not escape our notice what the real state of the case is and that we ourselves may be able to refute if another person uses speech unjustly."[41] To do the work of popular rule, the populace needed the benefit of persuasive expertise. The skilled political communicator enabled citizens to deliberate, and citizen deliberation was integral to the ethical ideals upon which democracy was founded. Taking persuasion seriously is an ethical service to self and others.

In Sum

The ancient Greeks celebrated the power of human speech for shaping lives and societies. Rival educators, philosophers, and politicians debated how best to cultivate this human power to make democracy successful and how much of political life should be dependent on persuasion. Some thinkers, such as Protagoras, Gorgias, Aristotle, and Isocrates, believed that persuasive speech is the glue of political life because other sources of political knowledge—

such as the gods, science, or philosophy—cannot solve the toughest issues of justice and policy. Other thinkers, such as Socrates and Plato, doubted that persuasive speech could achieve the highest ideals of human political life, but even they embraced speech as indispensable for seeking knowledge and influencing citizens. Despite deep disagreements, the vigorous intellectual debates among these ancient Athenians produced shared commitments to ethical political communication.

Democracy Now

We cherish democracy not for its own sake but for its unique capacity to balance our need for cooperative sociality with individuated self-interest. Our political communication—whether digital or face-to-face, whether verbal or nonverbal, whether produced by career politicians or by "ordinary" citizens—should sync with the ethical ideals of democratic governance.

Based on the principles of ethical political persuasion, how ought we to communicate?

- *Expand the resources for judgment:* Ethical political communicators welcome diverse viewpoints and competing positions. Citizens should advocate for their views, but that advocacy ought to be persuasive for diverse audiences and not limited to mere cheerleading for one's treasured positions. Advocacy flourishes when citizens have abundant resources available to build arguments, debate options, and seek creative solutions. Thus, advocacy does not silence opponents through threats, coalitions, or deceptions.
- *Cultivate the virtues of self and society:* Ethical political communicators respect each other's freedom of inquiry and the freedom to build convictions. This requires that advocates weigh alternative views and cooperatively participate in the deliberation of those views. Citizens should open themselves to the persuasion of others and in turn offer their own persuasion as a courageous expression of social commitment. The more persuasion takes root within a citizenship, the more the ideals of human excellence and democratic flourishing can grow.
- *Sharpen techniques for citizen deliberation:* Ethical political communicators look for ways to improve their persuasive abilities and to advance the quality of persuasion throughout society. Citizens should not shy away from appreciating technical accomplishments in equipping them to make decisions, which is a human capacity that fuels a democracy. Indeed, skillfully crafted political communication is a citizenly commitment to the quality of shared social life. Importantly, though, this skill ought to be directed toward the goal of citizen judgment; political communication that is fine-tuned to achieve political dominance

or "groupthink" comformity is closer to coercion and authoritarianism than to democratic persuasion.

Democracies today differ greatly from the direct popular rule of the Athenian city-state, which complicates any comparison between the classical and the contemporary. The sheer size of a modern citizenry requires elected representatives, and the greatly expanded resources of advanced technology, global media, international commerce, transportation, and information—to name only a few of the myriad changes—make it much harder to balance the aggregation, alignment, and codification of knowledge. Furthermore, and importantly, we have abolished slavery and extended citizenship to women and all born on US soil. Yet Athenians built their ideals of ethical communication within a culture of persuasive practice that was not completely unlike ours. They struggled with greedy politicians, corrupt lawyers, and citizens who were more interested in entertainment and pleasure than in wise political decision making. Plato, Isocrates, and Aristotle all condemned those political communicators who used spin, distraction, and deception to keep their own power and build their own wealth. Therefore, considering the ethical ideals of the ancients might provide us with the courage and insight needed to battle our own political demons and envision more admirable persuasion.

Notes

1 The story is recounted in J. F. Dobson, *The Greek Orators* (London: Methuen and Co., 1919), available online at www.perseus.tufts.edu (section 1.5). Most contemporary scholars reject the authenticity of the story. The best historical evidence indicates that Corax was either fictitious or a nickname for Tisias himself, and that the story is a fabrication perhaps intended to belittle Tisias's persuasive strategies that he exported to Athens. See the brief overview in George A. Kennedy, *A New History of Classical Rhetoric* (Princeton, NJ: Princeton University Press, 1994), 33–34.

2 My account of classical Athens, including most of the data about political structure and history, relies heavily on Josiah Ober, *Democracy and Knowledge: Innovation and Learning in Classical Athens* (Princeton, NJ: Princeton University Press, 2008). I supplemented Ober's analysis with Harvey Yunis, *Taming Democracy: Models of Political Rhetoric in Classical Athens* (Ithaca, NY: Cornell University Press, 1996), and Thomas R. Martin, *Ancient Greece: From Prehistoric to Hellenistic Times*, 2nd ed. (New Haven, CT: Yale University Press, 2013).

3 Josiah Ober, *The Rise and Fall of Classical Greece* (Princeton, NJ: Princeton University Press, 2015), 3.

4 Ober, *Democracy and Knowledge*; and Ober, *Rise and Fall*.

5 See, e.g., Ober, *Rise and Fall*, 45–47.

6 Ober, *Democracy and Knowledge*, 84–97.

7 Ober, *Democracy and Knowledge*, 108.

[8] Ober, *Democracy and Knowledge*, 3–6.

[9] Athens's theater, located on the hillside of the Acropolis, seated up to fourteen thousand people; Martin, *Ancient* Greece, 166.

[10] Aeschylus, *The Eumenides*, in *The Oresteia*, trans. Robert Fagles (Toronto: Bantam Books, 1982), lines 922–923. When citing primary sources, I use standard section numbers unless the particular translation or edited collection is best referenced by page numbers/line numbers.

[11] Aeschylus, *The Eumenides*, lines 913–920.

[12] For this overview of Protagoras, I rely on Edward Schiappa, *Protagoras and* Logos: *A Study in Greek Philosophy and Rhetoric*, 2nd ed. (Columbia: Unversity of South Carolina Press, 2003).

[13] Michael J. O'Brien, trans., "Protagoras," in *The Older Sophists*, ed. Rosamond Kent Sprague (1972; reprinted, Indianapolis, IN: Hackett Publishing Company, 2001), 18.

[14] Nicole Loraux, *The Invention of Athens: The Funeral Oration in the Classical City*, trans. Alan Sheridan (New York: Zone Books, 2006).

[15] Most likely the speech we have was rewritten by the historian Thucydides, whose account of Pericles's eloquence does not presume to be a word-for-word transcription; see Yunis, *Taming Democracy*, 59–67.

[16] "Thucydides: Pericles' Funeral Speech," in *Greek Political Oratory*, trans. A. N. W. Saunders (New York: Penguin Books, 1970), 34.

[17] On Plato's coining of the term "rhetoric," see Schiappa, *Protagoras and* Logos, 44–49.

[18] Plato's analogy linking flattery with the art of persuasion is in *Gorgias*. Plato, *Lysias-Symposium-Gorgias*, trans. W. R. M. Lamb, Loeb Classical Library (Cambridge, MA: Harvard University Press, 1925), 465c.

[19] Josiah Ober, *Political Dissent in Democratic Athens: Intellectual Critics of Popular Rule* (Princeton, NJ: Princeton University Press, 1998), 245.

[20] Aristotle, *On Rhetoric: A Theory of Civic Discourse*, 2nd ed., trans. George A. Kennedy (New York: Oxford University Press, 2007), 1358b.

[21] Aristotle, *On Rhetoric*, 1356a.

[22] For an excellent overall introduction to Isocrates and his place in ancient Athens, see Terry L. Papillon, "Isocrates," in *A Companion to Greek Rhetoric*, ed. Ian Worthington (Malden, MA: Blackwell Publishing, 2007), 58–74.

[23] Isocrates, *Antidosis*, in *Isocrates I*, trans. David C. Mirhady and Yun Lee Too, The Oratory of Classical Greece series (Austin: University of Texas Press, 2000), sect. 254.

[24] Isocrates, *Antidosis*, sect. 256.

[25] Isocrates, *Antidosis*, sect. 256.

[26] On Demosthenes's principled opposition to Philip and the tragedy of his successful persuasion, see the summary in Kennedy, *A New History of Classical Rhetoric*, 73–76.

[27] For an excellent discussion of the classical virtues, see Helen F. North, "Canons and Hierarchies of the Cardinal Virtues in Greek and Latin Literature," in *The Classical Tradition: Literary and Historical Studies in Honor of Harry Caplan*, ed. Luitpold Wallach (Ithaca, NY: Cornell University Press, 1966), 165–183.

[28] "Thucydides: Pericles' Funeral Speech," 36.

[29] J. S. Morrison, trans., "Antiphon," in *The Older Sophists*, 136–163.

[30] Morrison, "Antiphon," 147–156.

[31] Christopher W. Tindale, *Reason's Dark Champions: Constructive Strategies of Sophistic Argument* (Columbia: University of South Carolina Press, 2010), e.g., 71, 74, 79.

[32] Plato, *Phaedrus*, in *Euthyphro—Apology—Crito—Phaedo—Phaedrus*, trans. Harold North Fowler, Loeb Classical Library (Cambridge, MA: Harvard University Press, 1914), 228c; the dialogue between Socrates and Phaedrus in *Phaedrus* revolves around the relationship of discourse to the soul.

[33] Isocrates, *Against the Sophists*, in *Isocrates I*, sect. 22.

[34] Isocrates, *Antidosis*, sect. 276–280.

[35] Aristotle, *Politics*, trans. B. Jowett, in *Aristotle's Politics: Writings from the Complete Works*, ed. Jonathan Barnes (Princeton, NJ: Princeton University Press, 2016), 1253a.

[36] Aristotle, *On Rhetoric*, 1378a.

[37] On the "magic" of Gorgias's persuasion, see Jacqueline de Romilly, *Magic and Rhetoric in Ancient Greece* (Cambridge, MA: Harvard University Press, 1975).

[38] I rely on the translation by George A. Kennedy in "Appendix I: Supplementary Texts, A. Gorgias' *Encomium of Helen*," in Aristotle, *On Rhetoric*, 251–256.

[39] Edward Schiappa, "Gorgias's *Helen* Revisited," *Quarterly Journal of Speech* 81 (1995): 310–324.

[40] Kennedy, "Appendix I: Supplementary Texts, A. Gorgias' *Encomium of Helen*," par. 6.

[41] Aristotle, *On Rhetoric*, 1355a.

2

Ethics and the Ends of Rhetoric

Janet M. Atwill

The relationship between rhetoric and ethics in Western traditions has been debated since Plato (ca. 427–ca. 347 BCE) named the teaching of political discourse *rhētorikē*.[1] Plato's assertion that rhetoric offered only a semblance of true knowledge, divorced from virtue, put rhetoric on the defensive from the start. Historically, two versions of rhetoric's relationship to ethics emerged from these debates: rhetoric as character and rhetoric as *technē*, or art.[2] While this distinction oversimplifies the complexities of histories of rhetoric, it offers a starting point for exploring what—if anything—Western history has to us teach about rhetoric and ethics.

According to one tradition, ethics was literally ethos (*ēthos*), or character, not an externally defined set of values or standards. The Greek *ēthika*, which sounds most like our term "ethics," could refer to an ethical treatise, such as Aristotle's *Nicomachean Ethics*.[3] But the precise concerns of ethics in antiquity were generally handed over to philosophers. Even when Aristotle (384–322 BCE) refers to rhetoric in the *Nicomachean Ethics*, it is largely to distinguish it from and subordinate it to the study of politics. The most important measure of character was the esteem or honor in which the rhetor was held by the audience or polis. While persuasive success was *an* end of rhetoric, those who adhered to this tradition maintained that success was impossible without moral character. Indeed, for Quintilian (ca. 35–100 CE), in some cases character itself was the end of rhetoric. For the sake of clarity, I call this tradition "rhetorical ethics as character."

An alternative tradition maintained that successful persuasion was the end of rhetoric. Rhetoricians in this tradition usually express some preference for rhetorical appeals grounded in truth. Standards of truth and ethics were again handed over to the specialists: philosophers. This tradition was centrally concerned with teaching the art of rhetoric, and that art was composed of strategies and sample speeches that "worked." Thus, rhetorical success was the end of rhetoric. I call this tradition "rhetoric ethics as *technē*, or art."

While these traditions were never consistently distinct, they are evident in rhetorical treatises and pedagogies. Of course their historical contexts were vastly different from our own. Before the era of mass media, rhetors spoke before a political assembly or the polis,[4] audiences with similar values and on a much smaller scale. Even the terms are rather alien. Today the word "character" is generally identified with an actor on TV or in film. And "honor" is likely to be associated with an academic achievement or a military guard. So can these traditions offer any insights for the political culture of today, one dominated by mass media and governed by statistical analytics? This chapter explores that question.

Rhetorical Ethics as Character

In Plato's dialogue, *Protagoras*, Socrates interrogates the young man Hippocrates, who is intent on studying with the sophist after whom the dialogue is named.[5] Using analogies of other arts, from medicine to sculpture, Socrates asks what the young man expects to become by studying with this teacher. For example, if Hippocrates were to pay a fee to study medicine, the young man agrees he would become a doctor. And if he were to study with a famous sculptor, Hippocrates would become a sculptor himself (311b–c).[6] Finally, Socrates asks what Hippocrates hopes to become by studying with Protagoras. The young man acknowledges that he would become a sophist (312a). Eventually, Socrates and Hippocrates meet the Sophist himself. Protagoras gives two responses to Socrates's question concerning what Hippocrates will take away under the sophist's instruction. First, every day, the Sophist asserts, Hippocrates "will go home a better man" (318a). Second, Hippocrates will learn "good judgement in his own affairs, showing how best to order his own home; and in the affairs of his city, showing how he may have the most influence on public affairs both in speech and in action" (318e–319a). Socrates agrees with Protagoras that the sophist teaches "the art of politics [*tēn technē politikēn*]," which promises to "make men good citizens [*politas*]" (319c). But because Protagoras is not centrally concerned with the dialectical examination of truth,[7] Socrates implies that Protagoras's instruction is inadequate, if not harmful. Socrates insists that Hippocrates should know the soul of his teacher and be confident his teacher can distinguish good from evil. The philosopher warns Hippocrates that his soul is at risk because his knowledge does not adhere to philosophical standards. However, both Socrates and Protagoras appear to agree that knowledge is not something one can carry in a parcel; it is something one *becomes*. Thus, the end of rhetorical instruction is "character."

Isocrates (436–338 BCE) similarly ties rhetoric to character, offering insights into the classical conception of honor. Though Isocrates invokes such virtues as goodness and faithfulness, the model for these virtues is the polis, *not* a discrete set of standards or an internal moral plum line. Isocrates's description of the rhetor's process of invention suggests a permeable membrane between the city and the soul: "[T]he same arguments which we use in persuading others when we speak in public, we employ also when we deliberate in our own thoughts; and, while we call eloquent those who are able to speak before a crowd, we regard as sage those who most skillfully debate their problems in their own minds" (*Antidosis* 256–257). The very word for deliberation, *bouleuein*, is related to the name of the democratic Boule, the Council that served the citizen Assembly. The measure of knowledge and goodness in Isocrates's paradigm is deliberation in the polis: "[T]he power to speak well is taken as the surest index of a sound understanding, and discourse which is true and lawful and just is the outward image of a good and faithful soul" (*Antidosis* 255–256). The polis provides the model for the soul; indeed, it is in the polis that virtue is most important: "It behoves states much more than individuals to cultivate the virtues and shun vices; for a man who is godless and depraved may die before paying the penalty for his sins, but states, since they are deathless, soon or late must submit to punishment at the hands both of men and of the gods" (*On the Peace* 120).

For Isocrates, to teach the art of rhetoric is to be concerned with the construction of character, and character is measured by the respect one earns from one's peers: "[T]he stronger a man's desire to persuade his hearers, the more zealously will he strive to be honourable and to have the esteem of his fellow-citizens" (*Antidosis* 278). Isocrates's sense of character is essentially rhetorical, tied to social and political exigencies. The goal of Isocrates's pedagogy is successful intervention in the affairs of the polis, and in those acts of intervention the rhetor's *ēthos* is both a tool and a product.

In Roman rhetoric, this sense of the *ēthos* emerges in the concept of eloquence. Cicero (106–43 BCE) and Quintilian (35–ca. 96 CE) explicitly acknowledge the role of art and liberal education in the formation of the orator. Eloquence is the expression of character that education produced.[8] Cicero writes in *De Oratore*:

> Eloquence is one of the supreme virtues . . . which after compassing knowledge of facts, gives verbal expression to the thoughts and purposes of the mind in such a manner as to have the power of driving the hearers forward in any direction in which it has applied its weight; and the stronger this faculty is, the more necessary it is for it to be combined with integrity and supreme wisdom, and if we bestow fluency of speech on persons devoid of those virtues, we shall not have made orators of them but shall have put weapons into the hands of madmen. (III.xiv.55)

If there is an external standard by which the orator is evaluated, it is neither an ethical measuring stick nor success in rhetorical endeavors. The orator is judged by the esteem of audiences: "Our orator must carefully see to it, that he not only contents those whom it is necessary to satisfy, but is wonderful as well in the eyes of such as have the right to judge freely" (I.xxvi.119).

Quintilian most explicitly makes character the end of rhetoric. He fears that Cicero did not adequately define the character that should be the product of a rhetorical education. In *The Institutes of Oratory*, he promises to make up for Cicero's deficiencies by outlining what is necessary "to form my orator's character and to teach him his duties" (XII. pr. 4). Quintilian stipulates that the true orator must be a "good man" (XII.1.1). Even the honor accrued by eloquence may be an inadequate standard since the "powers of eloquence" can be used for good and ill (XII.1.1). He bemoans the fact that he cannot control how students use their rhetorical knowledge—that the labors of his teaching may have forged "weapons not for a soldier, but for a robber" (XII.1.1). Quintilian wants to avoid this possibility by uniting character with virtue: "For I do not merely assert that an ideal orator should be a good man, but I affirm that no man can be an orator unless he is a good man" (I.1.13). Since the ideal orator must be gifted with intelligence, no such person "on being offered the choice between the two paths of virtue and vice choose the latter" (XII.1.3). Quintilian goes so far as to identify moral standards with human characteristics. "Oratory is in the main concerned with the treatment of what is just and honorable" (XII.1.8). Thus, only the person possessing justice and honor can bear the title of orator. While Quintilian acknowledges the significance of art, he is perfectly willing to sacrifice art's power to protect the character of the orator: "My orator, and the art that I have defined, do not depend on the outcome. The speaker certainly aims to win; but when he has spoken well, even if he does not win, he has fulfilled the demands of his art" (II.17.23).

Rhetorical Ethics as *Technē*

In contrast to Quintilian, those who held to the tradition of rhetorical ethics as *technē* firmly believed that the end of rhetoric was persuasive success. This is not to say that they were necessarily averse to moral concerns, but they were far more committed to distributing the art through teaching, and they expected their students to succeed in rhetorical endeavors. The *Dissoi Logoi,* or *Opposing Arguments*, is considered to be a sophistic treatise. Along with small sample speeches, the *Dissoi Logoi* includes arguments on both sides of a question. Of course, this appalled those who followed Plato's standards of truth. But the practice became standard in rhetorical training, especially training for law.

For those who viewed rhetoric primarily as art, knowledge was something one "has," not something one "is." And rhetorical art, in this sense, could be used for any moral or ideological end. Aristotle offers useful examples. He maintains rigorous standards for truth in the domain of philosophy.[9] Moreover, in Book One of the *Rhetoric,* Aristotle posits that "the true and the just are naturally superior to their opposites" (1355a). However, he does not hold rhetoric to standards of truth or justice. Indeed, the *Rhetoric* offers the following advice to those practicing in the courts: "As for contracts, argument may be used to the extent of magnifying or minimizing their importance, of proving that they do or do not deserve credit. If we have them on our side, we must try to prove them worthy of credit and authoritative; but if they are on the side of our opponent, we must do the opposite" (1376b).

Aristotle's treatment of contracts is an apt example of an instrumental rhetoric: a strategy that can be used in a variety of contexts with the end being rhetorical success. It may be unfair to suggest that all of Aristotle's rhetoric is an instrumental means to an end. Such strategies, however, are characteristic of rhetoric as a *technē*. Rhetorical art is transferable, not bound to a specific epistemological or ethical end.

Though Plato and Protagoras agree that knowledge produces a person, Protagoras uses rhetoric's transferability to argue his support for the democratic structure of the Athenian polis. In the sophist's dialogue with Socrates, he offers another version of the Prometheus myth. This myth was always about the ways the arts shift the balance of power between humankind and the gods. Earlier versions of the myth are found in the *Works and Days* of Hesiod (fl. eighth century BCE) and *Prometheus Bound* by Aeschylus (523–456 BCE). These treatises deal with arts ranging from agriculture to written discourse. Protagoras, however, focuses on the art of politics.

Before Protagoras's retelling of the Prometheus myth, Socrates has already criticized the distribution of political art in the Athenian polis. He points out that in the democratic assembly, the city depends on experts to construct buildings and ships (319b–c). At the time, all Athenians were subject to participating in the Assembly because service was determined by the drawing of lots, much like our current jury system. Socrates criticizes decision making in the polis: "[W]hen they have to deliberate on something connected with the administration of the State, the man who rises to advise them on this may equally well be a smith, a shoemaker, a merchant, a sea-captain, a rich man, a poor man, of good family or of none" (319 c–d). Socrates affirms Plato's principle that the polis should be governed by an expert, which is to say a philosopher. Protagoras responds with his version of the Prometheus myth.

Protagoras begins with Zeus's creation of mortal creatures. The two Titans Epimetheus and Prometheus are given the responsibility of allotting distinctive features and abilities to all living creatures. Epimetheus takes over the task, distributing these features according to a principle of compensation: "To those which he invested with smallness he dealt a winged escape or an underground habitation; those which he increased in largeness he pre-served by this very means; and he dealt all the other properties on this plan of compensation. In contriving all this he was taking precaution that no kind should be extinguished" (320–321). Epimetheus then equips them with appropriate protection from the elements and means of sustenance (321b–c). Given that the distinctive characteristic of Epimetheus is the absence of forethought (epi-metheus: after thought), he dispenses the powers allotted to him by Zeus to the animals, leaving humankind "naked, unshod, unbed-ded, unarmed" (321c). To rectify Epimetheus's errors, Prometheus steals from Zeus fire, a symbol of the power of arts (*technai*). By means of the arts humankind acquires "a share in the portion of the gods" (322a). These arts enable humans to develop culture and rudimentary social organization. Humankind has the capacity "to establish altars and holy images" (322a) and the "skill to articulate speech and words, and to invent dwellings, clothes, sandals, beds, and the foods that are of the earth" (322a). However, they are still vulnerable to "wild beasts." When they seek safety by coming together and "founding cities," they still do "wrong to one another through the lack of civic art" (*politikēn technēn*) (322c). Zeus is forced to intervene by sending Hermes to distribute "respect [*aidōs*] and right [*dikē*]," mean-ing justice (322c). When Hermes asks if this political art should be distrib-uted like the other arts, on the principle of compensation, Zeus replies that they must be distributed to all: "Let all have their share: for cities cannot be formed if only a few have a share . . . (322d). There could never be cities if only a few shared in these virtues" (322d). Thus, Protagoras concludes that Athenians, at least, do not believe the political *technē* should be restricted to experts. Instead, "everyone must share in this kind of virtue; otherwise the state could not exist" (323).

A Compromise or Combination

Often the purpose of making this kind of distinction between ethics as character and ethics as art is to find a synthesis or combination of features that seemed previously unreconcilable. In our present political culture, it is unlikely that teachers and practitioners of political communication would find rhetorical ethics as character very useful. The end of political communi-cation is generally depicted as persuasive or political success, not character. Moreover, the model of character outlined in the chapter was shaped by gender, class, and cultural forces that we are more likely to challenge than endorse.[10] At the same time, if we hold *only* to rhetoric as *technē*, will we cre-ate a political community in which we want to live?

The compromise I propose resides in the civic art (*politikēn technēn*) Zeus commanded Hermes to distribute to all. That political art consisted of respect (*aidōs*) and right (*dikē*) (usually translated "justice"). I suggest that these two qualities can be flexible ethical standards that have no pre-determined end. Douglas Cairns notes that the Greek concept of *aidōs* was embedded in the culture of honor, which was related to the culture of shame.[11] In Cairns's discussion of Protagoras's Prometheus narrative, he describes *aidōs* as a "valued disposition or trait of character encompassing a sense of the ways in which one's own honour and status are bound up with those of others" (1993, 356). *Aidōs* is thus an attitude of respect toward others that is tied to the respect on can expect from others. Cairns describes *aidōs* as an "inhibitory emotion" that further explicates the relationship between it and shame:

> The notions of shame and respect are not totally unrelated, to feel inhibitory shame . . . is to picture oneself as losing honour, while to show respect is to recognize the honour of another. . . . [T]o be concerned with one's own honour is to envisage oneself as one among others, also bearers of honour; thus to limit one's own claim to honour is to accept one's status vis-à-vis others, to inhibit self-assertion is to recognize how such conduct would impinge upon the honour of others. (13)

Aidōs is thus the product of both an attitude and a relationship. The attitude of *aidōs* assumes that one does not have all the answers, that one's perspective is by definition partial. As an attitude, *aidōs* seems to bridge character and ethics. Though scholars will continue to debate the forms that justice should take, it is worth considering at least tempering our discourse with *aidōs*.

Notes

1 For a discussion of Plato's coining of the term *rhētorikē*, see Cole (1991) and Schiappa (1990).

2 A number of scholars have worked with similar distinctions. See, for example, Kimball (1986).

3 Liddell, Scott, and Jones (1940).

4 "Polis" is the Greek term for a city or city-state.

5 In the fourth century BCE, "sophist" could refer simply to a "wise man," but in modern scholarship it generally refers to a rhetorician, a teacher of the art of political discourse or, simply, rhetoric. In *Protagoras,* the sophist claims to teach the "political art" (*tēn technē politikēn*).

6 All quotations from classical sources are taken from *Loeb Classical Library* (1911–).

7 Platonic dialectic was concerned with the definition of important terms by means of classification and division.

8 For in-depth treatments of *ēthos*, see May (1988) and Wisse (1988).

9 See Aristotle's *Metaphysics.*

10 See Atwill (1998).

11 See Cairns (1993).

References

Atwill, Janet. 1998. *Rhetoric Reclaimed: Aristotle and the Liberal Arts Tradition.* Ithaca, NY, and London: Cornell University Press.

Cairns, Douglas L. 1993. *Aidōs: The Psychology and Ethics of Honour and Shame in Ancient Greek Literature.* Oxford: Clarendon.

Cole, Thomas. 1991.*The Origins of Rhetoric in Ancient Greece.* Baltimore, MD: Johns Hopkins University Press.

Kimball, Bruce. 1986. *Orators and Philosophers: A History of the Idea of Liberal Education.* New York: Teachers College Press.

Liddell, Henry George, Robert Scott, and Henry Stuart Jones. 1940. *A Greek-English Lexicon.* Rev. ed. (Reprint with supplement, Oxford: Clarendon Press, 1968).

Loeb Classical Library. 1911–. Cambridge, MA, and London: Harvard University Press.

May, James. 1988. *Trials of Character: The Eloquence of Ciceronian Ethos.* Chapel Hill: University of North Carolina Press.

Schiappa, Edward. 1990. "Did Plato Coin Rhētorikē?" *American Journal of Philology* 3: 460–473.

Sprague, Rosamond Kent, ed. 1972. *The Older Sophists.* A complete translation by several hands of the Fragments in *Die Fragmente der Vorsokratiker*, edited by Diels-Kranz. Columbia: University of South Carolina Press.

Wisse, Jacob. 1988. *Ethos and Pathos from Aristotle to Cicero.* Amsterdam: Hakkert.

3

Communication Ethics in Machiavelli

Alexander S. Duff

Niccolò Machiavelli (b. 1469; d. 1527) served the Florentine Republic as an important diplomat from 1498 to 1512. He was then expelled from office by the Medici family, tortured for his supposed involvement in a plot against them, and finally returned to their patronage as a writer. He produced works of poetry, political philosophy, and drama throughout the latter period of his life. Niccolò Machiavelli, Florentine, was in the crucial sense a man *in* the Renaissance but not *of* the Renaissance, or in what perhaps amounts to the same thing, was of a different renaissance than his contemporaries.[1]

What we refer to as the Renaissance consisted in the revival—literally the rebirth—within European Christendom of the art, architecture, engineering, rhetoric, poetry, science, and philosophy of the pre-Christian period centered in Greece and extending west to Rome and east to the Hellenic empires and satrapies. Centered in Italy in the fourteenth, fifteenth, and sixteenth centuries, this revival was initiated by the rediscovery of a wealth of lost manuscripts by Cicero, Polybius, Plutarch, Sallust, Livy, and a host of other literary luminaries from the classical, Hellenistic, and Roman periods—many recovered from monasteries—and then accelerated by the arrival of an abundance of material culture—sculpture, other plastic arts, codices—as the flight from Byzantium reached its apogee in the mid-fifteenth century.[2] Machiavelli was reared and educated in this milieu.

Inasmuch as this renaissance also included the resuscitation of classical moral and political philosophical reflections, including their aspiration to offer moral and political guidance for the conduct of statecraft at the highest levels, Machiavelli dissented in characteristically pungent but effective terms. He rejected the theoretical or philosophical principles of the revival of classical political and rhetorical theory because he objected to the manifest political results of attempting to live and conduct politics according to these understandings. In plain terms, Machiavelli thought that bad practice followed

from bad theory; he sought to correct this by offering an altogether different account of the ground of political life and action and therefore inspiring
altogether more beneficial political action. This is particularly evident in his
correction of classical understandings of political speech or reasoning and its
place in political life, which his contemporaries—Renaissance humanists, men
of letters, many of them holding important governmental offices in the leading cities of Italy—had been attempting to revive and give force to for almost
two centuries before Machiavelli wrote.

To understand Machiavelli's view of the place that discourse and morality
should have in properly understood and conducted political life, it is helpful
to understand the position against which he set himself, one broadly adopted
and expressed by the humanists of the Renaissance but that was stated most
clearly by its ancient originators, Aristotle and Cicero.

What is the discourse ethos of the Renaissance humanists whose views
Machiavelli is trying to displace? It would be preposterous to say that
Renaissance humanists such as Leonardo Bruni or Coluccio Salutati, whom
Machiavelli objected to, were boy scouts, devoted to an idea of the nobility
of politics and therefore to the place of good, sober honesty as being central
to its conduct. It did not take Machiavelli to introduce to the Renaissance
mind the idea that politics might be conducted by poison and steel. Yet the
Renaissance humanists were oriented to the view that through the contest
of opinions that constituted political existence, it was necessary that politics
itself be a stage on which controversies concerning true and false opinions of
good policy were tested. For this reason, with Cicero, they held that *oratio*
exhibited or was guided by *ratio*, and that therefore politics was an endeavor
formed centrally by a kind of reason.

Deliberation is central to the very being of political life, according to
both the original and the revival of this view. In Aristotle's presentation of
the bodies that make up the political community in his *Politics*, he insists that
the center of what makes a *political* community *what it is*, and not simply
a contract or common location of people, is a shared—imperfectly shared,
but shared—moral commitment to a given opinion or holding of justice.
As such, the citizens of a city (Aristotle's political community in the precise
sense) will dispute with uncommon passion precisely that which they hold in
common, a notion of justice. This dispute will be characterized, it seems of
necessity and always, by characteristic biases concerning justice, which may
even obscure from the perspective of the various partisans of the city the fact
that they have something in common with their brother citizens, who contend with one another as if sworn enemies. But as Aristotle himself teaches
in the work of the *Politics*, the parts of the city can, at least in principle, be
brought to see what they share with their fellow citizens, and therefore this
remains the orienting goal of what might be called their ethic of communi-

cation. Having in common such a notion of justice certainly remains more than the tacit goal of meliorative statecraft within that political community.

In Machiavelli's view, however, political communities are not so constituted, and therefore the possibility of their divisions being improved through deliberation concerning the things they hold in common is impossible; moreover, the hope that this might be so is a pernicious dream. In each of his three major works—*The Prince*, the *Discourses on Livy*, and the *Florentine Histories*—Machiavelli presents an account of the fundamental makeup of political communities that is conspicuously different than that transmitted by the ancient political philosophers and their Renaissance students. As Machiavelli tells it, every political community is composed of two fundamentally distinct "humors" (*umori*): one desires to rule and command, the other desires *not* to be ruled and *not* to be commanded (P 9, D I.4, FH 3.1).[3] Political life is therefore fundamentally unharmonious, composed of the rule of one part of a community over another, but without any common element or shared notion of justice to bind them together. All that binds the community together is the successful application of force and manipulation of one segment of the community by another. The community so understood is therefore composed of desires rather than opinions. This seemingly slight difference in presentation is rich in capturing the profoundly changed sense for Machiavelli of what political speech is and is capable of, and therefore of what ethic of communication is appropriate to political life. Machiavelli still recognizes that politics is manifestly conducted, often if not always, by means of speech. But speech on such an understanding therefore has a different character. To the extent that it consists of debates about justice or the moral issues that emerge in political life, these are not opinions capable of being clarified through correction and dispute. Rather, they are post hoc justifications or rationalizations—more or less deceitful appeals to acceptable principles that would attain the assent of relevant powerful bodies in the large body politic. Their criteria are not whether they are true, partially true, or false, but whether they are useful or functional in curbing or guiding political action.

Machiavelli is not simply "against" the moral views of the ancient political philosophers and their Renaissance humanist students and in favor of "realism" instead, a view that is sometimes attributed to him. What he insists on is clarity about both the true motivations at work in political life and the characteristic human temptation to be unclear about such motivations or to obscure them for the sake of satisfying self-aggrandizement or self-satisfaction. What has gone wrong, in his view, is that the seduction of thinking oneself noble has confused political actors with respect to the true necessities of political existence.

To really see Machiavelli's difference, it is necessary to look closely at his writings. In particular, because it is explicitly directed to the political actor with the greatest capacity, his small book *The Prince* is indispensable for seeing the new and franker role of communication ethics in political life prescribed by Machiavelli. *The Prince* is written to benefit its reader in the act of seeking and maintaining political status. Machiavelli professes in the letter that introduces it to the reader that it is a work of modest size and pretention, "not ornamented . . . [or] filled with fulsome phrases nor with pompous and magnificent words" (P Dedicatory Letter). Machiavelli thus presents himself as a blunt, straight-shooting adviser. As this self-presentation develops throughout the work, and he does not balk at considering even the grisliest dimensions of politics, he further assures the reader of his hard-boiled bona fides. Machiavelli can hardly be accused of prettifying politics.

At several junctures in his major writings, Machiavelli takes issue with a class of people he refers to as "the writers" or "those who have written," a sweeping category that seems to include his humanist contemporaries as well as older philosophers and even historians from the classical-Christian tradition. This is more than just boasting on Machiavelli's part to emphasize the novelty or originality of his own position; it actually reflects very deeply his own sense of his purpose in writing. These writers, he implies, have mistaken the characteristic attractiveness of the results of political action—pleasing, calm, perhaps even seemingly noble in their way—for the awful violence that is required to bring such a condition into being, or else they have simply misrepresented the same. Writing contributes to a general forgetfulness or oblivion of the violence and unpleasantness in the foundational levels of political action. This pattern exhibits itself in his discussions of the historical figures Cyrus the Great and Scipio Africanus in *The Prince*.

In chapter 14 of *The Prince* we learn about the need for a prince to imitate his most illustrious forebears: Alexander the Great, who imitated Achilles, and Caesar, who imitated Alexander. Machiavelli also mentions the great Roman general Scipio, who he says learned from Cyrus, but as Machiavelli repeats his point for emphasis, he references particularly the writer who communicated to Scipio about Cyrus, Xenophon: "And whoever reads the life of Cyrus *written by Xenophon* will then recognize in the life of Scipio how much glory that imitation brought him, how much in chastity, affability, humanity, and liberality Scipio conformed to what had been *written of Cyrus by Xenophon*" (P 6, 60; emphasis added). Twice in a short line Machiavelli references Xenophon the writer as intermediary between the political actor Cyrus and his imitator, Scipio. When the reader attentively notes Scipio's next appearance in Machiavelli's book, though, just a few pages later, he or she can hardly miss the odd payoff: Scipio emerges as inferior to his typological rival, Hannibal. What did Scipio learn from Xenophon the writer? Not enough, it would seem. Machiavelli juxtaposes the ease or noble grace with which Scipio attempted to rule his Roman army with the infamous cruelty and terror—"and infinite other virtues," per Machiavelli—

employed by Hannibal in his rule over a fearsome army. Despite—indeed the reader must wonder, rather because of—what he learned from Xenophon the writer, Scipio blundered in his rule. His troops rebelled against him, whereas Hannibal's management of his army was quite literally ruthlessly efficient. Machiavelli's choice of Scipio to make this point is not meant to be narrowly historical (though Cicero also reports that Xenophon's Cyrus was a formative text for Scipio). Rather, he is summing up the moral-political orientation of Xenophon and the classically inspired "writers" as such as a key source for misunderstanding the true nature of politics. To select Scipio to make this point is especially cutting, because for generations of humanists—themselves already echoing Cicero and St. Anselm—Scipio had been taken as exemplifying the highest possible harmony of moral-political virtue and philosophical inquiry, to which they aspired and to which standard they held political actors in Renaissance Italy.[4]

There is another crucial element in the failure typical of the writers—those representatives of the approach to history, politics, morals, and philosophy from the classical tradition, which his humanist contemporaries were trying to revive—namely, their cowardice. Machiavelli uses the example of "the writers'" treatment of Caesar to make this point. They have been obsequiously flattering to Caesar and his successors—the emperors of Rome—for no reason but their cowardice. No one, Machiavelli writes,

> should deceive himself because of the glory of Caesar, hearing him especially celebrated by the writers; for those who praise him are corrupted by his fortune and awed by the duration of the empire that, ruling under that name, did not permit writers to speak freely of him. But whoever wishes to know what the writers would say of him if they were free should see what they say of Catiline. Caesar is so much more detestable as he who has done an evil is more to blame than he who has wished to do one. He should also see with how much praise they celebrate Brutus, as though, unable to blame Caesar because of his power, they celebrate his enemy. (D I.10.3)

The writers under the Roman Empire said openly about Catiline—a failed usurper and would-be tyrant—what they would not dare say about Caesar. The results of Caesar's victories then obscure the truth, which is that Caesar is like Catiline, the same type of daring, frustrated, would-be tyrant. Machiavelli argues that the consequences of such cowardice for political understanding are dire, and this ultimately translates to political practice. Real political accomplishment is not well-understood; it looks easier, less messy, less violent than it is. This encourages a kind of laxness or easiness among rulers, and this laxness passes for generosity or ease for charm. But real tyranny is misunderstood as well; its results are admired, even glorified. Such misunderstandings are ultimately translated into political practice. Accordingly, Machiavelli says, "in ordering republics, maintaining states, governing kingdoms, ordering the military and administering war, judging subjects, and increasing empire, neither prince nor republic may be found that has recourse to the examples of the ancients" (D preface 6), and Italy is subject to barbarians (P 26). Thus no one really understands politics, and the widespread humanist impulse to imitate the revival of the other arts and sciences of antiquity promises simply to repeat all the errors Machiavelli is diagnosing.

It is fair to ask, then, how Machiavelli understands his own project in light of his condemnation of these other writers. In the *Discourses on Livy* he says he is motivated by benefaction: "that natural desire that has always been in me to work, without any respect, for those things I believe will bring common benefit to everyone, I have decided to take a path as yet untrodden by anyone" (D preface 5). He aims to avoid the "results-oriented" writing of others and instead capture the real and grim business of politics. As such he does not flatter princes: "[I]t appears to me I have gone outside the common usage of those who write, who are accustomed always to address their works to some prince and, blinded by ambition and avarice, praise him for all virtuous qualities when they should blame him for every part worthy of reproach" (D ed, 3). In *The Prince* he places himself among the people (P ed, 4).

Understanding the confusion of political results with means in this way provides some helpful context for understanding Machiavelli's cardinal advice to princes and would-be rulers, namely, to join him in going "directly to the effectual truth of the thing." Machiavelli distinguishes such an approach from that which was prescribed by "many who have written" of political matters, who take their bearings by "the imagination" of the truth. As he elaborates famously, "many have imagined republics and principalities that have never been seen or known to exist in truth" (P 15, 61). Being oriented by the effectual truth will mean being less fascinated by beautiful impressions or imaginations and being more attuned to useful effects. This turns out to involve dispensing with a great many pleasantries about the moral potential of political action. In the same chapter, Machiavelli lists a series of "qualities"—a studiously neutral term—that may bring praise or blame to a prince, for example, cruelty and mercy. According to Machiavelli, it is not the case that one of these (cruelty?) is a vice and the other is a virtue. Rather, the way Machiavelli raises the issue, one is invited to think not simply that mercy may sometimes cause one trouble—"blame"—in the course of ruling, but more positively that cruelty might be the source of "praise." The same applies to the qualities "breaker of faith" and "faithful": someone might find that breaking faith—breaking promises, but also implicitly violating religion—earns praise, or that it earns blame, or that being faithful can earn praise but also blame. Machiavelli reveals that when one abjures any orientation to the "imagined" truth of things, such as is typically celebrated by the writers, the full and dizzying range of political possibilities and therefore even necessities is altogether liberated from customary notions of moral direction or restraint. One must indeed learn "not to be good."

Machiavelli baptizes the would-be prince into a world where appearances and what may be said of them are so far from in truth representing what is what that the primary demand on a prince is that "he be so prudent as to know how to avoid the infamy of those vices that would take his state from him and to be on guard against those that do not, if that is possible; but if one cannot, one can let them go on with less hesitation" (P 15, 62). Perhaps still more impressive is that "one should not care about incurring the fame of those vices without which it is difficult to save one's state; for if one considers everything well, one will find something appears to be virtue, which if pursued would be one's ruin, and something else appears to be vice, which if pursued results in one's security and well-being" (P 15, 62). The radical separation that Machiavelli introduces between appearances and reality, or between how things seem to be and how they really are, is perhaps the core of what makes his ethics of communication so distinctively "Machiavellian." For no one needed Machiavelli to teach politicians that lying, cheating, and stealing might be to their advantage, or indeed that politics was a deadly sport, played for the highest stakes. What makes Machiavelli distinctive is his insistence that what *looks like* virtue need not *be* virtue.

Machiavelli brings many of these themes, central to the problem of communication ethics, into focus in his advice offered to a prince in chapter 18 of *The Prince*, even the title of which is evidently important: "In What Mode Faith Should Be Kept by Princes." Here Machiavelli brings crystalline clarity to his differences with his contemporaries, taking issue with the advice of their authority, the Roman republican statesman Cicero, while also articulating his own deepest sense of the unreliability of appearances and words and the need for a prince to seize every opportunity to dissemble. In this chapter of *The Prince*, Machiavelli commends to his reader the necessity of lying, "getting around men's brains with astuteness," as he puts it. In saying this, he refers to two well-known motifs from Cicero's *De officiis*, which was the single most widely distributed piece of literature in the Italian Renaissance, with the exception of the Bible. In this work, Cicero argues that the noble and the advantageous can be harmonized, but that central to doing so is the necessity of orienting oneself by moral principles, in particular by foreswearing deception. Machiavelli's setup is this: there are two modes of doing combat, one with laws, the other with force. The first of these is unique to humans, the second characteristic of beasts (brutes). But because the first mode of combat is usually inadequate, one should be prepared for the second. It is in regard to the second—combat by force—that Machiavelli counsels a would-be prince to "know well how to use" the fox and the lion. That is, each of these images or methods is an expression of needed "force." What could this mean? Is not the fox an expression of fraud and the lion an expression of force?

As always with Machiavelli, the devil is in the textual details. The lion, he says, "does not defend itself from snares"; it is susceptible to being trapped, duped. The fox, however, does not defend itself from wolves; it is not strong enough on its own. One therefore "needs to be a fox to recognize snares and a lion to frighten the wolves." This teaching is particularly poorly understood by lions. Only foxes understand the need for deception in politics; they see its need because they themselves are capable of detecting deception. One could read Machiavelli to be saying that, indeed, more important than strength or force in the crude sense is for political leaders to be shrewd and devious. As he remarks, "[T]he one who has known best how to use the fox has come out best. . . . [I]t is necessary to know well how to color this nature, and to be a great pretender and dissembler."

The reason dissembling and dishonesty are so important is that the world itself is constituted of such shifting and transforming ground and is populated entirely by people eager to believe falsehoods, that it is simply impossible to maintain high political office and satisfy the various moral expectations that one might wish, even demand, a leader to evince—including such demands as one might make of oneself, for why else would Machiavelli need to emphasize this with a would-be prince? What to do then? Machiavelli is emphatic: "This has to be understood: that a prince, and especially a new prince, cannot observe all those things for which men are held good"—all faith, charity, humanity, religion, decency, and so forth—"since he is often under a necessity to maintain his status. . . . And so he needs to have a spirit disposed to change as the winds of fortune and variation of things command him . . . to know how to enter into evil when forced by necessity" (P 18, 70). It is necessary to appear virtuous—full of the admirable, praiseworthy qualities that are generally desired from rulers—yet impossible truly to be all of these things, given the press of necessity at the peak of political life. For Machiavelli, in this way politics is truly distinct from ethics, inasmuch as ethics consists of a concern for truly being good.

Machiavelli's reasons for thinking this way about freeing politics, and therefore also political communication, from ethical restraint is that the world itself, in its fundamental organizing principles, is hostile to the communication of the truth. What might be called Machiavelli's political "epistemology" entails a strong sense of the distance between impressions or appearances and the reality underneath. Awareness of this and the capability to manage it are truly what distinguish the princely from the general run of humanity. That is, far more than the democratic notions that inform more recent understandings of politics, Machiavelli's advice is offered—plainly and in the open, as it were—to those who are interested in distinguishing themselves from the multitude. Most people, he claims, "judge more by their eyes than by their hands, because seeing is given to everyone, touching to few" (P 18, 71). In Machiavelli's epistemology, the sense of touch is more refined than the visual sense. The latter is easily deceived, dazzled even; the former is more sure, more certain in its orientation to the tangible. "Everyone sees how you appear, few touch what you are; and these few dare not oppose the opinion of many." Machiavelli's precise formulation of the order of strength here is very telling of his more general understanding of politics. Few may genuinely get a sense, a grasp of who the prince is and how things work—the few who are more intelligent about matters than the general run of people who make up the body politic—but even these intelligent few are subject to the force majeure of the many, who are subject to appearances. So master these appearances: lie, dissemble, conceal, deceive. This is the path to enlisting the great many on your side in political contests, and they have the numbers. Politics for Machiavelli, despite his rigid hierarchical sense of who knows and understands versus the great rabble of the body politic, is therefore in no sense "aristocratic" or "noble." It is a work, quite literally, of force, and in any community the large body of the people are stronger than the more refined few. As such, "the vulgar are taken in by the appearance and the outcome of a thing, and in the world there is no one but the vulgar; the few have no place there, when the many have somewhere to lean on" (P 18, 71).

This ambiguity in Machiavelli's political epistemology points to the final important ingredient in his communication ethics that must be reckoned with: his fundamentally populist or "democratic" impulse. It comes out, once again, with special clarity when it is contrasted with the disposition of those Renaissance humanists who sought to revive the approach of classical political philosophy of the Ciceronian or Aristotelian mode. In his account of the characteristic division of the body politic, Machiavelli inclines to favor, and advises his readers to favor, the larger part, the *popolo* or people. This is in opposition to the more aristocratic bent of classical political philosophy, which saw the contribution of the "nobles" to the political community as being part of justice. In Machiavelli's view, though, these notions of justice and its aristocratic prejudice depended on a stronger bond between appearances of justice and the common good and the true being of justice and the common good. That is, the aristocratic disposition of the classical political philosophers and their Renaissance students depended on a view of the intelligibility and therefore ultimate beneficence of the natural order that Machiavelli ultimately rejected as untrustworthy and hostile. In *History of the Florentine People* Leonardo Bruni expresses a version of the classic vision, which is that good, orderly government is a reflected expression of good, orderly character, which in turn is favored by Nature herself:

Because there were certain powerful individuals who seemed inordinately given to civil discord, the government of the city was handed over to a quiet and peace-loving sort of person who was more inclined to carrying on business in peacetime than to engaging in war and strife. . . . [T]hey enjoyed popular approval and preference because they were neither predatory nor seditious, but frugal and peace-loving persons each exercising his own métier (for the lazy have to feed off the goods of others). That this magistracy under the same name has lasted in the city up to the present day, one hundred and thirty-eight years later, is a sign that it was excellently designed. Even when human beings cannot do so, time and Experience, the mistress of nature, show harmful things to be wrong-headed and do not allow them to enjoy long life. (Bruni 2001, 3.59)

Machiavelli's fundamental orientation, however, is not toward favoring "good character" in office, a traditional orientation in political theory that had privileged the well-born, not to say the rich. In his analysis, politics is about benefiting the largest number among the population, principally, the large body of the *popolo*. Thus he advises political leaders, when faced with favoring either "the great" in a community—those who love to command and oppress—or "the people"—those who desire neither to be commanded nor to be oppressed—to favor the people. Their desires are more "decent," he says—*onesto*, he writes in Italian, a cognate of the Latin *honestum* or honorable, noble—but perhaps more important, "a prince can never secure himself against a hostile people, as they are too many" (P 9, 39).

In the *Discourses* Machiavelli's reasoning in "favor" of the populist democratic element in a community is even stronger.[5] He argues in this work that a political order is better served if the "guard of freedom" is established among the people rather than among the great. The desire of the people, as he sees it, is more conducive to a free and civil way of life, the spirit of living peaceably and secure among one's neighbors, unthreatened by violence or dispossession. The primary sort of people that the bulk of a society needs to worry about being violent or dispossessing them are the "great," those whose principal desire, whose fundamental political passion, is the impulse to "command and oppress." To counterbalance this impulse, Machiavelli reasons, it is better to empower the people in a constitutional arrangement with offices or institutions that will protect them from the great; this is what the term "guard of freedom" refers to.

The deepest reason, though, for this inclination to prefer the popular element in a political body is that "the multitude is wiser and more constant than a prince." Machiavelli is fully aware, as the classical tradition holds and relates in numerous particulars, of the fickleness and violence of mobs, a characterization that informs a long tradition of political reflection. Yet after weighing all sides of the matter, he concludes that "a people that commands and is well ordered will be stable, prudent, and grateful no otherwise than a prince, or better than a prince, even one esteemed wise" (D I.58.3). Moreover, a people is a good judge of the oratory of leaders. Machiavelli holds that a candid, brave orator who speaks with decision and dignity to a people will earn their respect (D 58.4, 54.1). Here he contrasts his own view of the matter implicitly with Cicero, himself famous for his oratory: "For a licentious and tumultuous people can be spoken to by a good man, and it can easily be returned to the good way; there is no one who can speak to a wicked prince, nor is there any remedy other than steel" (D I.58.4). This appears to be the maturation of Machiavelli's earlier point that "nothing is so apt to check an excited multitude as is the reverence for some grave man of authority who puts himself against it" (D I.54.1). Machiavelli's populism or democratic inclinations do not arise—as should now be perfectly clear—from an idealistic notion of the goodness of people or from a love of equality. He himself favors and instructs political leaders to favor the people because, as the famous dictum has it, this is *less bad* than the alternatives. To accomplish this, he needs political leaders not to flatter the multitude but to speak to them candidly—indeed, he suggests that the evident bravery of doing so will impress the people. Because the ends of politics are not in principle controversial, because they consist in the satisfaction of widespread material needs, the greatest danger to their satisfaction is not the moral vulgarity of the large body of the people but the unlicensed desire for rapacity and cruelty so characteristic of ruling classes always and everywhere. His wish that leaders speak truthfully to the people is not informed, as should now be clear, by high expectations of the morality or decency of either the speakers or the audience, but rather from the expectation that the audience is sufficiently capable of understanding the elementary realities of political life, should they be offered the opportunity to do so.

Machiavelli's ethic of communication, is thus built on what might be called a low but solid expectation of the possibilities of political life. He sees debates about justice, however well-intentioned, as aiming too high or mistaking the true possibilities—indeed, the necessities—of political life. In general, the love of nobility that characterizes the political tradition against which he sets himself misleads political leaders and even encourages them to expect too much of themselves or to hope for too perfect a combination of morality and political accomplishment. This is the background to his famous dubiousness about the merit of political morality, of which his celebration of deception is a critical element. That celebration, moreover, must be set against his equally profound though less notorious sense that political leaders will do best who speak with some gravity and candor to the large body of the people. In assessing Machiavelli's communication ethics, one must conclude by wondering what to make of his own advice, his own candid instruction to would-be leaders—what to make of this communication, through writing, by such an adviser to political leaders.

Notes

1 For more on Machiavelli's life and thought, the reader should consult Honeycutt (n.d.). For a splendid biography of Machiavelli, see the peerless Viroli (2000).
2 On the Renaissance more generally, see Kristeller (1961).
3 The items in parentheses are references to Machiavelli's works. P designates *The Prince*, D designates *Discourses on Livy*, and FH designates *Florentine Histories*. Each is followed by standard section or chapter and paragraph indications, then by page number of the English translations listed in the references.
4 On Machiavelli's presentation of Scipio and Hannibal in his critique of Xenophon, see Newell (1988).
5 The best account of Machiavelli's populist inclinations is in Zuckert (2017), a welcome correction of and deepening of themes partly explored by McCormick (2011).

References

Bruni, Leonardo. 2001. *History of the Florentine People*. 3 vols. Edited and translated by James Hankins. Cambridge, MA: Harvard University Press.
Honeycutt, Kevin. n.d. "Niccolo Machiavelli." *The Internet Encyclopedia of Philosophy*. Accessed October 1, 2019. https://www.iep.utm.edu/machiave/.
Kristeller, Paul Oskar. 1961. *Renaissance Thought: The Classic, Scholastic, and Humanist Strains*. New York: Harper and Row.
Machiavelli, Niccolò. 1988. *Florentine Histories*. Translated by Laura F. Banfield and Harvey C. Mansfield Jr. Princeton, NJ: Princeton University Press, 1988.
———. 1996. *Discourses on Livy*. Translated by Harvey C. Mansfield Jr. and Nathan Tarcov. Chicago: University of Chicago Press.
———. 1998. *The Prince*. Translated by Harvey C. Mansfield. Chicago: University of Chicago Press.
McCormick, John P. 2011. *Machiavellian Democracy*. Cambridge, UK: Cambridge University Press.
Newell, Waller R. 1988. "Machiavelli and Xenophon on Princely Rule: A Double-Edged Encounter." *Journal of Politics* 50, no. 1: 108–130.
Viroli, Maurizio. 2000. *Niccolò's Smile: A Biography of Machiavelli*. New York: Farrar, Straus and Giroux.
Zuckert, Catherine. 2017. *Machiavelli's Politics*. Chicago: University of Chicago Press.

4

Toward an Idealistic Political Theory of American and Global Politics in an Era of Ascendant Incivility

Benjamin Voth

The Critical Problem in Political Communication Ethics

There is a widespread understanding among political commentators that both in the United States and in the world abroad there is a shared concern about declining ethics in political communication.[1] In any thorough study of history there is an observable recurring pattern of ascendant idealism versus descendant cynicism. The challenge in current circumstances is how to engineer a more ideal outcome. Despite the current malaise, there is a real possibility and probability of (1) apprehending a moral and ethical schema for better political communication, (2) applying that schema to better understand and improve political communication, and (3) realizing a better world consequent to better political communication.

Toward a Better Schema: Discursive Complexity

The most globally well-known distillation of that American political project known as the US Constitution is the First Amendment.[2] Within those five civil rights spelled out in the first of all amendments is freedom of speech. The freedom of speech is both textually and as a matter of communication practice a beacon of ethics in our theoretically troubled times. Postmodern theorists of communication often ask: What is truth? This is offered as an academic death knell to ethics. Despite the pedantic pattern of late-twentieth-century offerings in political communication ethics, the articulation of freedom of speech in 1791 has had two hundred years in effective praxis alongside a profound and deep global admiration among humanity's most oppressed. The First Amendment's distillation of Jesus's profound observation, recorded in the Gospel of John—"the truth will set you free"— remains a practical basis for discerning truth from untruth. That which is untrue must be protected by censorship and systems of propaganda. What is true does not need such systemic defense. This simple guide can be practically described as discursive complexity: the capacity of a group, society, or even an individual to both entertain and allow multiple points of view to be expressed. The more discursive complexity we have, the better. The less discursive complexity we have, the worse for us all. Here I appropriate a simple yet empirical ethical yardstick for measuring political communication: To what extent are those touched by a given piece of political communication free to challenge and interrogate the rhetorical artifact? This question can establish at both informal and formal levels a test for ethical quality. The American precept of free speech is one of the most validated theories of communication ever offered in human history. The ability to freely challenge political utterances has for more than two hundred years elevated a small band of rebels against monarchy to the third most populous nation on the earth, with the largest economy and all-volunteer military every achieved in human history. Moreover, the adversaries of the United States who have most committed themselves to an innate political rejection of this notion have committed some of the most profound human ethical atrocities in history. Such atrocities in the twentieth century include, in order of magnitude: communism, Shinto supremacism, and Nazi fascism. Communism killed no fewer than 150 million people across the world in the twentieth century. Shinto supremacism as politically engineered in Japan killed 10 to 14 million people,[3] and German Nazi supremacism killed more than 10 million people. All three of these political projects made a specific and profound point of rejecting American notions of free speech and relying on systemic propaganda to suppress political truths and consequent ethical misconduct within their political ranks. Many more ethical case studies in genocide can and should be explored to further validate the political communication theory of discursive complexity.[4]

Encountering Our Rhetorical Problem: Postmodernism and Social Fracture

Most scholars and students will readily recognize the First Amendment and its high-value kernel of free speech. Moreover, we tend to agree that it is a social good and worthy of admiration and respect. However, many scholars remain skeptical of its ongoing reformative power in light of the tremendous political disjunctions that prevail not only in spite of the First Amendment but perhaps because of it. After all, the filibuster in the US Congress is an imperative political tool that largely guarantees the probability of frustrating and aggravating federal government shutdowns when Congress cannot agree in the course of political debate to approve an annual budget. More broadly, the American political system presently is so shrill and divisive that more free speech seems a likely barrier to improvement rather than a therapeutic aid. My colleague and friend, Dr. Robert Denton, commented on and diagnosed this condition in our 2017 book, *Social Fragmentation and the Decline of American Democracy*.[5] The path forward in the twenty-first century is to gain a better intellectual mapping of where we are with regard to political intransigence and frustration. Put simply, we are nowhere near both historical and even relatively contemporaneous levels of political frustration. Of course the inception of the United States under the ideal rubric of the Constitution was bound by political cynicism and raw violence. Duels that pitted gunslinging politicians in mortal combat in order to settle political disputes were not uncommon. More contemporaneously, the year 1968 stands out as an extraordinary era of profound anger and cynicism. The assassinations of Robert Kennedy and Martin Luther King Jr. and major riots in dozens of American cities made that presidential election year a nightmare compared to our present situation. These observations should not cause us to accept as benign our present frustrated state. In fact, we ought to examine with some intellectual penetration how these miasmic moments were overcome within the American model.

Here again, the path forward is simple and clear. Our theoretical and methodological approaches to politics are dominated by an ethic of cynicism. Pessimism is now doctrinaire as a matter of political communication study. A recent study of political affiliation among communication professors at the top forty universities in the United States found that there were 108 faculty members of one political party and not a single faculty member registered to the opposing political party.[6] It does not matter which political party was preferred in this 2018 study; if the other party had enjoyed the same status, we would still recognize the same intellectual condition: propaganda. The raw cynicism and pessimism among those practicing communication study are profoundly disconcerting. Communication studies was one of only two disciplines found to have not a single opposing member of the two major political parties in the United States. Not a single discipline among more than a dozen reviewed was found to have a preponderance of members from the opposing party. The average disparity among all academic disciplines was roughly 20 to 1. This is both profoundly good news and profoundly bad news. The good news is that almost *any* fundamental reconsideration of communication theory as presently understood is likely to improve our condition of discursive complexity. The bad news is that the entrenched ideological forces not only ensure but increase bad conditions for any individual student or faculty member. Systemic ostracism and tactics such as doxing generally await individuals resisting the present order.

Some intellectual mapping of how we came to be in such an absurd academic position in political communication theory is important for any effort to ameliorate this ethically toxic environment. The year 1968 does stand out as a rather profound moment in US political history, as already noted. Approximately fifty years ago, the advent of activist notions of pessimism began to displace the political project of American idealism. King, who was assassinated on a Memphis balcony on April 4, was the leader of a "Beloved Community." His idealistic, integrated view of race relations was already being displaced by an Afro-pessimist view of race relations known as black power.[7] Additional pessimist views of geopolitical relations began to romanticize socialism and communism and demonize the American military as the incorrigible opponent of the Good. Within our economy, enviro-pessimist notions of poison and overpopulation began to displace the ideas of economic growth, prosperity, and human thriving. The essential practical political strategy text for these interconnected notions of pessimism is Saul Alinsky's *Rules for Radicals*. At its theoretical heart, Alinsky's tome on tactics for radicals supposes that all aspects of American idealism can be overcome by simply overloading any idealist with an adherence to principle that becomes self-defeating. All idealists should be intensively taunted in a cynical public manner designed to "expose" the idealist as a fraud and unworthy of public respect. This rather simple theory was elaborated into a methodology of twelve rules detailed by Alinsky. The book remains at the heart of most pessimist projects dedicated to decimating the American political experiment in human freedom. The empirical success of the book and its adherents is difficult to deny.

Nonetheless, it is also difficult to deny that America and the world have rebounded from perilous conditions like these with far fewer resources than we presently find ourselves with in twenty-first-century society. First, we should familiarize ourselves with Alinsky's precepts, not with the goal of adhering to them but with an informed desire to overcome them. Second, we must adopt our own code of response. Put simply, we must become singularly cynical about cynicism. We must understand our American ideals well, and in a complementary manner, we must prepare to be cynical of cynics in a way that overloads their system of praxis. In so doing, we can achieve the same implosion of the pessimist model that was achieved after 1968 with the American idealist model.

In an effort to model and enact the precepts offered here, in the next section I present a rhetorical analysis of American political communication designed to resurrect dead moral clarity in our political discourse and juxtapose it against the cynical traditions of political communication as offered by twentieth-century scholars. In performing this study of political communication, I hope to establish a scholarly pattern that can be followed by other scholars and students of political communication to heighten discursive complexity and improve the ethical conditions of all of humanity.

The Political Communication of President Woodrow Wilson versus President Calvin Coolidge

Rankings of American presidents suggest that Woodrow Wilson is among the top ten greatest presidents in all of American history.[8] Wilson was president for eight years, from 1913 to 1921. He is considered a foundational progressive in American politics. His reification as one of America's greatest presidents speaks to the corruption of our intellectual life, which is designed to cynically denigrate the enduring idealism of the United States found in the Constitution and replace it with rejectionist politics affectionately termed "progressivism." The term should be ironically understood—we should cynically understand its cynical application to Wilson—as an affirmation of one the most regressive notions of human politics: racism. Though racism received a considerable boost from intellectual science heroes such as Charles Darwin, who titled his seminal work *Origin of Species by Means of Natural Selection, or the Preservation of Favoured Races in the Struggle for Life*—racism is in fact a diminution of human worth as a practical matter of political idealism. Wilson thoroughly endorsed racism as a necessary political practice within American governance and one that would lead to "progress" for our society.[9] The federal workforce was explicitly segregated on the basis of race by Wilson because he believed whites would better advance the human condition as part of his larger belief in progressivism. As president of Princeton, Wilson told a black applicant to the school that it was "altogether inadvisable for a colored man to enter Princeton." Wilson's academic textbook *A History of the American People* described Reconstruction-era efforts to free the South from "the incubus of that ignorant and often hostile" black vote. The efforts to sanitize and isolate Wilson's cynical racist assumptions about America are rooted in equally cynical contemporary efforts to play politics with American presidential rhetoric and valorize through subversive means the inherently racist notions of progressivism that continue to the present day.

Standing in sharp and direct contrast to President Wilson is President Calvin Coolidge who was president from 1923 to 1929. I sometimes joke with undergraduates by asking them how many have visited the Coolidge memorial in Washington, DC. Inevitably someone raises a hand, and I must explain that there is no such memorial to Coolidge.[10] This hiding of Coolidge and exalting of men like Wilson and Franklin Delano Roosevelt is part of a painful ideological suppression designed to create an arc of history in the direction of the blue privilege[11] practiced broadly in academia. Coolidge is ranked number 28 among 45 American presidents in the most recent ranking by scholars.[12] Coolidge's Christian humanist upbringing at Amherst College laid the foundation for an exceptional American idealist to begin reversing the "progressivism" of Wilson and defend the dignity of African Americans in the United States. Coolidge's political rhetoric on race in America is remarkable and stands as an ethical beacon of discursive complexity within our intellectual webs of deceit attached to contemporary studies of political rhetoric. Several key incidents of Coolidge's political communication demonstrate the American ethical model.

Coolidge made a point of speaking at Howard University in 1924 for the commencement ceremonies not long after being elevated from the vice presidency in August 1923. Howard was and is arguably the preeminent historically black college or university in the United States. His remarks there stand as a stark clarion call against the outrageous racism of Wilson:

> The nation has need of all that can be contributed to it through the best efforts of all its citizens. The colored people have repeatedly proved their devotion to the high ideals of our country. They gave their services to the war with the same patriotism and readiness that other citizens did. The propaganda of prejudice and hatred which sought to keep the colored men from supporting the national cause completely failed. The black man showed himself the same kind of citizen, moved by the same kind of patriotism as the white man. They were tempted, but not one betrayed his country. They came home with many decorations, and their conduct repeatedly won high commendation from both American and European commanders.[13]

Coolidge's remarks echoed rhetoric offered before the U.S. Congress in 1923:

> Numbered Among our population are some 12,000,000 Colored people. Under our Constitution their rights are just as sacred as those of any other citizen. It is both a public and a private duty to protect those rights.[14]

Coolidge's remarks stand in sharp contrast to those of South Carolina governor Strom Thurmond, who more than twenty years later in 1947 described Wilson's practice of segregation this way:

> I want to tell you, ladies and gentlemen, that there's not enough troops in the army to force the southern people to break down segregation and admit the nigger race into our theatres into our swimming pools into our homes and into our churches.[15]

Coolidge's stance on race was not strategic, cynical, or manipulative. It was consistent with an idealistic notion of American rights and clearly juxtaposed against the increasingly entrenched racist premises of progressivism. Coolidge's ethical stance on race was clear in public remarks he chose to make against members of his own political party. In 1924 political leaders in New York City demanded that a black man not be allowed to run for public office on the basis of his race. President Coolidge wrote the following letter, published in a Brooklyn paper:

> My dear sir,
>   Your letter is received, accompanied by a newspaper clipping which discussed the possibility that a colored man may be the Republican nominee from one of the New York districts. Referring to this newspaper statement, you say:
>
>> "It is of some concern whether a Negro is allowed to run for Congress anywhere, at any time, in any party, in this, a white man's country. Repeated ignoring of the growing race problem does not excuse us for allowing encroachments. . . ."
>
>   Leaving out of consideration the manifest impropriety of the President intruding himself in a local contest for nomination, I was amazed to receive such a letter. During the war 500,000 colored men and boys were called up under the draft, not one of whom sought to evade it. They took their places wherever assigned in defense of the nation of which they are just as truly citizens as are any others. The suggestion of denying any measure of their full political rights to such a great group of our population as the colored people is one which, however it might be received in some other quarters, could not possibly be permitted by one who feels a responsibility for living up to the traditions and maintaining the principles of the Republican Party.
>   Our Constitution guarantees equal rights to all our citizens, without discrimination on account of race or color. I have taken my oath to support that Constitution. It is the source of your rights and my rights. I purpose to regard it, and administer it, as the source of the rights of all the people, whatever their belief or race. A colored man is precisely as much entitled to submit his candidacy in a party primary, as is any other citizen. The decision must be made by the constituents to whom he offers himself, and by nobody else. You have suggested that in some fashion I should bring influence to bear to prevent the possibility of a colored man being nominated for Congress. In reply, I quote my great predecessor, Theodore Roosevelt: ". . . I cannot consent to take the position that the door of hope—the door of opportunity—is to be shut upon any man, no matter how worthy, purely upon the grounds of race or color."
>   Yours very truly, etc.
>   Calvin Coolidge[16]

Coolidge's American idealism with regard to race in 1924 was light years ahead of many political utterances on race made since that time. The fact that this political communication took place in opposition to the local politics of his own party highlights that Coolidge's rhetoric was not motivated by political pragmatism. This political communication, now almost one hundred years old, indicts contemporary studies of Coolidge that have ignorantly supposed that he was "among America's most racist Presidents."[17] Such appellations reveal a blue privilege bias within our intellectual culture that is cynically committed to perpetuating partisan stereotypes that hurt rather than help race relations. Coolidge's public stances were not without moral effect. Coolidge scholar Amity Shlaes documents a significant decline in lynchings during the presidential era of Coolidge. According to *Historical Statistics of the United States: From Colonial Times to the Present* (1975), there were fifty-one racial lynchings reported in the United States in 1922 after reaching a peak of seventy-seven in 1919. By the time Coolidge left office in 1929, reported lynchings had declined to an average seven per year. There were nearly 90 percent fewer lynchings in the United States at the end of Coolidge's presidency than there were at the height of the Wilson presidency.

The lessons of this political communication study are profound, discernible, and actionable: (1) a forgotten hero of the American presidency was a champion advocate against racism, (2) America is not intrinsically committed to racism, as theorized by contemporary Afro-pessimist scholars, and (3) rediscovering "lost" history can enable a true path forward on moral questions such as racism today. Saul Alinsky provided the theoretical pretext for much of our contemporary political tactics, which so often aim to silence sources rather than adding to a conversation. In the current Alinsky-fueled era of censorship in the form of removing names and taking down statues, the discursive complexity model argues radically that we should rather supplant current rhetorical shortcomings with "forgotten" figures. These figures have been deliberately forgotten by our cynical Alinsky-driven intellectual culture in order to cripple the American political system. Coolidge is not alone as a resurrecting figure. Great leaders on the question of race who have been forgotten include Harry Hosier, James Meredith, and James Farmer Jr. These men span American history with incredible idealistic political communication that should be given the same kind of attention given here to President Coolidge. Similarly, we should take a clearer look at women, who are more easily overlooked in history. Great women like Sojourner Truth, Fannie Lou Hamer, and Lula Farmer can provide as great or greater illumination in this moral cause than men. We need to take a theoretically strategic view of the current culture of political cynicism and look for the figures who allow us to be cynical about cynicism and resurrect American political ideas as articulated in discursive complexity.

Operationalizing an Ethical Theory of Political Communication

Unfortunately, human societies are prone to ideological reductionism, leading to propaganda. The systemic removal of ideal figures in American political communication and their replacement with figures of cynicism requires a renaissance of diligence to reverse this course. There must be a systemic and sustained reversal of our intellectual culture, which seeks to tell a dystopian story of America in favor of a cynical Platonic Republic, in which freedom will be the narrow vale and experience of an elite, privileged few, rather than the dramatic expansion to millions of a life of freedom in the United States. Several intellectual precepts need to be embraced to improve our ethical condition both in the United States and globally.

1. A Renunciation of Secular Privilege

One of the enduring Jacobin precepts undermining American idealism is secular privilege. Secular privilege is the intellectual notion that reality is best understood from a secular point of view. To be secular is to view reality as inherently without theology. Put more directly and in plain language: God has no role in our thinking. The idea that discourse must be conducted without reference to religion is a praxis that has gained dominance within public education and higher education in the United States. Sociologically, the growth of a group recognized as "the nones" is focused among young people receiving the most contemporaneous education. Of course theology is a profound source of idealism that suggests human resources exist beyond the limits of our individual experiences. The revocation of secular privilege should not be conflated with a notion that individuals cannot choose to be secular in their views. It does require that we acknowledge as a community of knowledge that we do not require the shedding or exclusion of theological thought in public reasoning. Theological reasoning is predominant globally and is increasing rather than decreasing in Europe and much of the United States. There is in fact a profound global demographic trend toward belief in God and against agnosticism. Becoming comfortable with this view requires finding fault with one of the central cynical assumptions of secular privilege: religious people are especially intolerant. This slur against religious persons is without empirical foundation. In fact, the most secular intellectual paradigm—communism—is the most deadly human practice of politics in history. Moreover, with regard to the ongoing problem of genocide, the religious Muslim, Christian, Jew, or Hindu is more likely to be a target of extermination than a secular individual. The ongoing war against all religions in China today is a clear clarion call on this moral point. That war is conducted in full deference to the pathological hatred of religion held by cult leader Mao Tse-tung. The claim that the "extermination of religion" will liberate the human mind is traceable to violent fantasies of the French Jacobins and detectable in a wide range of more recent violent incidents, including anti-Semitic attacks in Pittsburgh, anti-Christian attacks in Charlottesville, and anti-Muslim attacks led by groups like ISIS. Religious communities can easily navigate interfaith dialogues toward greater discursive complexity. Here again, the inspiring leadership of Christian men like James Farmer Jr. and Martin Luther King Jr. easily collaborated with Hindu precepts delivered and practiced by Gandhi, debated productively with inspiring Muslim men like Malcolm X, and relied upon the Jewish ethics of martyrs like Mickey Schwerner. Ridding ourselves of the false pretense of "intolerance" as a matter of intellectual bigotry toward those who are religious will open our minds to greater resources of idealism and a capacity to overcome the grip of intellectual cynical gravity. Here again, Coolidge's political rhetoric about Christmas is instructive of how far afield we are from useful optimism and practical ethics: "Christmas is not a time or a season, but a state of mind. To cherish peace and goodwill, to be plenteous in mercy, is to have the real spirit of Christmas."

We need to release ourselves from the false fear that "not everyone is of the same religious persuasion." That is true in every realm of thought—including religion. That cannot and should not prevent any intellectual rally against cynicism and toward idealism from drawing from all productive roots, with discursive complexity as our guide.

When Malcolm X began his departure from the dogmas of Afro-pessimism, he provided this preliminary map of his departure from supporting segregation to cautiously endorsing racial integration as espoused by King and Farmer:

> I say again that I'm not a racist, I don't believe in any form of segregation or anything like that. I'm for the brotherhood of everybody, but I don't believe in forcing brotherhood upon people who don't want it. Long as we practice brotherhood among ourselves, and then others who want to practice brotherhood with us, we practice it with them also, we're for that. But I don't think that we should run around trying to love somebody who doesn't love us.[18]

Malcolm X's renunciation of segregation based on race was a renunciation of his former position, stated in a debate with James Farmer Jr. at Cornell University in 1962.[19] In the following week, Malcolm's apparent break with the Black Muslim movement led to his being assassinated in New York City. The interfaith friendship of Farmer and Malcolm X nonetheless positively altered Malcolm's Afro-pessimist view of America and enabled him to begin advocating for a constructive American solution to racism. This ethical transition in political communication points to similar opportunities today.

2. Affirmation of Idealist-Based Empirical Economic Education

The popularity of socialism among American college students is one of the most plainly pathological convictions to arise in the past twenty-five years. Economic pessimism is an important theoretical premise, unleashed by radicals like Alinsky fifty years ago against our free market system. Neo-Marxist terms such as "capitalism" and "socialism" are freely transacted in communication as polarized moral valances. American socialist Bernie Sanders is among the most popular politicians in America today because of a false pessimistic vision of American and global economics. This transition is taking place in the midst of the largest reduction in poverty in human history. Tens of millions of people are being lifted out of poverty and into reasonable economic conditions by the conditions of freedom in economics engineered by the American model. This empirical reality is denied by a strong percentage of American college students, cynically led by an academy dominated by socialist-sympathizing faculty. Because students falsely believe that the American market is the cause of inequity and poverty, millions of people are being suspended in needless economic suffering as they await the complete collapse of the worst economic system devised since the Enlightenment: communism. The plain suffering and abuse evident in socialist communities like Venezuela do not permeate an intellectual culture dedicated to proving the faulty conviction that American economic practices are unfair and cruel to humanity. Among the most absurd warrants in communication analysis today is the celebration of political rhetoric like that offered by Senator Sanders, which falsely asserts that the government can reasonably pay for almost any conjured desire of the public. Socialist features of political argument are given positive reviews while American business models are demonized and tagged as hurtful to the public.

3. Rejection of Ecological Pessimism

One of the most actively deadly paradigms of communication analysis is the pathological notion that humanity is killing the earth. Since the time of Thomas Malthus and beyond, Platonic intellectuals have spun up dystopian fantasies of how the ecology cannot sustain humanity much longer. Our ecological vulnerability requires a dramatic surrender of human freedom in favor of self-selected philosopher kings who will guide us back to ecological abundance. Empiricism is the enemy of these tall tales. Among the more contemporary examples of these dystopian fantasy themes are Rachel Carson's *Silent Spring* and Paul Ehrlich's *Population Bomb*. Both academic tomes falsely portended the probable extinction of humanity due to economic development. Carson's anti-pesticide screed remains arguably one of the deadliest fantasies of our day. Mosquito-borne diseases like malaria continue to kill more than one million people every year.[20] This happens in deference to Carson's unethical rhetorical demonization of DDT—a pesticide effective in reducing and eliminating malaria in much of the world. Arguably, this ongoing permission to allow malaria to kill so many is excruciatingly racist. Africa is maintained as a rhetorical ecological museum wherein we may observe the more "ideal and progressive" world free of pesticidal constraints on insect-based killing. The passive killing of millions of Africans by refusing to allow intensive aerial spraying is unethical and inhumane. More recently, Ehrlich's false warnings about there being "too many people" on the planet made the loss of human life a passive social good for social engineers. Whether through starvation or disease, in the 1970s and 1980s our intellectual leaders became passive about vectors of human death because they falsely believed that the "carrying capacity" of the earth was being exceeded and human death was not only necessary but useful. Ehrlich's predictions are plainly and empirically false. His science about food supplies was defeated by dramatic human innovations such as genetically modified grain—a product also now being demonized by pseudo-scientists. Arguably one of the greatest lifesavers in history was Bourlaug's genetic modifications of wheat, which allowed the global food supply to be dramatically increased and turned highly populated nations like India into food exporters instead of food importers as predicted by the ecological pessimism of Ehrlich.

Climate change is the contemporary scientific certitude determined to blunt human progress and allow for the engineering of human suffering. False claims of deforestation are plainly contradicted by empirical evidence of forest expansion encouraged by the plant growth stimulation provided by CO_2. The world is experiencing record crop yields despite increasingly disproven scientific theories that a warmer earth will destroy all life. We find ourselves on this topic within a perilous ethic of low discursive complexity—anyone who questions these threat allegations is publicly referenced as a "denier"—an inappropriate allusion to Holocaust denial that trivializes that horrible crime by the Nazis. More specifically, the demand that no contrary evidence be allowed is intrinsically antithetical to the essential nature of science. An important principle of scientific study is that results are in fact falsifiable. Scientific studies of warming show that warmer temperatures have saved millions of human lives because cold kills many more people than excess heat.[21] Individuals are seven times as likely to die from cold weather as warm weather. Allowing discursive complexity into our discussions of climate change will improve not only the science surrounding the question but the more pervasive human condition.

Rethinking Political Communication Through Idealistic Empiricism

Idealism as a model can often lead to the intellectual accusation of wishful thinking. Individuals and groups can simply wish they are better off than they actually are. This is described as a lack of realism. Realistic idealism as a theoretical center recognizes this risk and utilizes empiricism to organize our understanding of an answer to which political communication is most ethical. Two prominent idealist empiricists stand out as examples of this approach: Stephen Pinker and Hans Rosling. Both professors demonstrate that idealism is both practical and verifiable.

Pinker's research makes the compelling case that the worst aspects of human existence—war, murder, crime, genocide, and disease—are all on demonstrable declines for the global human family. Understanding this reality is not a prerequisite to dismissing threats or the disingenuous rhetoric that often drives the most undesirable of human behaviors—violence. In fact, Pinker's empirical approach can help us understand local interruptions to this global trend. His empiricism can also help us better understand how to accentuate and even accelerate these positive trends for humanity. Pinker is a cognitive psychologist who sees tremendous positive potential in humanity from his secular vantage point. His most recent book, *Enlightenment Now: The Case for Reason, Science, Humanism, and Progress*, illuminates how the intellectual habits of the Enlightenment contribute to positive human outcomes. The book follows his scholarly tradition of defending optimism. The *New York Times Review of Books* provided this summary:

> Much of the book is taken up with evidence-based philosophizing, with charts showing a worldwide increase in life expectancy, a decline in life-shattering diseases, ever better education and access to information, greater recognition of female equality and L.G.B.T. rights, and so on—even down to data showing that Americans today are 37 times less likely to be killed by lightning than in 1900, thanks to better weather forecasting, electrical engineering and safety awareness.[22]

This highlights how we as communication scholars can utilize empiricism to document a better world. The wider dissemination of information through freedom of speech allows all of humanity to make better and safer choices that minimize harms. Pinker's work is a good model for our own.

A great researcher who unfortunately passed away in 2017, Hans Rosling is another excellent model of idealistic empiricism. He was a Swedish physician, academic, and statistician who was largely unsurpassed in his capacity to make data illuminating and visually compelling. His TED Talks demonstrated rather forcefully and empirically that the human condition is improving, along the same lines described by Pinker. We should continue the type of work pioneered by Rosling to make the case for how the world gets better. His specific ability to localize global data and help us see how distinct regions were doing better or worse in terms of economic poverty or life expectancy have profound political implications for our pursuit of the ethical condition known as discursive complexity.

Within the United States there exists a compelling constitutional clue about what forms of political communication are most ethical and desirable: federalism. The relatively unique American notion that each of the fifty states is relatively free to design autonomous political systems for its residents provides a provocative empirical gateway for testing political communication. Which states have the best political conditions? Much like our own local search for the best restaurants, we can look in the state parking lots to see where all the cars are. Federalism helps us answer where the best politics are. On the global level, human migration tells us where political situations are good and where political situations are bad. At present, arguably the best state in the United States is Texas. More people migrate to Texas than any other. Within the realms of choosing, they are preferring to live in the political order of Texas. Reciprocally, states like New York and Illinois are losing residents, who apparently do not like the politics. In global politics, the United States continues to dwarf all nation-states as the most ideal. The most recent surveys show more than 150 million people would have liked to come the United States in 2019.[23] While this desperate desire is infused with one of the most contentious political issues of our time—immigration—it also tells us about American politics and the surrounding global reception to our national practice. We are the global ideal. Empiricism helps verify this fact. Canada is the second most popular choice and attracts less than one-third as many people as the United States. Human migration is a clear measure for discerning politically ideal circumstances. This can be observed at the city, state, or national levels, and we ought to use this empiricism to build new theories of political communication that emphasize the ethical.

Life expectancy is another important empirical measure, one that is uniquely disconcerting for American politics and the ethics of our current political communication theory. For the first time in almost one hundred years, life expectancy declined for three consecutive years, from 2015 to 2017. Climbing life expectancy is one of the hallmarks of global idealism. As an example, Rwanda has powerfully recovered from genocide by increasingly the average life expectancy from around twenty-seven at the height of the genocide in 1994 to a life expectancy of sixty-four in 2019. This is among the highest on the continent and a profound testament to the emergence of a more ideal and ethical praxis of politics. The decline in life expectancy in the United States and Great Britain is one of the more disconcerting ethical matters of our time. Apparently there are two major explanations for this decline: suicide and opioid abuse. The premature deaths of Americans are dramatically impacting our life expectancy. Some of the most profound locations of these impacts are Ohio and Kentucky, where the economically oppressed coal-mining areas and larger rust belt regions are besieged by a sense of despair and hopelessness. These dramatic health impacts occur in spite of and perhaps because of the largest change to the US medical system since the introduction of Medicare: the Affordable Care Act. Despite more than ten to twenty million people gaining health care insurance since the passage of the act, American life expectancy began to decline as this law began to take effect. The refusal of our intellectual ruling classes to deeply critique the ACA displays a painful and deadly recalcitrance regarding how the law may have deformed health insurance in a way that discourages individuals from going to the doctor. Insurance deductibles and premiums have increased dramatically. The conditional expansion of Medicaid within some states appears to correlate with the opioid crisis. In any case, the lack of serious probing analysis of health impacts worse than AIDS and a great number of other medical crises points to a collapse of the discursive complexity necessary to heal the American condition. The effort to leave the ACA as a settled political "success" for the blue privilege community of academics is killing red state America. This is an unethical condition that needs research and deliberation.

Conclusion

This chapter argues for an operational redesign of political communication theory that can bring a refreshing air of critical thinking to the study of American and even global politics. Students and colleagues who decide to take up this model of discursive complexity as a moral compass should understand and work upon the following precepts:

1. We must become cynical about cynicism and build ideal models of communication.
2. We can find models of communication in "forgotten" history of political communication.
3. We must recognize and overcome the precepts of the Alinsky model for American political deconstruction.
4. We can utilize empiricism to resist various intellectual strands of political pessimism dampening human opportunity.
5. We can utilize the constitutional premise of federalism to verify dimensions of political contrast that describe the most beneficial political circumstances for humanity.

6. We must personally adhere to an ethic of discursive complexity wherein we encourage and respect dissent to our ideas and research while refusing to surrender to a community of silence when Jacobins become overzealous in seeking cynical political ends through doxing and group intimidation.

If we adhere to these precepts, we can rebuild an American political communication model that is both civil and ethical. More than two hundred years of American history demonstrate the enduring resilience of the model and provide the compelling empirical backdrop for renewing the American dream from generation to generation.

Notes

1 Following is a sample of sources citing these data: "Feeling of Alienation among Americans Reaches Highest Point on Record," Harris Poll, January 20, 2015, accessed July 1, 2019, https://theharrispoll.com/this-years-midterm-elections-brought-a-bitterly-fought-campaign-across-many-states-soon-after-these-elections-the-harris-poll-revisited-a-long-term-trend-looking-at-how-alienated-americans-feel-th/; Carroll Doherty, "7 Things to Know about Polarization in America," Pew Research, June 12, 2014, accessed July 1, 2019, https://www.pewresearch.org/fact-tank/2014/06/12/7-things-to-know-about-polarization-in-america/; Justin McCarthy, "Majority in U.S. Still Say Moral Values Getting Worse," Gallup, June 2, 2015, accessed July 1, 2019, https://news.gallup.com/poll/183467/majority-say-moral-values-getting-worse.aspx; Mark Gerzon, *The Reunited States of America* (Oakland, CA: Berret Kochler Publishers, 2016); and Andrew Eil, "Disdain: The Root of Our Diseased Politics," *Observer*, May 3, 2016, accessed July 1, 2019, https://observer.com/2016/05/disdain-the-root-of-our-diseased-politics/.

2 Peter Moore, "First Amendment Is the Most Important, and Well Known, Amendment," YouGov, April 12, 2016, accessed July 7, 2019, https://today.yougov.com/topics/politics/articles-reports/2016/04/12/bill-rights.

3 Rudolph Rummel, *Death by Government* (London: Transaction Publishers, 2004); and Rana Mitter, "The World's Wartime Debt to China," *New York Times*, October 17, 2013, accessed July 8, 2019, https://www.nytimes.com/2013/10/18/opinion/the-worlds-wartime-debt-to-china.html.

4 Ben Voth, *The Rhetoric of Genocide: Death as a Text* (London: Lexington, 2014).

5 Robert Denton and Ben Voth, *Social Fragmentation and the Decline of American Democracy* (London: Palgrave Macmillan, 2017).

6 Mitchell Langbert, "Homogenous: The Political Affiliations of Elite Liberal Arts College Faculty," *Academic Questions* (Summer 2018), accessed July 30, 2019, https://www.nas.org/academic-questions/31/2/homogenous_the_political_affiliations_of_elite_liberal_arts_college_faculty.

7 Stokely Carmichael, "Black Power," *Voices of Democracy*, accessed September 22, 2019, https://voicesofdemocracy.umd.edu/carmichael-black-power-speech-text/.

8 Brandon Rottinghaus, "Measuring Obama against the Great Presidents," Brookings Institute, February 13, 2015, accessed July 2, 2019, https://www

.brookings.edu/blog/fixgov/2015/02/13/measuring-obama-against-the-great-presidents/; Jennifer Schuessler, "Woodrow Wilson's Legacy Gets Complicated," *New York Times*, November 29, 2015, accessed July 18, 2019, https://www.nytimes.com/2015/11/30/arts/woodrow-wilsons-legacy-gets-compli cated.html; and Brennan Weiss, "RANKED: The Greatest US Presidents, According to Political Scientists," *Business Insider*, February 18, 2019, accessed July 10, 2019, https://www.businessinsider.com/greatest-us-presidents-ranked-by-politi cal-scientists-2018-2.

9 Schuessler, "Woodrow Wilson's Legacy Gets Complicated."

10 I am pleased to report that this is about to change, as the Coolidge Foundation is seeking to purchase a property in Georgetown to become a center for Coolidge history in the DC area: "Coolidge in Washington," Coolidge Presidential Foundation, accessed July 22, 2019, https://www.coolidgefoundation.org/uncatego rized/coolidge-in-washington/.

11 Blue privilege is a notion of social control rooted in a rhetorical capacity to utilize contradictory symbols to manipulate the public toward ideological ends. This process is described in Ben Voth, "Blue Privilege," *American Thinker*, July 11, 2013, accessed September 22, 2019, https://www.americanthinker.com/arti cles/2013/07/blue_privilege.html.

12 Weiss, "RANKED."

13 Quoted in Kurt Schmoke, "The Little Known History of Coolidge and Civil Rights," *Coolidge Quarterly* 1, no. 3 (November 2016), accessed June 21, 2019, https://coolidgefoundation.org/wp-content/uploads/2017/01/TheCoolidge Quarterly_October2016.pdf.

14 President Calvin Coolidge, First Annual Message to Congress on the State of the Union, December 6, 1923.

15 Quoted in T. Coates (2013). "Bigotry and the English Language," *The Atlantic*, December 3, 2013, accessed February 15, 2020, https://www.theatlantic .com/national/archive/2013/12/bigotry-and-the-english-language/281935/.

16 Cited in David Pietrusza, "Calvin Coolidge and Civil Rights—the Rest of the Story," *The Blaze*, May 16, 2013, accessed June 21, 2019, https://www.theblaze .com/contributions/calvin-coolidge-and-civil-rights-the-rest-of-the-story.

17 Ibram X. Kendi, "The 11 Most Racist U.S. Presidents," *Huffington Post*, May 28, 2017, accessed July 10, 2019, https://www.huffingtonpost.com/ibram-x-kendi/ would-a-president-trump-m_b_10135836.html.

18 Malcolm X, "Speech at Ford Auditorium," Detroit, February 14, 1965, accessed September 22, 2019, https://www.blackpast.org/african-american-history/ speeches-african-american-history/1965-malcolm-x-speech-ford-auditorium/.

19 Ben Voth, *James Farmer Jr.: The Great Debater* (Lanham, MD: Lexington, 2017).

20 Debora MacKenzie, "Malaria May Kill Far More People Than We Thought," *New Scientist*, February 3, 2012, accessed July 10, 2019, https://www.newscientist .com/article/dn21424-malaria-may-kill-far-more-people-than-we-thought/.

21 Doyle Rice, "Study: Cold Kills 20 Times More People Than Heat," *USA Today*, May 21, 2015, accessed July 20, 2019, https://www.usatoday.com/story/ weather/2015/05/20/cold-weather-deaths/27657269/; Antonio Gasparrini et al., "Mortality Risk Attributable to High and Low Ambient Temperature: A Multicountry Observational Study," *The Lancet* 386, no. 9991 (2015): 369–375,

accessed July 20, 2019, https://www.thelancet.com/journals/lancet/article/PIIS0140-6736(14)62114-0/fulltext.

[22] Sarah Bakewell, "Steven Pinker Continues to See the Glass Half Full," *New York Times*, March 2, 2018, accessed July 10, 2019, https://www.nytimes.com/2018/03/02/books/review/steven-pinker-enlightenment-now.html.

[23] Neli Esipova, Anita Pugliese, and Julie Ray, "More Than 750 Million Worldwide Would Migrate If They Could," Gallup, December 10, 2018, accessed July 22, 2019, https://news.gallup.com/poll/245255/750-million-worldwide-migrate.aspx?g_source=link_WWWV9&g_medium=related_insights_tile1&g_campaign=item_245255&g_content=750%2520Million%2520Worldwide%2520Migrate.

Bibliography

Bakewell, Sarah. "Steven Pinker Continues to See the Glass Half Full." *New York Times*, March 2, 2018/ Accessed July 10, 2019. https://www.nytimes.com/2018/03/02/books/review/steven-pinker-enlightenment-now.html.

Carmichael, Stokely. "Black Power." *Voices of Democracy*, Accessed September 22, 2019. https://voicesofdemocracy.umd.edu/carmichael-black-power-speech-text/.

Coolidge, Calvin. First Annual Message to Congress on the State of the Union, December 6, 1923, in Kurt Schmoke, "The Little Known History of Coolidge and Civil Rights," *Coolidge Quarterly* 1, no. 3 (November 2016), accessed June 21, 2019, https://coolidgefoundation.org/wp-content/uploads/2017/01/TheCoolidgeQuarterly_October2016.pdf.

Denton, Robert, and Ben Voth. *Social Fragmentation and the Decline of American Democracy*. London: Palgrave Macmillan, 2017.

Doherty, Carroll. "7 Things to Know about Polarization in America." Pew Research, June 12, 2014. Accessed July 1, 2019. https://www.pewresearch.org/fact-tank/2014/06/12/7-things-to-know-about-polarization-in-america/.

Eil, Andrew. "Disdain: The Root of Our Diseased Politics." *Observer*, May 3, 2016. Accessed July 1, 2019. https://observer.com/2016/05/disdain-the-root-of-our-diseased-politics/.

Esipova, Neli, Anita Pugliese, and Julie Ray. "More Than 750 Million Worldwide Would Migrate If They Could." *Gallup*, December 10, 2018. Accessed July 22, 2019. https://news.gallup.com/poll/245255/750-million-worldwide-migrate.aspx?g_source=link_WWWV9&g_medium=related_insights_tile1&g_campaign=item_245255&g_content=750%2520Million%2520Worldwide%2520Migrate.

"Feeling of Alienation among Americans Reaches Highest Point on Record." Harris Poll, January 20, 2015. Accessed July 1, 2019. https://theharrispoll.com/this-years-midterm-elections-brought-a-bitterly-fought-campaign-across-many-states-soon-after-these-elections-the-harris-poll-revisited-a-long-term-trend-looking-at-how-alienated-americans-feel-th/.

Gasparrini, Antonio, Yuming Guo, Masahiro Hashizume, Eric Lavigne, Antonella Zanobetti, Joel Schwartz, Aurelio Tobias, et al. "Mortality Risk Attributable to High and Low Ambient Temperature: A Multicountry Observational Study." *The Lancet* 386, no. 9991 (2015): 369–375. Accessed July 20, 2019. https://www.thelancet.com/journals/lancet/article/PIIS0140-6736(14)62114-0/fulltext.

Gerzon, Mark. *The Reunited States of America*. Oakland, CA: Berret Kochler Publishers, 2016.

Kendi, Ibram X. "The 11 Most Racist U.S. Presidents." *Huffington Post*, May 28, 2017. Accessed July 10, 2019. https://www.huffingtonpost.com/ibram-x -kendi/would-a-president-trump-m_b_10135836.html.

Langbert, Mitchell. "Homogenous: The Political Affiliations of Elite Liberal Arts College Faculty." *Academic Questions* (Summer 2018). Accessed July 30, 2019. https://www.nas.org/academic-questions/31/2/homogenous_the_political_ affiliations_of_elite_liberal_arts_college_faculty.

MacKenzie, Debora. "Malaria May Kill Far More People Than We Thought." *New Scientist*, February 3, 2012. Accessed July 10, 2019. https://www.newscientist .com/article/dn21424-malaria-may-kill-far-more-people-than-we-thought/.

McCarthy, Justin. "Majority in U.S. Still Say Moral Values Getting Worse." Gallup, June 2, 2015. Accessed July 1, 2019. https://news.gallup.com/poll/183467/ majority-say-moral-values-getting-worse.aspx.

Mitter, Rana. "The World's Wartime Debt to China." *New York Times*, October 17, 2013. Accessed July 8, 2019. https://www.nytimes.com/2013/10/18/opin ion/the-worlds-wartime-debt-to-china.html.

Moore, Peter. "First Amendment Is the Most Important, and Well Known, Amend-ment." YouGov, April 12, 2016. Accessed July 7, 2019. https://today.yougov .com/topics/politics/articles-reports/2016/04/12/bill-rights.

Pietrusza, David. "Calvin Coolidge and Civil Rights—the Rest of the Story." *The Blaze*, May 16, 2013. Accessed June 21, 2019. https://www.theblaze.com/con tributions/calvin-coolidge-and-civil-rights-the-rest-of-the-story.

Rice, Doyle. "Study: Cold Kills 20 Times More People Than Heat." *USA Today*, May 21, 2015. Accessed July 20, 2019. https://www.usatoday.com/story/ weather/2015/05/20/cold-weather-deaths/27657269/.

Rottinghaus, Brandon. "Measuring Obama against the Great Presidents." Brook-ings Institute, February 13, 2015. Accessed July 2, 2019. https://www .brookings.edu/blog/fixgov/2015/02/13/measuring-obama-against-the -great-presidents/.

Rummel, Rudolph. *Death by Government*. London: Transaction Publishers, 2004.

Schmoke, Kurt. "The Little Known History of Coolidge and Civil Rights," *Coolidge Quarterly* 1, no. 3 (November 2016), accessed June 21, 2019, https://coolidge foundation.org/wp-content/uploads/2017/01/TheCoolidgeQuarterly_Octo ber2016.pdf.

Schuessler, Jennifer. "Woodrow Wilson's Legacy Gets Complicated." *New York Times*, November 29, 2015. Accessed July 18, 2019. https://www.nytimes.com/ 2015/11/30/arts/woodrow-wilsons-legacy-gets-complicated.html.

Voth, Ben. "Blue Privilege." *American Thinker*, July 11, 2013. Accessed September 22, 2019. https://www.americanthinker.com/articles/2013/07/blue_privilege .html.

———. *James Farmer Jr.: The Great Debater*. Lanham, MD: Lexington, 2017.

———. *The Rhetoric of Genocide: Death as a Text*. London: Lexington, 2014.

Weiss, Brennan. "RANKED: The Greatest US Presidents, According to Political Sci-entists." *Business Insider*, February 18, 2019. Accessed July 10, 2019. https:// www.businessinsider.com/greatest-us-presidents-ranked-by-political-scien tists-2018-2.

X, Malcolm. "Speech at Ford Auditorium." Detroit, February 14, 1965. Accessed September 22, 2019. https://www.blackpast.org/african-american-history/ speeches-african-american-history/1965-malcolm-x-speech-ford-auditorium/.

5

Civil Religion as an Ethical Foundation for Political Communication

Peter Loge

Those who engage in political communication have an obligation not to undermine, and when possible to promote, the system that allows that communication. Further, political communicators have an obligation to a prophetic version of America's civil religion.

Introduction

We all participate in our national political conversation in one way or another. For most of us that usually means posting what we hope are clever comments on social media and arguing with family at the holidays. For some, including a number of authors in this volume, engaging in our national political dialogue is how they pay the bills (sometimes that includes me). Our national public political commons is crowded and raucous. Everyone in the crowd, everyone adding to the noise, has an obligation to that shared political commons. The social media newbie with four followers has the same responsibility as a president's spokesperson. Just because dump trucks carry more garbage than you do, does not mean it is okay to toss your empty wrapper on the sidewalk. Trash is trash.

We can all more or less agree on what should go in the garbage, even if the rules about recycling and composting can get confusing. The question of ethical political communication is trickier. It is easy to say that lying and bribery are bad, but what about lying to protect someone's safety? Does it matter how big the lie is and how many people are in danger? When does spinning (or explaining something from a favorable angle) become a lie? Can a campaign take money from a developer in exchange for preferential treatment if that money will help defeat an opponent who would sell out to the developer and worse?[1] The list of questions quickly gets longer and tougher.

Rather than try to imagine every scenario and an appropriate solution or attempt to develop a code that is specific enough to be useful and broad enough to be relevant, I suggest that the foundation of political communication ethics should be a prophetic version of American civil religion.

To make this case I argue that the United States (like all countries) is at least as much a rhetorical construction as it is a geography, offer a brief overview of civil religion, explain the faith tradition I have in mind, and demonstrate how it can be applied to contemporary political communication.

Nation as a Rhetorical Construction

We are, in Walter Fisher's (1984) words, *homo narrans*. We are storytellers and sense-makers. Our world is big, complicated, and confusing. We cannot possibly understand all of it, all of the time, from every possible angle. We make sense of this complexity by telling ourselves and each other stories about what is happening and why, and what will therefore likely happen next. Narratives—stories—are "a distinctive and distinctively important means of giving meaning to events" (Lewis 1987, 288).

The objective truth of these stories matters. One cannot tell a story (even a really good story) that gravity makes things fall up rather than down and hope that it will fly. But the story matters a great deal.

Most of what we encounter is less certain than gravity (and for physicists, gravity is far from certain). Most of what we encounter is a lot of things all at once. The chair on which you may be sitting is sometimes a table, a stool, or a coat rack. It is a collection of plastic, metal, or wood, and it is former natural resources and future garbage. But when you sat down you probably only thought "chair." We cannot conceive of everything it could be, and even if we could, we would not have time to say all of it.

Ideas are less fixed than furniture. The chair has a function in a moment regardless of what you call it, and it will remain when you stand up and leave the room. But ideas only have themselves or other ideas to which they can refer; even a Platonic ideal is a perfect idea, not a rock. Events happen and are gone. All descriptions of ideas or events are necessarily only partially true because they only include parts of what is being described. In deciding what *to* call something, we are simultaneously deciding what *not to* call it. All leaving in requires some leaving out. As Kenneth Burke writes, "Even if any given terminology is a *reflection* of reality, by its very nature as a terminology it must be a *selection* of reality; and to this extent it must function as a *deflection* of reality" (in Bizzell and Herzberg, 1990, 1035). This leaving in and out matters because it shapes how we see and respond to our world. As Burke notes, "[M]uch of what we take as observations about 'reality' may be but the spinning out of possibilities implicit in our particular choice of terms" (in Bizzell and Herzberg, 1990, 1035).

Think about this in the context of politics. For example, what is the difference between a death tax and an estate tax? One's estate is taxed when one dies, making both descriptions accurate. But people tend to be angrier about being taxed for dying than they are about estates being taxed, in part because for most of us estates are where people like Bruce Wayne live, not a term for all the stuff one possesses.

A good description of an idea or story about an event has to be true enough to account for reality (gravity matters) but also sound and feel right in accounting for the parts that we cannot easily or comfortably measure, or to which we do not want to draw attention. "The perception of truth," Lewis notes, "depends upon the story as a whole rather than upon the accuracy of individual statements" (1987, 289).

For Burke, one function of rhetoric is a "putting together" or creating an "us" (1962, 546). Rhetoric is a sense-making act that helps us understand who we are individually and as a group. In this light, political reality matters in the context of the story of that reality. Our political reality, who we imagine ourselves to be as a polity, is a description of that polity and our role in it. That rhetorical construction has to sound or feel true but cannot ever be entirely accurate.

It is easy to think about this in the context of your life. For example, you may be reading this for a college or university course (and if not, odds are good you are now or were once a student). Think about your college or university: What is it? It is probably a tax-exempt organization that takes your money in exchange for improving your intellectual ability, providing you with professional and life skills, and helping you get a job that pays more over time than you are paying for school. But it is often much more than that. Colleges and universities have traditions, mascots, and inside jokes. In addition to paying tuition and buying books like this one, you probably also bought a sticker for your (or your parents') car, a T-shirt, or other things that identify you as one of "us." Your school probably has portraits of its presidents and other important leaders hanging in prominent places. There are stories of great alumni from the past, and a story of how the school grew from an idea to its current exalted state (it is always in an exalted state; no school's motto is "Faded Glory," and no brochure brags that it is "not great but still accredited"). You may be in a fraternity or sorority or other organization with its own history, rituals, and apparel. You are part of a description of an idea, and that description of an idea helps you tell the world—and yourself—who you are.

The place needs to be there. It matters that I am writing this at my desk in the Media and Public Affairs building at The George Washington University. This is a physical structure. But it is also more than that. GW is a hippo statue with its own story, a logo, and other rhetorical and narrative elements that give GW meaning beyond the brick and mortar. In some measure, we take our meaning from and give our meaning to the physical place and legal documents that "are" the School of Media and Public Affairs and The George Washington University.[2]

You can apply this thinking to sports (Red Sox Nation), civic organizations (the Rotary), and so on. Rhetoric is constantly putting us together and pulling us apart, reminding us who we are, where we came from, and therefore what we should do next.

Which brings us to the idea of a nation. A nation is not just lines on a map, in part because, like gravity, borders only seem clear when you don't look closely. For example, in 2017 some people in South Carolina learned they were actually residents of North Carolina (WRAL 2018) and the Georgia legislature voted to reopen a one-hundred-year-old border dispute with its neighbor to the north (Niessee 2019). Internationally, the issue of what "counts" as a country is even more complicated. Borders are lines we agree to draw on maps, and maps are images of places. A borderline is an efficient way of saying "your bit stops there and my bit starts here." But there is nothing a priori or fixed about any of it.

We do not sing (or sit out) the national anthem in celebration of a map or because we like the tune, and we do not pledge allegiance to the flag (or sit it out) because we are especially fond of Betsy Ross's aesthetic choices or have a thing for cloth rectangles. We sing and pledge (or not) because of the ideas and actions for which those tunes and colors stand. These actions and ideas are part of a narrative or story that lives through and helps give life to the anthem and flag.

Borders matter, even if they are somewhat imprecise. Among other things, they determine the taxes one pays, the social services available, the type of government one has, and a range of other items big and small. Similarly, anthems, flags, and other symbols matter because they stand in for complex sets of ideas that tell us who we are and what we should do. But they are not themselves meaningful absent something for which they stand. A nation is the story it tells about itself. As people and as "a people" we are our own stories about ourselves. As Wallwork and Dixon write, nations are "imagined as entities possessing a geographic and historical 'reality' that somehow exceeds their human membership" (2004, 22). And as Bruner explains, "national identity is incessantly produced through rhetoric" (2005, 309).

In his article, "In Search of 'the People': A Rhetorical Alternative," Michael McGee argues:

> One begins with the understanding that political myths are purely rhetorical phenomena, ontological appeals constructed from artistic proofs and intended to redefine an uncomfortable and oppressive reality. Such myths are endemic in the human condition and, though technically they represent nothing but a "false consciousness," they nonetheless function as a means

of providing social unity and collective identity. Indeed, "the people" *are* the social and political myths they accept. (1975, 247)

When we talk to each other about the United States, we are telling each other the story of who we are. We implicitly and explicitly remind each other where we came from as a means of explaining where we are, and therefore what we should do next. If America was "conceived in liberty" (Lincoln 1863), then our political moment will be seen as fulfilling or countering that conception, and our next actions must move toward liberty. If on the other hand our nation is based on the "original sin of slavery," then our political conversations will be in the context of redemption. "Make America great again" (a phrase used by Ronald Reagan, Bill Clinton, and others [Dangremond 2018]) implies first that America was once great, second that America is no longer great, and third that "we" can re-create that greatness. The red hat from 2016 with the letters MAGA told a complete and familiar story of someone who fought for or was born to greatness and success, who squandered that success or had it taken away, and who through hard work and moral force returned to greatness. This is about as American a story as one can write (McAdams 2004).

Our American story, like all stories, is necessarily incomplete, and parts of it are made up. But in the context of the explanatory power of the narrative, that is inevitable. The point of the story is not to accurately and completely capture everything at once; the point is to make sense of the present based on an explanation of the past that offers a direction for the future. As Richard Rorty writes, "Stories about what a nation has been and should try to be are not attempts a[t] accurate representation, but rather attempts to forge a moral identity" (1998, 13). The story has to be true to life, or true enough, but it cannot be completely complete and factual.

Think about your university again. The story about your school or alma mater is not entirely accidental. Much of it is an attempt to create an idea of the sort of place it wants to be and the sort of person it wants you to be. Your school was built, in part, to look like what you imagine a college or university should look like. There is likely a quad, or something that passes for a quad.[3] The brochure you got in the mail almost certainly included a picture of someone sitting under a tree and reading. There is nothing essentially "college" about any of this. One can read anywhere (when was the last time you sat under a tree and read?). Yet you bought it, literally and figuratively.

Events happen, and we search for meaning for those events and locate ourselves within that meaning. Enterprising political communicators point to events and say "this means such and such and therefore you must . . ." Advocates, candidates, and commentators describe events and people in ways that make sense; they tell political stories. Descriptions of events—and therefore one's role in those events and what one should do about them—are political acts. As Murray Edelman points out, "It is language about political events and developments that people experience; even events that are close by take their meaning from the language used to depict them. So political language *is* political reality; there is no other so far as the meaning of events to actor and spectators is concerned" (Edelman 1985, 10). The success or failure of these stories, which need to be true enough but cannot be completely accurate, helps determine the success of a candidate or cause.

The success or failure of the story of a nation can similarly determine the success or failure of a nation itself. Hammer draws on Anderson to explain that "nations should be understood as *imagined communities* since the fundamental requirement to make a nation in the modern era is a narrative that tells the members of a community too large to truly know one another to 'image' themselves as a nation" (2010, 269). Similarly, Roof writes, "Myths are the means by which a nation affirms its deepest identities and frames its rationale for political action; they are the elementary, yet profound, stories giving meaning and purpose to the collective life of a people; they evoke the imagination, so crucial to national self-understanding" (Roof 2009, 287).

This national narrative is not fixed, but rather "incessantly negotiated through discourse" in "an ongoing rhetorical process" (Bruner 2002, 1, 7). We are always creating and re-creating meaning, locating ourselves in the context of a complex world around us. To the extent that we can all share an evolving narrative and therefore an image of who we are and who we continue to become, we can call ourselves a nation.

Seen in this light, the question is not whether we should engage in identity politics; we can't not do so because politics is largely about constructing collective and individual identities. The question is which identity or identities we should create.

Civil Religion

The concept of civil religion was first articulated by Jean Jacques Rousseau in the *Social Contract* (1968, 187). A lot of people have spent a lot of time writing about civil religion since then (e.g., Bailey and Linholm 2003; Bellah 1967; Carlson 2017; Gorsky 2017; Liu 2019).[4] Most of that writing has applied to the United States, but some have applied the concept elsewhere as well (e.g., Arnoff 1981).

Robert Bellah popularized civil religion in his 1967 essay, "Civil Religion in America." Bellah opens his essay by stating, "While some have argued that Christianity is the national faith, and others that church and synagogue celebrate only the generalized religion of 'the American Way of Life,' few have realized that there actually exists alongside of and rather clearly differentiated from the churches an elaborate and well-institutionalized civil religion in America" (1967, 1).

As Gorski puts it, Bellah's civil religion "provides a conceptual framework for thinking about the American project" (2017, 16). Bellah writes, "What we have, then, from the earliest years of the republic is a collection of beliefs, symbols, and rituals with respect to sacred things and institutionalized in a collectivity" (1967, 8). Civil religion draws on Judeo-Christian traditions and something outside of or other than ourselves. It is not hostile to a person's view of a creator; it exists alongside private faith (or lack thereof) in a god or gods.

John D. Carlson explains that civil religion "is the moral backbone of our body politic. It is the collective effort to understand the American experience of self-government in light of higher truths and through reference to a shared heritage of beliefs, stories, ideas, symbols, and events. For a country of immigrants and diverse peoples—where national identity is based not upon ethnic or tribal belonging or cultural homogeneity—civil religion provides a shared basis for citizenship" (2017, 1).

Like all faiths, our civil religion has an origin story. We have our sacred documents (the Declaration of Independence, the Constitution) and sacred places (the US Capitol, the Supreme Court, the Lincoln Memorial). We have rituals and holidays, including Thanksgiving, the Fourth of July, Election Day, and presidential inaugurations. And we have our saints and martyrs, George Washington, Abraham Lincoln, John F. Kennedy, and Martin Luther King Jr. among them.

Every four years, hundreds of thousands of people gather on the National Mall in Washington, DC, for the inauguration of the president of the United States. Spectators have no role in the event, the weather is often miserable, and most people get a terrible view. It makes much more sense to watch the event from the sofa at home, where it is warm and you can see and hear the speeches. But like countless others, I have stood in the rain and cold to watch the ritual, once flying cross-country to do so. I wanted to be at those events for the same reason I go to weddings: to bear witness to a sacred ritual recognizing a moment and honoring an ideal for which the ritual stands. I am there because that moment takes meaning from, and gives meaning to, the larger rhetorical construction of which it is a part.

We were conceived as a "shining city upon a hill"[5] and a "new Jerusalem" before the Pilgrims founded the Massachusetts Bay Colony. Fleeing religious persecution and general awfulness, the Pilgrims came to the New World to start afresh in a promised land.

America has faced hardship and "times of trial" and come out stronger (Bellah 1967). Early settlers faced serious hardship, and through belief and hard work overcame all obstacles. The trials of Williamstown, stories of sacrifice, heroism, faith, and triumph, were the first stories of the founding of the republic.[6] We had a civil war in the late 1800s and civil strife in the 1960s. Now in the first third of the twenty-first century we are again facing challenges to our national faith.

Our civil religion is, of course, a myth. It is an explanation, not a box of facts. Like all explanations, it leaves in and leaves out. The explanation expresses a point of view. The "New World" was only new to the Europeans; to those living here it was already home. Religious freedom meant freedom for everyone who was more or less Protestant; Catholics were very much unwelcome in most early colonies. The faiths of the Iroquois, Navajo, and others whose land the Europeans stole were not even worth considering by the early settlers. We then chased Native Americans off their lands or we killed them. Women had no formal or institutional power. The man who wrote the phrase "all men are created equal" owned slaves, and slavery remains our nation's original sin. The list goes on.

Those facts matter. People were treated cruelly and murdered. Much of the awful origins of America continue to echo today. We live the story, not the facts. As Richard Rorty writes, "You cannot urge national political renewal on the basis of descriptions of fact. You have to describe the country in terms of what you passionately hope it will become, as well as what you know it to be now. You have to be loyal to a dream country rather than to the one to which you wake up every morning" (1998, 101). The story is what tells us who we are and what we should do next in ways facts alone cannot; the facts need to be assembled into something coherent, and it is that coherence that matters. As Rorty puts it, "We should face up to unpleasant truths about ourselves, but we should not take those truths to be the last word about chances for happiness, or about our national character. Our national character is still in the making" (1998, 106). To borrow Nikole Hannah-Jones's (2019) example from the *1619 Project*, we need to fly the flag for the country we can become, if not for the country we are.

Our story is as yet unfinished. Sexism remains real and a real problem. Even so, women are increasingly holding positions of power. Racism is baked into every corner of our society. The Stonewall uprising, which many argue was the launch of the modern gay rights movement, happened not that long ago, and members of the LGBTQ community still face legal discrimination. The list of things about which we need to do better goes on from there. But things are better and will continue to get better if we continue to work on them.

Carlson explains that our civil religion "affords a model for forging consensus based upon founding principles that transcend differences in ethnicity, race, gender, religion, and political party. The promise of unity this vision holds out-based on convictions that we are created equal, endowed with certain inalienable rights, and share common dreams and pursuits—is greater than any individual" (2017, 2). This civil religion "gives voice to moral convictions and values beyond crude economic and political interests" (2017, 2).

There is danger in claiming such moral high ground. To borrow from Lincoln, it is easy to slip from being concerned about being on God's side to assuming God is on ours. The former is humble and always working to improve, the latter assumes greatness has already been bestowed and therefore anything the country does is great—the only sin is questioning, because questioning assumes that we may not be perfect, and since perfection is our nature, humility (which assumes one might be wrong) is wrong.

This strain of civil religion may seem dominant, but it is not the only strain of the faith available. Carlson (2017), Gorski (2017), and others argue for a prophetic version of civil religion. In this version, there is a "propensity to instill humility. Its prophetic strands presume a nation can be called to account for its wrongs—even punished, as Lincoln interpreted the woe of war inflicted on North and South alike for the offense of slavery" (2017, 3).

For Gorski, civil religion "is fed by biblical as well as philosophical sources, specifically prophetic religion and civic republicanism" (2017, 18). The prophetic piece of the faith draws on God's demand for "individual righteousness and social justice" (Gorski 2017, 20). Civic republicanism generally holds that "free institutions are inherently fragile and cannot survive very long without a virtuous citizenry to support them" (Gorski 2017, 25). This stands in contrast to what he calls religious nationalism, which is rooted in blood sacrifice and is ultimately apocalyptic (Gorski 2017, 21–23). For Gorski, this vision is a "red-hued canvas in heavy oils, filled with the blood and fire of war and Apocalypse, and replete with battle scenes in which the forces of good and evil square off on land, on sea, and in the air" (2017, 34).

Ethics

The prophetic version of civil religion should serve as a basis for political communication ethics. This has several elements. It is inclusive and rooted in the self-evident truth that all people are created equal. It is fundamentally humble; our ideals may be grand, but they are acted on by people, and sometimes people do stupid and awful things. Finally it is optimistic; we are not doomed by our failures. This vision holds that no person (or nation) is defined by its best or worst moment—America is no more eternally great than it is permanently stained. Ours is, in Gorski's words, a "righteous republic" that is "the dream of a free people governing themselves for the common good" (Gorski 2017, 223). At the core of this vision is "an ethic of social justice and human equality that requires that we be willing to abridge ourselves for the sake of others" (2017, 224).

Because our republic is inhabited and run by people and people are flawed, we need institutions to keep our worst instincts in check and help keep us moving in a better direction. Those institutions include easy access to voting, fair and open elections, a free (if sometimes frustrating) press, institutional checks and balances, and a commitment from all of us to speak and act on behalf of the ideal of the nation over the urges of the moment. These institutions need our rhetorical as well as legal support if they are to work and survive.

This vision is not the same as civility. Calls for greater civil discourse and respect are important. We could all do with a little less shouting and a little more decency. But one can politely lie, and not everyone has earned our respect. We can, and should, be loud, partisan, and rude when the situation demands it. It is worth recalling that Dr. Martin Luther King Jr.'s March on Washington was seen in a much different light in 1963 than it is today (Younge 2013). Dr. King—one of the martyrs of America's civil religion—praised increasing tension and argued against too much civility in his "Letter from a Birmingham Jail" (King 1963).

We should engage in political debate in ways that reflect this prophetic understanding of America. For example, suggesting someone is unqualified or ill-equipped to speak or hold office because of that person's race, faith, gender identity, or anything other than a commitment to a shared American ideal is wrong. Go hard after ideas with which you disagree. Be funny, clever, biting, whatever it takes, but stick to the idea and not the person. Rhetoric that pits people against each other as if the American ideal were a pie to be divided rather than a vision to be shared is wrong.

Do not attack the press as an institution. The press can be a real pain. Reporters are not always nice, some reporters and media outlets are biased, and some reporting is wrong or unfair. But the alternative to a free and open press is worse. Attacks on the press as an institution are wrong.

Do not attack the constitutionally established institutions through which we govern ourselves. It is popular and easy to attack Congress or Washington as abstract villains, made up dragons in a faraway land that only the righteous can slay. That is not how democracy works. Congress is not a dragon, and people who live in Washington are not the dragon's minions. Congress is a collection of people from all over the country who come together to solve shared problems and address shared needs. Washington, DC, is home to nearly three-quarters of a million people, most of whom have nothing to do with politics. Some members of Congress are corrupt or bad at their jobs. Some rules in Congress may be unfair and need fixing. But the institution itself is critical, and the District of Columbia is my home. Communicate in ways that strengthen the institution (or at least that do not undermine it) and do not attack an entire city because you disagree with some of the people who work there.

Those who engage in political communication should acknowledge our flaws and call on all of us to do better. Be civil and respectful when you can, and be loud and rude when necessary to advance the promise of a more perfect union. Strengthen our shared civil religion.

The United States is not a place, a person, or a moment. It is an idea and an ideal. Those who engage in political communication have an ethical responsibility to that idea and to moving us toward that ideal.

Notes

Special thanks to School of Media and Public Affairs undergraduates Hunter Ihrman, Halle Kendall, Conor Kilgore, and Ben Pistora who provided invaluable insights and edits of this chapter.

1 The "dirty hands" problem applied to politics (Miller and Medvic 2002, 25).
2 That I teach at *The* George Washington University, not merely *a* George Washington University, makes this point pretty well.
3 Urban campuses still refer to the idea of a quad with phrases like Emerson College's "campus on the Common."
4 My treatment of civil religion is necessarily short. Those interested in learning more should check out *American Covenant: A History of Civil Religion from the Puritans to the Present* (Gorski 2017).
5 To quote President Reagan quoting Reverend John Winthrop, who used the term in a sermon before arriving in the Massachusetts Bay Colony in 1630: "We shall be as a city upon a hill, the eyes of all people are upon us."
6 I know there was much more to it, including exploitation of Native Americans whose land the settlers stole. The incompleteness of the story is inherent in the story; the point is not to be accurate, the point is to create a compelling narrative and instructive that is "fact based" if not entirely factual.

References

Arnoff, Myron J. 1981. "Civil Religion in Israel." *RAIN* (Royal Anthropological Institute of Great Britain and Ireland) 44: 2.
Bailey, Michael E., and Kristin Linholm. 2003. "Tocqueville and the Rhetoric of Civil Religion in the Presidential Inaugural Addresses." *Christian Scholar's Review* 32, no. 3: 259–278.
Bellah, Robert. 1967. "Civil Religion in America." *Deadalus* 96, no. 1: 1–21.
Bizzell, Patricia, and Bruce Herzberg. 1990. *The Rhetorical Tradition: Readings from Classical Times to the Present.* Boston: Bedford Books.
Bruner, M. Lane. 2002. *Strategies of Remembrance: The Rhetorical Dimensions of National Identity Construction.* Columbia: University of South Carolina Press.
———. 2005. "Rhetorical Theory and the Critique of National Identity Construction." *National Identities* 7, no. 3: 309–327.
Burke, Kenneth. 1962. *A Grammar of Motives and a Rhetoric of Motives.* Cleveland, OH: Meridian Books.

Carlson, John D. 2017. "Losing Our Civil Religion." *Religion & Politics*, September 26. Accessed June 24, 2019. https://religionandpolitics.org/2017/09/26/losing-our-civil-religion/.

Dangremond, Sam. 2018. "Who Was the First Politician to Use 'Make America Great Again' Anyway?" *Town & Country*, November 14. Accessed August 27, 2019. https://www.townandcountrymag.com/society/politics/a25053571/donald-trump-make-america-great-again-slogan-origin/.

Edelman, Murray. 1985. "Political Language and Political Reality." *PS* 18, no. 1: 10–19.

Fisher, Walter R. 1984. "Narration as a Human Communication Paradigm: The Case of Public Moral Argument." *Communication Monographs* 51, no. 1: 1–22.

Gorski, Philip. 2017. *American Covenant: A History of Civil Religion from the Puritans to the Present*. Princeton, NJ: Princeton University Press.

Hammer, Stefanie. 2010. "The Role of Narrative in Political Campaigning: An Analysis of Speeches by Barack Obama." *National Identities* 12, no. 3: 269–290.

Hannah-Jones, Nikole. 2019. "Our Democracy's Founding Ideals Were False When They Were Written: Black Americans Have Fought to Make Them True." *New York Times Magazine*, August 14. Accessed August 27, 2019. https://www.nytimes.com/interactive/2019/08/14/magazine/black-history-american-democracy.html.

King, Martin Luther Jr., Dr. 1963. "Letter from a Birmingham Jail." African Studies Center–University of Pennsylvania. April 16. Accessed July 1, 2019. https://www.africa.upenn.edu/Articles_Gen/Letter_Birmingham.html.

Lewis, William F. 1987. "Telling America's Story: Narrative Form and the Reagan Presidency." *Quarterly Journal of Speech* 73, no. 3: 280–302.

Lincoln, Abraham. 1863. "The Gettysburg Address." Abraham Lincoln Online. November 19. Accessed June 25, 2009. http://www.abrahamlincolnonline.org/lincoln/speeches/gettysburg.htm.

Liu, Eric. 2019. *Become America*. Seattle, WA: Sasquatch Books.

McAdams, Dan P. 2004. "Redemption in American Politics." *Chronicle of Higher Education* 51, no. 15: B14–B15.

McGee, Michael C. 1975. "In Search of 'the People': A Rhetorical Alternative." *The Quarterly Journal of Speech* 61, no. 3: 235–249.

Miller, Dale E., and Stephen K. Medvic. 2002. "Civic Responsiblity or Self-Interest?" In *Shades of Gray: Perspectives on Campaign Ethics*, edited by Candice J. Nelson, David A. Dulio, and Stephen K. Medvic, 18–38. Washington, DC: Brookings Institution Press.

Niessee, Mark. 2019. "Georgia Lawmakers Vote to Reignite Border Dispute with Tennessee." *AJC*, April 2. Accessed June 24, 2019. https://www.ajc.com/news/state-regional-govt-politics/georgia-lawmakers-vote-reignite-border-dispute-with-tennessee/FzdgCMsR5LSVXr0g9f1v7H/.

Roof, Wade Clark. 2009. "American Presidential Rhetoric from Ronald Reagan to George W. Bush: Another Look at Civil Religion." *Social Compass* 56, no. 2: 286–301.

Rorty, Richard. 1998. *Achieving Our Country*. Cambridge, MA: Harvard University Press.

Rousseau, Jean-Jacques. 1968. *The Social Contract*. Translated by Maurice Cranston. London: Penguin Books.

Wallwork, Jodi, and John A. Dixon. 2004. "Foxes, Green Fields and Britishness: On the Rhetorical Construction of Place and National Identity." *British Journal of Social Psychology* 43: 21–39.

WRAL. 2018. "Between the Lines: Changes to the Border Leave Residents Frustrated." July 13. Accessed June 24, 2019. https://www.wral.com/changes-to -the-border-between-states-leave-residents-frustrated/16565449/.

Younge, Gary. 2013. "The Misremembering of 'I Have a Dream.'" *The Nation*, August 14. Accessed July 1, 2019. https://www.thenation.com/article/misre membering-i-have-dream/.

6

The Rhetoric and Ethics of Political Communication

Freedom Summer as a Case Study in Moral Leadership

Mark L. McPhail

This chapter examines the 1964 Mississippi Freedom Summer Project as a case study in ethical political communication. Drawing upon contemporary studies in rhetorical, moral, and political philosophy and theory, it provides an examination of Freedom Summer and the legacy of racial justice and reconciliation it created to offer a definitive account of ethical political communication. The definition I propose illustrates the transformative possibilities of moral coherence and ethical courage in the service of political engagement and social justice, as well as the limitations and liabilities of established theories of ethical leadership and political communication.

The study of ethical leadership offers important insights into the relationship between theory and practice and the extent to which philosophical knowledge can be translated into social and political action. "Much has been written about ethics and leadership from a normative or philosophical perspective, suggesting what leaders should do," note Michael E. Brown and Linda K. Trevino. "But, a more descriptive and predictive social scientific approach to ethics and leadership has remained underdeveloped and fragmented, leaving scholars and practitioners with few answers to even the most fundamental questions, such as 'what is ethical leadership?'"[1] Brown and Trevino define ethical leadership as "the demonstration of normatively appropriate conduct through personal actions and interpersonal relationships, and the promotion of such conduct to followers through two-way communication, reinforcement, and decision-making."[2]

Almost a decade later, Joanne B. Ciulla responded to their call in her edited book *Ethics: The Heart of Leadership*. Ciulla integrates the insights of ethical leadership researchers and practitioners to answer the questions raised by Brown and Trevino, yet her conclusions, I argue, succeed only in complicating the issue of ethical leadership. She summarizes the essays in her book in the introduction by suggesting that "the morality of leadership depends on the particulars of the relationship between people. It matters who the leaders and followers are, how well they understand and feel about themselves and each other, and the context of their relationship."[3] Far from providing a principled account of ethical leadership reflected in concrete practices, Ciulla's summary suggests that it is contingent and relative, eluding any definition that transcends temporal, cultural, or relational differences or distinctions.

This chapter challenges Ciulla's account and answers the call advanced by Brown and Trevino to answer comprehensively the question "What is ethical leadership?" Drawing upon several perspectives on leadership that complement and extend their analysis, I offer a definitive account of ethical political leadership by focusing on its role in race relations, specifically the 1964 Mississippi Freedom Summer Project and the leadership of Mississippi politician and activist Dick Molpus. I argue that a focus on race relations requires a reframing of our understanding of what constitutes political communication and who is or is not a politician and reveals essential principles of ethical leadership that are not contingent upon time, place, outcome, or expediency. A focus on race also provides clarification on the ethical foundations and obligations of our society, the necessity of ethical action in social and political life, and how we might determine whether the words and deeds of political communicators are ethical.

I begin by examining the historical relationship between rhetoric, ethics, and politics and illustrate the value for leadership theory and practice of "rhetorical coherence," a theoretical perspective on communication that has important practical implications for defining ethical political leadership. Next I consider several perspectives on leadership that point to the role of rhetorical coherence in establishing a principled and concrete definition of ethical political communication. Drawing upon these theoretical perspectives, I offer an analysis of the relationship between rhetorical coherence and ethical leadership as these are expressed and enacted in the struggles for civil rights, social justice, and racial reconciliation in American society, and conclude that a definitive account of ethical leadership and communication in politics is characterized by *self-sacrifice and moral courage in service to others.*

Rhetoric, Politics, and Ethics:
A Trilogy for Moral Leadership

The term "rhetoric" is widely misunderstood as negative and pejorative, but rhetorical communication is at the heart of the legal and political institutions that sustain our cultural values and practices. Rhetoric is at the root of what Christopher Lyle Johnstone describes as "an Aristotelian trilogy," and he argues that Aristotle's rhetoric must be understood in relation to his writing on both politics and ethics. He maintains that "when we inquire into the relationship between ethics and politics in Aristotle's philosophy, we are led to a unifying vision of the arts of ethics, politics, and rhetoric."[4]

At the heart of this vision is *practical reasoning*, which guides how discourse and deliberation is understood and enacted in our relationships with others. "When we honestly submit to others the conclusions and justifications that are consequent upon our own practical reasonings, we implicitly recognize the possibility of our own error. To speak in this context, then, is fundamentally an act of humility."[5] He notes that engaging in rhetorical discourse is not only an act of humility but "is also one of courage; for to consider and present arguments is to disclose to others what is finally one of our most personal and treasured possessions: the wisdom to which we have been led by our own experience."[6] His focus is not only on the persuasive aspects of rhetoric, but also on its dialogic potential. "Rhetoric, as the counterpart of dialectic, functions to promote a dialogical exchange of moral perspectives, and thus to establish a common moral perspective upon which cooperative behavior can be based," concludes Johnstone. "The moral truths thus discovered and clarified become a basis upon which genuine community can be founded."[7]

Johnstone's emphasis on the relationship between moral knowledge and the establishment of a community of shared values is echoed in the notion of rhetorical coherence, a contemporary theory of rhetoric that integrates its productive and critical elements to illustrate and illuminate communicative contexts in which moral contradictions limit or inhibit the persuasive potential of communication.[8] The theory defines rhetoric as "the capacity to integrate diverse conceptions of reality"[9] and measures rhetorical effectiveness in terms of the alignment between theory and practice, words and deeds, and expressed and enacted values. Communication scholars writing in the areas of political discourse and racial reconciliation have utilized the theory to address situations in which the creation of genuine community is hampered by rhetorical practices that fail to reconcile divisions and negative differences.[10] In Western classical and modern political philosophy and theory, the moral truths that characterize genuine community are expressed in ethical leadership that affirms and confirms the ideals of the social contract.[11]

The extent to which those ideals are realized in ethical action has been increasingly analyzed and scrutinized by contemporary leadership and communication theorists and practitioners. "Today we face a crisis in leadership in many areas of public and private life," explains Ronald Heifetz, which requires "a different idea of leadership and a new social contract that promote our adaptive capacities rather than inappropriate expectations of authority. We need to reconceive and revitalize our civic life and the meaning of citizenship."[12] Heifetz notes that how we define and practice leadership "involves our self-images and moral codes" and is thus value laden. "We cannot talk about a crisis in leadership, and then say leadership is value free," he explains, nor can we define leadership only in terms of established organizations and institutions or limit its definition to those individuals who by formality or convention are granted the authority to influence and mobilize others. "The contradiction in our common understanding clouds not only the clarity of our thinking and scholarship, it shapes the quality of leadership we praise, teach, and get."[13]

In response to this limited understanding of leadership, Heifetz offers an alternative approach. "Rather than define leadership either as a position of authority in a social structure or a set of personal characteristics, we may find it a great deal more useful to define leadership as an *activity*."[14] At the heart of that activity is an awareness and understanding of the ethical values that shape the participants, interactions, and outcomes of leadership and a willingness to move beyond fixed and rigid beliefs to solve problems and meet challenges that seem irreconcilable. Heifetz defines these problems as "adaptive" and offers a theoretical perspective that "examines the usefulness of viewing leadership in terms of adaptive work."

> Adaptive works consists of the learning required to address conflicts in the values people hold, or to diminish the gap between the values people stand for and the reality they face. Adaptive work requires a change in values, beliefs, or behavior. The exposure and orchestration of conflict—internal contradictions—within individuals and constituencies provide the leverage for mobilizing people to learn in new ways.[15]

Placing adaptive work at the heart of leadership challenges both our definitions of leadership and our understanding of *who can be a leader*. In addition, it illustrates the limitations of our common understanding of the social contract: "The concept of social contract may be one cornerstone of democracy, yet democracy is not so easily achieved in light of our inclination to look to authority with overly expectant eyes" Heifetz explains. "In part, democracy requires that average citizens become aware that they are indeed the principles and that those upon whom they confer power are their agents."[16] Leadership, for Heifetz, cannot be reduced to a technical account of the relationship between those upon whom it has been conferred and those they influence, but must also consider the moral and ethical values of that relationship. This view is echoed in Robert Greenleaf's notion of "servant-leadership."

Greenleaf coined the term "servant-leader" in the early 1970s to describe a management philosophy that departs from traditional hierarchical approaches and is characterized by an "Ethic of Strength." "One of the difficulties of using the word *strength* as the symbol for a primary object of ethical striving is that it has meanings and connotations that distract."[17] In giving strength a "special meaning," Greenleaf directly addresses the relationship between leadership, ethical action, and individual motives. "We are concerned here with doing right, doing what is ethically sound." He defines *strength* as "the ability to see enough choices of aims, to choose the *right* aim, and to pursue that aim responsibly over a long period of time."[18] *Strength*, in Greenleaf's view, is characterized by "*responsible pursuit*," a phrase "used in the sense that the person who has chosen an aim thinks, speaks and acts as if personally accountable to all who may be affected by his or her thoughts, words, and deeds. This is a large and seemingly impossible order. But nothing short of this as a goal will do."[19] *Strength*, in Greenleaf's view, cannot be expedient, relative, or simply transactional, but must express in word, thoughts, and deeds essential qualities of competence, character, and humility. These qualities lie at the heart of Greenleaf's concept of servant-leadership.

Servant-leadership "begins with the natural feeling that one wants to serve, to serve first. Then conscious choice brings one to aspire to lead." Like Heifetz, Greenleaf challenges and redefines traditional conceptions of leadership based on authority, power, and individual self-interest, noting that a servant-leader "is sharply different from one who is *leader* first, perhaps because of the need to assuage an unusual power drive or to acquire material possessions."[20] In clarifying this difference, Greenleaf explains the ethical impulses that characterize servant-leadership, as well as its ultimate aims and outcomes:

> The difference manifests itself in the care taken by the servant—first to make sure that other people's highest priority needs are being served. The best test, and difficult to administer, is this: Do those served grow as persons? Do they, *while being served*, become healthier, wiser, freer, more autonomous, more likely themselves to become servants? *And*, what is the effect on the least privileged in society? Will they benefit or at least not be further deprived?[21]

Greenleaf's reframing of both terms—servant and leader—has important implications for understanding the moral and ethical motivation required for addressing some of our most enduring problems of political leadership, especially *adaptive* problems, which Heifetz argues resist the *technical* solutions usually pursued by leaders, such as legislation, legal redress, and economic reform.[22]

Greenleaf's redefinition of the two terms also places the discussion of ethical political leadership squarely in the realms of power relations, distinctions between the legitimate and illegitimate uses of authority, and accepted definitions of leaders and followers. Lawrence Spears suggests that Greenleaf was concerned with "the reality of power in everyday life—its legitimacy, the ethical restraints upon it, and the beneficial results that can be attained through the appropriate use of power"[23] Spears points to the anxieties created by both terms in their everyday uses and suggests that Greenleaf's reframing of servant and leader invites an understanding of each term that points to fundamentally moral and ethical concerns. "For some people, the word servant may prompt an initial negative connotation due to the oppression that many people—especially women and people of color—have historically endured," he explains. "For others, the word leader may also carry a great deal of unfavorable historical baggage. However, upon closer analysis many come to appreciate the spiritual nature of what Greenleaf intended by the pairing of servant and leader."[24] Spears's suggestion that servant-leadership is rooted in spiritual impulses aligns it with a third perspective that directly addresses the ethical concerns and consequences of leadership: Keshavan Nair's examination of leadership in the life and words of one of history's most important moral leaders, Mohandas Karamchand Gandhi.

Nair attempts to "develop a leadership framework within which lessons drawn from Gandhi's life can be used to bring the moral and spiritual dimension to leadership and guide us to a higher standard."[25] This higher standard is offered in contrast to the "double standard of conduct" and "gospel of expediency" at the root of our contemporary leadership crises:

> The evidence that many subscribe to the double standard is everywhere. Politicians ask us to judge them on their legislative accomplishments, not on their personal conduct. Social activists who claim the high moral ground in their personal philosophy use violence to obtain results. Business executives do not want their conduct examined but ask instead to focus exclusively on the bottom line. And many journalists who maintain a personal commitment to the truth succumb to the pressures of wanting to be the first and, rather than wait for the whole study, publish half-truths.[26]

Nair argues that the example set by Gandhi for ethical leadership is reflected in five commitments: absolute values, acknowledgment of ideals, training of conscience, reducing attachments, and minimizing secrecy.[27]

Nair points to these spiritual beliefs and commitments as foundational principles of the standard of leadership that Gandhi embraced and enacted in his life. "While Gandhi's basis was undoubtedly religious, he embraced the fundamental directive basic to every religion and culture: to treat other human beings as ourselves."[28]

Living by a single standard of conduct, Nair suggests, "requires that we evaluate our actions in a moral framework" and "a trained conscience—the disciplined, moral reasoning that tells us what we ought to do."[29] Knowing what we ought to do, for Nair, must be translated into practical action, and thus the defining characteristic of ethical leadership is *moral courage*. "In the end, it is *moral courage* that determines the standard of leadership in the practical arenas of politics, business, academics, and the community."[30] As an expression of ethical leadership in action, moral courage is motivated by an "enduring spirit of service, driven by values"[31] and a willingness to "act in accordance with moral principles and to embrace the absolute values of truth and nonviolence and the universal code of conduct: to treat others as ourselves."[32] Nair's account of Gandhi offers an important starting point for redefining our understanding of the relationship between rhetoric, ethics, and politics and reframing our understanding and enactment of moral judgment in public contexts.

Heifetz describes Gandhi as an adaptive leader, noting also that his leadership invoked principles of rhetorical coherence in its attention to the lack of alignment between professed and enacted values. "Massive demonstrations, brutal beatings, nationwide strikes, hunger fasts, and years in jail were meant to dramatize to the British the gap between their espoused values—justice and self-determination—and their behavior—subjugation."[33] Although Gandhi was not an official political leader, his use of informal authority had a much greater impact than that of his contemporaries in Indian politics, whose oppositional strategies and tactics failed to address the historical influences of colonization. "Colonialism was a way of life not only to Britain but to India. Breaking up that way of life would require enormous adaptive work. The British could just leave India, as eventually they did, but getting them ready to leave and getting India ready to rule herself were adaptive challenges of the first magnitude."[34] Because attempts at practical reasoning and moral suasion had failed to induce cooperation in the British, Gandhi's rhetorical strategy went beyond established communicative practices to address the ethical incoherence of British political practices in India, while at the same time affirming the political ideals of Western moral philosophy:

> More than the formal authorities in India, Gandhi operated at the focal point of the nation's attention. His fasting mattered because, over the course of thirty years he had become the singular embodiment of the nation's hopes and pains. Indians and non-Indians granted him moral authority, not only because he used his own person to represent issues, but because he had the strategic ability to dramatize over and over again that the aspirations of his people were consonant with the moral underpinning of the West.[35]

Gandhi's influence, Heifetz concludes, was made all the more powerful by his position outside of established political structures and by a rhetorically coherent message that was embodied in personal acts of moral courage. "Outside the center, Gandhi had the freedom to present a focused and coherent message, and to embody it. He had only to meet the expectations of those who, believing in him already, provided a base for his challenge to the nation and to Britain."[36]

While Heifetz praises Gandhi's adaptive leadership qualities, Greenleaf offers a much less laudatory perspective. "Gandhi was probably the greatest leader of the common people the world has ever known. He brought freedom from colonialism to India, he hastened the end of that uncivilized practice everywhere, and he left a concept of a good society that will keep us stretched for centuries," he writes. "But there was a negative side. Gandhi was coercive, and the consequence of his coercion was violence, awful violence."[37]

Greenleaf argues that Gandhi's leadership led to "communal strife," within India, "chaotic quarreling" within other colonized nations in the process of liberating themselves from Western domination, and "the flaw of coercion in his tactics."[38] In contrast to Heifetz, he is especially critical of Gandhi's "ultimate tactic, the 'fast unto death.' In this he is saying, without equivocation, 'If you don't do as I say, I will commit suicide.'"[39] Greenleaf's understanding of persuasion offers important insights into his criticism of Gandhi's "coercive" tactics:

> Persuasion begins with an attitude toward the persons or groupings toward which the persuasive argument is directed. The attitude accepts that one is persuaded only when one arrives at a belief or action through one's own intuitive sense of the rightness of that action untrammeled by coercive pressure of any kind. One cannot embrace that attitude and employ the strategy of nonviolent coercion to which Gandhi, by 1915, was deeply committed.[40]

Greenleaf's argument ignores centuries of evidence that the persuasive efforts of colonized peoples were routinely disregarded by European colonizers and rests upon several problematic assumptions and beliefs. He assumes, for example, a rigid distinction between coercion and persuasion, that coercion directed against others is the same as a willingness to sacrifice one's life or livelihood in the service of others, and that the effectiveness of practical reasoning at the heart of the social contract is equally efficacious in situations involving domination and subordination.

The theory of rhetorical coherence addresses these beliefs and assumptions directly, interrogating distinctions between persuasion and coercion and pointing to the critical importance of *embodied knowledge* in facilitating social change and cultural transformation.[41] Although Greenleaf is critical of colonialism and recognizes its moral and ethical contradictions, as a beneficiary of its history his understanding of the experience is abstract and divorced from its actual effects and outcomes. The theory of rhetorical coherence interrogates this understanding by uncovering the epistemological assumptions upon which it is based and illustrates how those assumptions are complicit in systems of domination. While ostensibly guided by the *theoretical* principles of the social contract, Western moral philosophy and political *practice* has been defined by what Carole Pateman and Charles Mills characterize as "domination contracts."[42]

In his discussion of racial domination contracts, Charles W. Mills points to the moral incoherence between an abstract social contract and an empirical racial contract. While the social contract assumes moral neutrality, the racial contract reflects "a moral psychology (not just in whites but sometimes in nonwhites) skewed consciously or unconsciously toward privileging them, taking the status quo of differential racial entitlement as normatively legitimate, and not to be investigated further."[43] Mills's analysis provides an important foundation for understanding ethical political communication in one of its most challenging colonial contexts: the history of race relations in the United States. One of the most pronounced examples of that history, and the leadership strategies that emerged within in it, is the state of Mississippi, which for centuries reflected a politics defined and undermined by the racial contract.

For centuries the formal and informal political structures of the state justified and defended racial segregation as a way of life, as did the nation as a whole, but Mississippi's history reveals an especially egregious violation of the "inalienable" rights and principles of the social contract: freedom and equality. "The historic fact is that in Mississippi, between 1875 and 1890, inequality was effected by force and finally regularized by law, that is, by the constitution under which the state still operates," explains Mississippi historian James W. Silver. "By 1890 Negroes had long since learned that Mississippi freedom included neither political nor any other kinds of equality."[44]

Writing in 1964, Silver challenged the prevailing political culture in Mississippi, courageously questioning the moral commitments of its leadership. Quoting a professor from the University of Mississippi, he observes:

> Men of good will who are content to sit on their hands silently hoping that nothing will rock the boat are seemingly unaware that the use of their oars might stay the foundering craft; these men are not leaders, nor are they followers. Leadership nurtures on controversy, it matures on intellectual dissension, it mellows on the free exchange of provocative ideas.[45]

The quote echoes Johnstone's theoretical insights and points to another of his central concerns: *courage*. Indeed, it was moral courage that led to the transformation of race relations that occurred in Mississippi and across the nation in 1964, when the contradictions of the social contract and the ineffectiveness of persuasion were brought into sharp focus in the Mississippi Freedom Summer Project, also known as Freedom Summer.

Freedom Summer not only challenged and changed the history of race relations in the United States but also redefined our understanding of leadership, politics, and ethical communication. As a rhetorical case study, Freedom Summer and the legacy of racial justice and reconciliation it created offer an enhanced understanding of leadership that both illustrates the breadth of its formal and informal manifestations and points out the problems and possibilities of definitions of ethical leadership that are contingent on the dominant normative practices, values, and behaviors of leaders and followers. It also illustrates what I argue are the defining characteristics of genuine ethical political communication: *self-sacrifice guided by moral courage and enacted in the spirit of service to others.*

Leadership without Easy Definitions: The Rhetorical Legacy of Freedom Summer

In *Leadership without Easy Answers,* Ronald Heifetz offers a traditional and widely accepted account of the history of the civil rights movement: "The modern Civil Rights movement may be said to have started when Rosa Parks refused to surrender her seat on a Montgomery, Alabama, bus to a white man. The year was 1955, and Martin Luther King took up the cause." Heifetz suggests that King's leadership was informal, that its power was derived from "his extraordinary ability to mobilize ordinary people on behalf of what he believed was right and true," and that his influence and effectiveness "revealed how in this country at that time grass roots activity could compel significant social change."[46] Heifetz presents a commonly accepted definition of leadership in the civil rights movement, one that emphasizes the role of prominent individuals mobilizing their followers to engage in civic actions and activities to challenge existing political structures and institutions. However, a second tradition of leadership emerges from the movement that more accurately describes the collective actions of its participants and reveals the limitations of existing definitions of politics, ethics, and communication: the organizing tradition.

Freedom Summer emphasized a conception of leadership that "was not limited to a drive for personal freedom, or even freedom for the Negro in the South. Repeatedly it was emphasized that the movement was concerned with the moral implications of racial discrimination for the 'whole world' and the 'Human Race.'"[47] This view of leadership was most eloquently articulated by Ella Baker who, in her speech "Bigger Than a Hamburger," emphasized the notion that "it is important to keep the movement democratic and to avoid struggles for personal leadership."[48] The radical character of Baker's vision would shape the vision of leadership that emerged during Freedom Summer, a vision that would challenge the established attitudinal and institutional structures of American politics and fundamentally redefine the role of ethical communication in the struggle for freedom and human dignity. It would also motivate the leadership philosophy and efforts of her most important and influential student: Robert Parris Moses.

Richard Jensen and John Hammerback explain how Moses's vision of leadership exposed the limitations of traditional notions of politics and civic engagement, and they point to the central role of his moral courage in shaping and expanding the boundaries of ethical political communication. "Although Moses did not fit the conventional mold as an activist leader/rhetor in the 1960s, civil rights militants of that period bestowed legendary status on him," they explain.[49] Moses was widely respected despite his lack of formal political status, and he offered and embodied a definition of leadership that challenged and fell outside the boundaries of accepted political norms in the state of Mississippi. "Here, whites controlled powerful 'structures' of society, ranging from politics to education to the economy, and were determined to protect their racist civilization—even if it means murdering blacks who protested," explain Jensen and Hammerback. "The whites most resistant to challenges to the status-quo, and the ones most responsible for the plight of blacks, were elite politicians who used their power to maintain the dominance of whites and keep blacks politically powerless."[50] Because established norms and structures of political leadership excluded active participation by Mississippi's African American citizens, Moses recognized the need for an adaptive vision for political engagement that ensured that the least privileged members of society would no longer be deprived of the inalienable rights enshrined in the contractarian ideals of the US Constitution.

The significance of this vision of leadership has largely been lost in contemporary accounts of the civil rights movement, yet its importance cannot be ignored. Indeed, as Moses explains: 'Today's commentary and analysis of the movement often miss the crucial point that, in addition to challenging white power, the movement also demanded that Black people challenge themselves. Small meetings and workshops became the spaces within the Black community where people could stand up and speak, or in groups outline their concerns" (81). Moses goes on to describe how these spaces differed markedly from conventional depictions of the struggle for civil rights, which characterized the movement in terms of a more traditional conception of leadership that emphases the persuasive efforts of a few motivating the many to action. "In these meetings, they were taking the first step toward gaining control over their lives, and the decision making that affected their lives, by making demands on themselves," he explains. "This important dimension has been almost completely lost to the imagery of hand-clapping, song filled rallies for protest demonstrations that have come to define portrayals of 1960s civil rights meetings: dynamic individual leaders using powerful voices to inspire listening crowds."[51] These spaces became further invigorated when the local black struggle was expanded to include a critical mass of mostly white Americans, the volunteers who went to Mississippi in 1964 to assist with voter registration, teach in freedom schools, and work together with African Americans to create the Mississippi Freedom Democratic Party (MFDP).

The MFDP, established as an alternative to the segregated Mississippi Democratic Party, was committed to "a common set of values and aspirations" and the ideals that undergirded American democracy. It was in the pursuit of these shared values that they realized in practice a rhetoric of coherence, a transformative understanding of self and other. "This was true diversity, and although we sometimes had difficulty with one another, there was a true bond that we were in Mississippi together, risking our lives, putting our bodies on the line for justice," recalls Chude Allen. Her experience during Freedom Summer led her to develop new insights into the limitations of traditional political structures and practices for dealing with racial domination and discrimination. "My parents believed as I had when I left for Mississippi that the Deep South was an aberration, a cancerous growth on what was an otherwise good and just system," but after the summer of 1964, she found herself "beginning to question that. I'd seen the federal government do nothing to protect the lives of the people fighting for their civil rights. I'd seen the Democratic Party allow blatant discrimination. I'd seen cruelty and violence."

Allen's lived encounter with the racial conditions that constrained the lives of black Mississippians transformed the abstractions of otherness into an embodied understanding of the suffering of others. "This society vilifies the poor, especially the black poor," she concludes. "But . . . we white volunteers benefited so much from working with the black people of Mississippi, most of whom were poor. We struggled. We cared. We benefited. We developed into better human beings."[52] Her story is echoed in the experiences of many of the other white volunteers, whose lives are testaments to the power of moral courage, servant leadership, and rhetorical coherence in transforming a rational understanding of the ideals of the social contract into the embodied actions required to challenge and transform the racial contract.

Freedom Summer illustrates the importance of self-sacrifice in establishing a higher standard of ethical political leadership and communication, and effectively destabilizes rigid distinctions between leaders and followers, politics and activism, and persuasion and coercion. It also clarifies and challenges the definitions proposed by Brown and Trevino and summarized by Ciulla. It illustrates how "normatively appropriate conduct" for one political constituency can be antithetical to the inalienable rights of another and reveals how defining ethical political leadership based solely on relationships between leaders, followers, and contexts can result in essentially unethical and immoral behavior. Finally, it reveals how a higher standard of leadership can transform politics at the state and national levels and even positively influence the moral and ethical behaviors of individuals and institutions within existing political structures.

The 1964 Civil Rights Act and the 1965 Voting Rights Act were indirect and direct outcomes of the events of the summer of 1964, and Freedom Summer had a profound, albeit paradoxical, influence on the struggle for equality and justice well into the twenty-first century. As Doug McAdam observes, all of the major progressive movements that emerged in the wake of the civil rights movement were either directly or indirectly influenced by those who participated in the Mississippi Freedom Summer Project.[53] Yet none of those movements continued to support the black freedom struggle for racial justice that motivated and defined Freedom Summer, instead cultivating an "identity politics"[54] that confused rights with privileges and freedom with license. As a consequence of these and other factors, according to Robert C. Smith, "black politics has become largely irrelevent [*sic*] in terms of a politics and policies that would address effectively the problem of race in the post-civil rights era."[55] Indeed, despite the election of the nation's first African American president, resistance to racial justice and reconciliation continued to undermine the establishment of the "more perfect union" enshrined in the Constitution and idealized in the social contract. Yet the struggle for freedom continued, ironically, within Mississippi, fueled by the efforts of one of the state's native sons, Dick Molpus. Molpus challenged the norms of the culture in which he was born and raised and brought the lessons of moral courage and self-sacrifice he learned from Freedom Summer into mainstream politics.

The Price of an Apology: Rhetorical Coherence, Moral Courage, and the Ethical Political Leadership of Dick Molpus

Dick Molpus was born in Neshoba County, where in the summer of 1964, on the orders of the citizens' council, the Mount Zion Methodist Church was burned to the ground in order to draw into Mississippi Michael Schwerner, then a member of CORE and a participant in the Mississippi Freedom Summer Project. Schwerner, accompanied by James Chaney and Andrew Goodman, arrived in Mississippi on June 20, 1964, to visit with members of the church who had been beaten and harassed earlier by local officials and to inspect the remains of the destroyed sanctuary. On the way out of Philadelphia heading toward Meridian, Mississippi, the three men were stopped and detained by deputy Cecil Price and held in the Neshoba County jail until late that evening. They were then released, but as they continued on toward Meridian, they were stopped by Price and several Ku Klux Klansmen, who took them from their vehicles, beat them, executed them, and then buried their bodies in an earthen dam.

Several of the men involved were indicted and tried in federal court for violating the civil rights of Chaney, Goodman, and Schwerner, but none served more than six years for their crimes, and the majority of the men involved were acquitted of the charges. The trial of Edgar Ray Killens, which took place more than forty years after the crime, was the result of the efforts of a coalition of African, European, and Native Americans from Philadelphia, who came together to promote racial reconciliation and achieve racial justice.[56] The man who inspired the creation of that coalition was Dick Molpus, who from the time that he was a teenager growing up in Neshoba County had been haunted by the terrible crime committed in that summer of 1964 and troubled by the unwillingness of any of his fellow citizens of Philadelphia or Mississippi to do anything about it.

Molpus began his political career in the administration of Governor William Winter, and in 1989, while serving as Mississippi's secretary of state, Molpus became the first white Mississippi politician to apologize to the families of Chaney, Goodman, and Schwerner. Appearing at the annual memorial held for the three men at the Mount Zion Methodist Church, Molpus remarked:

> We deeply regret what happened here 25 years ago. We wish we could undo it. We are profoundly sorry that they are gone. We wish we could bring them back. Every decent person in Philadelphia and Neshoba County and Mississippi feels that way. The nation and the world thinks of the events of 1964 in Philadelphia in historical terms and the deaths of these dedicated young men as a pivotal event in a great national movement. Of course, this is true—but it is not the whole truth.[57]

Through moral courage and principled action, Molpus effectively transformed the tradition of leadership that had dominated political discourse in his community and across the state. Molpus, however, paid a price for his moral courage. Six years later he ran for governor of Mississippi and was defeated by Kirk Fordice, an avowed racist and supporter of David Duke. Not only was Molpus's apology used against him in the campaign for governor, but it served to benefit Fordice, whose refusal to apologize was seen as a badge of honor among his constituents.[58]

Yet Molpus continued to seek justice for the slain civil rights workers, drawing upon the organizing strategies he had witnessed during the summer of 1964 to influence the creation of a diverse coalition whose "members reflected the depth and breadth of the county with regard to economic, racial, and educational parameters. Among them were lawyers, newspaper publishers and editors, nurses, ministers, housewives, and roulette wheel operators."[59] Like the participants in the Mississippi Freedom Summer, the coalition revealed how ordinary people, working outside of established political structures, could achieve what legislators and lawyers could not.

In 2004 Molpus presented an address at a memorial held at the Neshoba County Coliseum, which offers a definitive example of ethical political communication. He invoked a higher standard of leadership that called for a collective commitment to accountability and responsibility and argued that all of the citizens of Neshoba County were bound by a "corporate responsibility" for the events that took place in that Freedom Summer. He engaged in the adaptive work of reinventing leadership and establishing a new social contract, demanding that the philosophical ideals of democratic engagement and political action be realized in social practices and actions that acknowledge and challenge "problems for which no adequate response has yet been developed—for example, poverty and racism."[60] His concluding words offer a powerful example of rhetorical coherence in action:

> To build a lasting monument to James Chaney, Michael Schwerner and Andrew Goodman we must face these issues with a clear, unblinking eye and say "no more." And finally, we Mississippians must announce to the world what we've learned in 40 years. We know today that our enemies are not each other. Our real enemies are ignorance, illiteracy, poverty, racism, disease, unemployment, crime, the high dropout rate, teen pregnancy and lack of support for the public schools. We can defeat all those enemies—not as divided people—black or white or Indian—but as a united force banded together by our common humanity—by our own desire to lift each other up. 40 years from now I want our children and grandchildren to look back on us and what we did and say that we had the courage, the wisdom and the strength to rise up, to take the responsibility to right historical wrongs . . . that we pledged to build a future together . . . we moved on . . . yes, we moved on as one people.[61]

One year later, Edgar Ray Killens was brought to justice, and while some argued that his conviction was too little and too late,[62] others saw within it the promise of a new social reality in which a renewed and reinvigorated vision of rhetoric, ethics, and politics might move us closer to a more perfect union. "With this reality," Howard Ball concludes, "there is at last the beginning of racial reconciliation."[63]

Reconciling the Ethics of Political Communication: Establishing a Higher Standard of Democratic Leadership

The legacy of leadership embodied in the examples of Freedom Summer and Dick Molpus exemplify the transformative possibilities of rhetorical coherence and moral courage in the service of democratic engagement and politics. They offer practical illustrations of adaptive work, servant-leadership, and a higher standard of leadership, as well as opportunities to expand our definitions of ethical political leadership by illustrating the importance of challenging established social norms, the value of self-sacrifice, and the limitations of established political structures and institutions. And perhaps most important, they bring to the study of leadership a focus on racial justice and reconciliation and provide a standard by which ethical political communication and leadership can be judged, measured, and theorized.

But this legacy need not be separate and distinct from existing political structures or institutions. Indeed, within the context of contemporary American politics, one political leader offered a practical example of its enduring presence and its potential for defining ethical political communication. I conclude with communication scholars Spoma Jovanovic and Roy V. Wood's assessment of then senator Barack Obama's "More Perfect Union" speech:

> How do we bring ethics into the world of politics? Presidential hopeful Barack Obama told us how in his primary season speech, "A More Perfect Union." Obama offered messages of hope, care and compassion as he communicated about the suffering in our country. He detailed how people and leaders can ethically interact about political matters if we keep our focus there. Obama spoke in a prophetic style, rooted in the Hebrew scripture, and rallied Americans around common values.[64]

David Frank offers an account of Obama's speech that situates it within the legacy of Freedom Summer and its emphasis on "multiethnic alliances as the political means of solving problems."[65] Like Jovanovic and Wood, Frank also recognizes the prophetic aspects of the speech: "At the core of the speech is the prophetic tradition, with its fundamental assumptions that all human beings are made in the image of God, that the traces of God are found in the face of the other, and that humans have an obligation to recognize and care for their brothers and sisters."[66] That tradition, characterized by sacrifice, courage, and service, offers a powerful point of departure for defining ethical political communication in new and transformative ways, offering what David L. Chappell describes as "a challenge to modern democracy."[67]

Chappell's use of the term "prophetic" offers a fitting end for my analysis and an important starting point for future research on ethical political communication. In the spirit of adaptive work, he suggests new ways of learning about old and persistent problems; in the spirit of servant-leadership he offers new ways of disrupting established divisions; in the spirit of a single standard of conduct he points to the power of moral courage; and in the spirit of rhetorical coherence he calls for an aligning of words and deeds. "As a young atheist years ago, I was drawn to the bravery of a few in the civil rights movement. Theirs was a kind of intellectual and moral as well as physical courage. Their courage held up under the scrutiny of research, indeed it deepened."[68] As researchers continue to define ethical political communication, perhaps they will do so in the spirit of intellectual courage exemplified by the prophets studied by Chappell, who "were skeptical about prevailing dogmas and practices—skeptical above all about faith in the human future. They rejected the view that voluntary, gradual progress would ever undo the evils of segregation and disenfranchisement."[69] If, as is often suggested, "more research is needed" to effectively theorize and practice ethical political leadership and communication, then a healthy skepticism of this kind is called for, one that challenges prevailing beliefs and opinions; resists the seductive promises of progress and gradualism; and looks carefully at the history of race relations and the traditions of self-sacrifice, moral courage, and service to others exemplified in the leadership strategies reflected in this history. Perhaps then we may well be able to envision the prophetic possibilities of self-sacrifice, moral courage, and service to others for reshaping, in Heifetz's words, "the quality of the leadership we praise, teach, and get."[70]

Notes

[1] Michael E. Brown and Linda K. Trevino, "Ethical Leadership: A Review and Future Directions," *Leadership Quarterly* 17 (2006): 595.

[2] Brown and Trevino, "Ethical Leadership," 595–596.

[3] Joanne B. Ciulla, ed., *Ethics, the Heart of Leadership*. Santa Barbara, CA: Praeger, 2014.

[4] Christopher Lyle Johnstone, "An Aristotelian Trilogy: Ethics, Rhetoric, Politics, and the Search for Moral Truth," *Philosophy and Rhetoric* 13 (1980): 13.

[5] Johnstone, "An Aristotelian Trilogy," 16.

[6] Johnstone, "An Aristotelian Trilogy," 16.

[7] Johnstone, "An Aristotelian Trilogy," 17.

[8] Christopher Johnstone and Mark Lawrence McPhail, "Balance, Coherence, and Moral Knowledge: A Dialogue" (paper presented at the Fourth National Communication Ethics Conference, Duquesne University, Pittsburgh, PA, 1996).

[9] See Mark Lawrence McPhail, *The Rhetoric of Racism* (Lanham, MD: University Press of America, 1994); and Mark Lawrence McPhail, *Zen in the Art of Rhetoric: An Inquiry into Coherence* (Albany: State University of New York Press, 1996).

[10] David A. Frank and Mark Lawrence McPhail, "Barack Obama's Address to the 2004 Democratic National Convention: Trauma, Compromise, Consilience, and the (Im)possibility of Racial Reconciliation," in *Race and the Obama Phenomenon: The Vision of a More Perfect Multiracial Union*, ed. G. Reginald Daniels and Hettie V. Williams (Jackson: University of Mississippi Press, 2014), 265–286. See also David Frank's comments on National Public Radio, "The State of the Election: Momentum and Rhetoric," February 20, 2008, 12:59 PM ET; and John Hatch, *Race and Reconciliation: Redressing Wounds of Injustice* (Lanham, MD: Lexington Books, 2008).

[11] See Mark Hulliung, *The Social Contract in America: From the Revolution to the Present Age* (Lawrence: University Press of Kansas, 2007).

[12] Ronald Heifetz, *Leadership without Easy Answers* (Cambridge, MA: Harvard University Press, 1994), 2.

[13] Heifetz, *Leadership without Easy Answers*, 14.

[14] Heifetz, *Leadership without Easy Answers*, 20.

[15] Heiftetz, *Leadership without Easy Answers*, 22.

[16] Heifetz, *Leadership without Easy Answers*, 61.

[17] Robert K. Greenleaf, *On Becoming a Servant Leader* (San Francisco: Jossey-Bass, 1996), 25.

18 Greenleaf, *On Becoming a Servant Leader*, 27.

19 Greenleaf, *On Becoming a Servant Leader*, 29; emphasis in original.

20 Robert Greenleaf, *Servant Leadership: A Journey into the Nature of Legitimate Power & Greatness* (New York: Paulist Press, 2002), 27.

21 Greenleaf, *Servant Leadership*, 27.

22 Heifetz distinguishes between technical and adaptive problems.

23 Lawrence Spears, "The Understanding and Practice of Servant Leadership" (paper presented at Servant Leadership Roundtable, School of Leadership, Regent University, August 2005), 3.

24 Spears, "The Understanding and Practice of Servant Leadership," 7.

25 Keshavan Nair, *A Higher Standard of Leadership: Lessons from the Life of Gandhi* (San Francisco: Berrett-Koehler, 1994), xii.

26 Nair, *Higher Standard of Leadership*, 15.

27 Nair, *Higher Standard of Leadership*, 17.

28 Nair, *Higher Standard of Leadership*, 19.

29 Nair, *Higher Standard of Leadership*, 33.

30 Nair, *Higher Standard of Leadership*, 49; emphasis added.

31 Nair, *Higher Standard of Leadership*, 75.

32 Nair, *Higher Standard of Leadership*, 137.

33 Heifetz, *Leadership without Easy Answers*, 189.

34 Heifetz, *Leadership without Easy Answers*, 190.

35 Heifetz, *Leadership without Easy Answers*, 191.

36 Heifetz, *Leadership without Easy Answers*, 194.

37 Greenleaf, *On Becoming a Servant Leader*, 133.

38 Greenleaf, *On Becoming a Servant Leader*, 134–135.

39 Greenleaf, *On Becoming a Servant Leader*, 133.

40 Greenleaf, *On Becoming a Servant Leader*, 135–136.

41 See Mark Lawrence McPhail, "A Question of Character: Re(-)signing the Racial Contract," *Rhetoric and Public Affairs* 7 (2004): 391–405.

42 Carole Pateman and Charles W. Mills, *Contract and Domination* (Cambridge, UK: Polity Press, 2015).

43 Charles Mills, *The Racial Contract* (Ithaca, NY: Cornell University Press, 1997), 40.

44 James W. Silver, *Mississippi: The Closed Society* (New York: Harcourt, Brace and World, 1966): 15.

45 Silver, *Mississippi*, 144.

46 Heifetz, *Leadership without Easy Answers*, 17.

47 Ella Baker, "Bigger Than a Hamburger," *Southern Patriot* (May 1960): 1, https://www.crmvet.org/docs/sncc2.htm.

48 Baker, "Bigger Than a Hamburger."

49 Richard J. Jensen and John C. Hammerback, "'Your Tools Are Really the People': The Rhetoric of Robert Parris Moses," *Communication Monographs* 65 (1998): 127.

50 Jensen and Hammerback, "'Your Tools Are Really the People,'" 130.

51 Robert P. Moses and Charles Cobb Jr., *Radical Equations: Civil Rights from Mississippi to the Algebra Project* (Boston: Beacon Press, 2001), 81.

[52] Chude Allen, "Why Struggle, Why Care?" (Interdisciplinary Lecture Series: Letters from Mississippi and Social Justice, Western College, Miami University, September 20, 2005), 14.

[53] Doug McAdam, *Freedom Summer* (New York: Oxford University Press, 1988).

[54] George Lipsitz, *The Possessive Investment in Whiteness: How White People Profit from Identity Politics* (Philadelphia: Temple University Press, 1998).

[55] Robert C. Smith, *We Have No Leaders: African Americans in the Post-Civil Rights Era* (Albany: State University of New York Press, 1996), 21–22.

[56] Howard Ball, *Justice in Mississippi: The Murder Trial of Edgar Ray Killen* (Lawrence: University Press of Kansas, 2006), 77–78.

[57] "Remarks by Secretary of State Dick Molpus," Ecumenical Memorial Service, Mount Zion Church, June 21, 1989. The Philadelphia Coalition, http://neshobajustice.com/molpus1989.htm.

[58] Ball, *Justice in Mississippi*, 15–17.

[59] Ball, *Justice in Mississippi*, 79.

[60] Barbara Kellerman, *Reinventing Leadership: Making the Connection Between Politics and Business* (Albany: State University of New York Press, 1999), 136.

[61] Donna Ladd, "Dick Molpus Raises the Roof in Neshoba County," *Jackson Free Press*, June 21, 2004, http://www.jacksonfreepress.com/news/2004/jun/21/dick-molpus-raises-the-roof-in-neshoba-county/.

[62] See, for example, C. W. Roberson, "Mr. Hood: Finish the Job You Started," Mississippi Political News Watch, http://mississippipolitical.com/house.htm.

[63] Ball, *Justice in Mississippi*, 207.

[64] Spoma Jovanovic and Roy V. Wood, "Barack Obama's Call to Restore Ethics in Politics," *Communication Currents*, October 1, 2008, National Communication Association, https://www.natcom.org/communication-currents/barack-obamas-call-restore-ethics-politics.

[65] David A. Frank, "The Prophetic Voice and the Face of the Other in Barack Obama's 'A More Perfect Union' Address, March 18, 2008," *Rhetoric & Public Affairs* 12 (2009): 190.

[66] Frank, "Prophetic Voice and the Face of the Other," 190.

[67] David L. Chappell, "Prophetic Religion: A Transracial Challenge to Modern Democracy," *Social Research* 76 (2009): 1261–1276.

[68] Chappell, "Prophetic Religion," 1273.

[69] Chappell, "Prophetic Religion," 1273.

[70] Heifetz, *Leadership without Easy Answers*, 14.

7

The Ethical Implications of the Presidential Speechwriter's Metaphors

Michael Gerson's "The First Sign of a Smoking Gun Might be a Mushroom Cloud"

David A. Frank

etaphors are condensed analogies.[1] They are often the speechwriter's most important tool and are powerful agents of persuasion.[2] In this chapter I seek to answer three questions: (1) What ethical responsibilities do presidential speechwriters think they have for the metaphors they create? (2) How do presidential speechwriters craft metaphors? (3) What ethical responsibilities should presidential speechwriters have for their metaphors? In addressing these questions, I focus on President George W. Bush's speechwriter Michael Gerson's hybrid metaphor "The First Sign of a Smoking Gun Might Be a Mushroom Cloud." This mix of two metaphors was featured in the Bush administration's rhetorical efforts between October 2002 and March 2003 to persuade the US Congress and people that the president of Iraq, Saddam Hussein, had used, possessed, and was planning to deploy weapons of mass destruction (WMD) against the United States. As a hybrid metaphor, it effectively joined the "a smoking gun" metaphor (that Iraqi leader Saddam Hussein had developed the capacity to use WMD) to the metaphor of an Iraqi nuclear attack on the United States ("mushroom cloud").

Gerson's hybrid metaphor was "vivid" and "a carefully constructed piece of rhetoric" that the Bush administration argued "perfectly captured the larger point" about the need to counter threats from terrorism.[3] The Bush administration offered two pieces of evidence in support of the "smoking gun" metaphor: (1) that Iraq had purchased uranium yellowcake and (2) that Iraq had obtained high-strength aluminum tubes. Both were necessary for the construction of WMD. "These were the two foundations of evidence," argues Russ Hoyle, offered in support of the claim "that Saddam was intent on acquiring nuclear weapons, and they would be pressed into service soon enough."[4] They were the two essential "whiffs" of smoke from Gerson's smoking gun, proving that the Iraqi government had the tools needed for the construction of WMD. This evidence constituted "a major part of the case made by the Bush administration before the Iraq war that Hussein represented a serious threat because of his nuclear ambitions."[5]

Gerson's hybrid metaphor is structured with the "smoking gun" coming first and then yielding to a "mushroom cloud" representing a nuclear holocaust. The "mushroom cloud" metaphor provides the ending point, collapsing the two into a coherent and sequential argument. Although a "smoking gun" does not prove a crime has occurred, by joining it to the "mushroom cloud" Gerson effectively leads the audience from a smoking gun to images of nuclear catastrophe rather than inviting it to assess the evidence offered to support the idea of a "smoking gun." The "mushroom cloud" metaphor primed what Spencer Weart has called "nuclear fear," a deep anxiety about the prospects of a nuclear holocaust.[6] "In the public mind," Weart argues, "nuclear terrorism does trump all," shutting down the rational assessment of risk.[7]

Gerson introduced the metaphor to the president's White House Iraq Group (WHIG) on September 5, 2002.[8] The metaphor was used in a front-page article written by Michael R. Gordon and Judith Miller of the *New York Times* and in a television interview with National Security Advisor Condoleezza Rice on September 8, 2002.[9] On October 5 and 6, the intelligence community presented Gerson and the administration with evidence-based judgments that Saddam Hussein did not have uranium yellowcake.[10] This evidence was ignored as President Bush used Gerson's hybrid metaphor to represent the purported threat posed by Iraqi WMD.[11]

Jean Edward Smith describes the metaphor as the "battle cry of the administration."[12] In assessing the influence of the metaphor, Frank Rich writes, "It was nuclear weapons, that much-brandished smoking gun that could come in the form of a mushroom cloud, that had been the most prized and effective tool for selling the war."[13] Weart concurs with Rich's conclusion: "The president and other officials spoke of the Iraqi tyrant developing every sort of 'weapon of mass destruction,' but they got the greatest impact when they warned specifically of a 'mushroom cloud.'"[14]

The Bush administration effectively sold the war by using Gerson's hybrid metaphor. On October 10, 2002, the US House voted 296 to 133, and on October 11 the US Senate voted 77 to 23, to authorize the use of military force against Iraq. A number of Democrats, including future presidential candidates John Kerry, Hillary Clinton, and Joe Biden, voted to authorize the Bush administration to attack Iraq. On March 19, 2003, the United States and three allies invaded Iraq. A Gallup poll released on March 24, 2003, revealed that 74 percent of Americans supported the war. With its superior military force, the United States and its allies easily defeated the Hussein regime.[15] The United States occupied Iraq until December 18, 2011.

In the wake of its victory and during the nine-year occupation, the United States did not find any WMD. By almost any measure, the war was a disaster. The most detailed study of the Iraq war, conducted by the US Army War College, concluded that the only victor in the war was the state of Iran; the Bush administration did not achieve the goals it sold to the US Congress and public.[16] The war cost over $1 trillion that could have been invested in US infrastructure and resulted in the deaths of 500,000 Iraqis and 4,500 Americans.[17] Gerson's hybrid metaphor, central to the Bush administration's effort to sell the war, had been effective, underscoring George Lakoff's conclusion that "metaphors can kill."[18]

The Bush administration was wrong to advocate for the war, and as Frank Rich concluded, Gerson's "smoking guns about Iraq WMDs were toy pistols."[19] A comprehensive bipartisan study conducted by the Select Committee on Intelligence revealed that Gerson and the Bush administration were presented with compelling evidence from the intelligence community before and during their prewar deliberations that Saddam Hussein did not have WMD, which was ignored.[20]

This chapter is divided into two sections, followed by concluding remarks. The first section is dedicated to addressing this question: What ethical responsibilities did Gerson assume when he proposed the hybrid metaphor to the Bush administration and the metaphor became its "battle cry"? The second section considers this question: How did Gerson's hybrid metaphor work to persuade? The chapter concludes by contemplating this question: How should we judge Gerson and his hybrid metaphor?

Michael Gerson's Ethical Responsibilities as Presidential Speechwriter

Presidential speechwriters play a role and are hired to do a job. They are paid to create messages for presidents and their administrations. They are not hired to make policy, nor are they paid to render ethical judgments on the messages they are employed to create. In a recent study of ethics and speechwriting, Knapp and Hulbert note that speechwriters craft words that are used by others.[21] Speechwriters do not deliver the speeches. The speaker is held responsible for the effects of the spoken words and for the words written for that speaker by the speechwriter. Some speechwriters, Knapp and Hulbart observe, see their role as serving a client who deserves their best work, regardless of the argument or message. Robert Oliver, a well-known speechwriter, contended that someone hired by the American Nazi Party to write speeches in support of the party would not be unethical, but that the speaker delivering these speeches would be. But Oliver also states that he would "resign rather than write against my basic and important convictions."[22]

When Oliver served as the speechwriter for President Syngman Rhee of South Korea, he both argued with his client about policy and threatened to resign when Rhee's policies went against Oliver's basic convictions. He did try to persuade the president to pursue negotiations rather than war. At the same time, he also actively supported the president by writing important speeches demonizing South Korea's enemy; he enjoyed the rewards and privileges of the position and was easily persuaded by the president to remain in his post.[23]

Michael Gerson was said by some to be the mouth of President George W. Bush; he crafted many of the words Bush spoke. How did he see his responsibilities? Bush called Gerson his "chief speechwriter and trusted adviser."[24] To illustrate, on November 18, 2002, Gerson attended a "policy time" meeting with President Bush's senior staff. The topic of the meeting was the President's Emergency Plan for AIDS Relief (PEPFAR), which would become the largest health initiative for a single disease in the world, intended to reduce new HIV infections and AIDS-related deaths. Gerson witnessed and participated in a policy-oriented discussion, one that included arguments against the plan. He reports that President Bush "went around the room, asking for conclusions. Most supported the plan; the keepers of the budget opposed. At the last, he came to me. 'Gerson, what do you think?' 'If we can do this, and we don't,' I said, 'it will be a source of shame.'"[25] Bush endorsed PEPFAR, and Gerson wrote the words that appeared in the 2003 State of the Union address announcing the program.

Gerson and the Bush administration deserve praise for the initiative, one that was vetted through argument. President Bush heard arguments from the Office of Management and Budget, members of the National Security Council, and the Centers for Disease Control contesting the viability of PEFFAR. Gerson, his speechwriter, heard these arguments as well, and having considered the opposition, he could then argue that PEPFAR was worth the risk. Gerson was right; PEPFAR has saved eleven million lives.[26]

The success of PEPFAR illustrates the core ethical principle necessary for political communication and presidential speeches: the policies and words in presidential rhetoric should be interrogated with argumentation before they are shared with the public. This core principle was in evidence when Robert Oliver argued with President Rhee about going to war against North Korea and when President Bush hosted the November 18, 2002, meeting to evaluate PEPFAR. By voicing and airing opposing points of view, presidents can avoid "groupthink" (the tendency of a majority opinion to determine an outcome because it is a majority opinion, not because it is the right decision) with meetings dedicated and advisers equipped to engage in authentic argumentation. Unfortunately, as Peter Loge has observed, "young political operatives seem to have no ethical mooring" because they believe "disagreement is somehow ignoble or worse." Argument, Loge continues,

> is at the heart of politics, That's sort of the point of politics. But we don't teach our students that the point of political argument is to find the best path forward and then how to engage in those arguments. That means we don't teach them that the path forward is about something greater than the win in the moment, that there is more at stake than the next election, numbers of clicks[.] . . . We don't teach them that, in Weaver's words, "ideas have consequences."[27]

Argumentation allows for the careful scrutiny and interrogation of claims, allowing those who participate to better judge the values and the consequences of a proposed action. Better ethical decisions are often the result of argumentation.[28]

If President Bush and Gerson deserve praise for engaging in critical argumentation on the PEPFAR program and credit for its success in saving millions of lives, they deserve significant criticism for their failure to do the same when faced with the question of WMD in Iraq, the primary justification for the American invasion. Gerson, in *Heroic Conservatism*, revealed how, in the wake of the 9/11 trauma, he and the Bush administration utterly failed to use argumentation to test the claim that Hussein possessed WMD.[29] The reason is that Gerson and the Bush administration first assumed the existence of WMD in Iraq and then looked for proof. "The pre-war debate," Gerson observes, "did not generally focus on the existence of Iraq's weapons of mass destruction, but on the most prudent method to deal with them."[30] Gerson and colleagues were infected with "imperative thinking." In his book *Rethinking Risk in National Security*, Michael Mazarr argues that American foreign policy is far too often driven by "imperative-driven thinking."[31] Such thinking inflects the preferred decision of the US foreign policy establishment with a sense of urgency, uses language loaded with emotional terms, focuses on action rather than deliberation, and establishes a culture that discourages dissent.

The Bush administration's justification for the 2003 invasion of Iraq was dominated by imperative-driven thinking. The available evidence, assessed by the Central Intelligence Agency (CIA) and other intelligence services, did not prove that Iraq had purchased the uranium yellowcake. The Department of Energy concluded that the high-strength aluminum tubes were purchased for rockets, not WMD.[32]

Key figures in the Bush administration, but not Gerson, admit that they erred in not giving weight to this evidence.[33] There is no evidence in the historical record that Gerson interrogated, assessed, or critically analyzed

Table 7.1. Use of and Challenges to the Hybrid Metaphor "The First Sign of a Smoking Gun Might Be a Mushroom Cloud"

Date	Source	Venue
Use of hybrid metaphor		
September 5, 2002	Gerson introduces hybrid metaphor	White House Iraq Group
September 8, 2002	Michael Gordon and Judith Miller	*New York Times* lead story
September 8, 2002	Condoleezza Rice	*Late Edition*, CNN
October 7, 2002	George Bush	Speech to nation
Argumentative challenges to hybrid metaphor		
October 5, 2002	CIA requests removal of yellowcake line from Cincinnati speech	Memo to Gerson and Hadley
October 6, 2002	CIA states Iraqi possession of uranium not true	Memo to Rice and Hadley

the two foundations of his hybrid metaphor. The two whiffs from Gerson's smoking gun metaphor were illusions. As table 7.1 illustrates, Gerson and the Bush administration were informed by the CIA (on October 5 and October 6) that the evidence supporting the claim that Iraq had purchased uranium yellowcake and high-strength aluminum tubes was weak, and that the president should not assert in his October 7 speech that Saddam had the capacity to launch WMD. Ignoring this evidence, Gerson had Bush use "The First Sign of a Smoking Gun Might Be a Mushroom Cloud" in the president's October 7, 2002, speech in Cincinnati. The invention of these yoked metaphors is a function of imperative thinking, which rushes to judgment, sidestepping argumentative interrogation.

The events of 9/11 were a national shock that moved the Bush administration to focus on a policy of preventing terrorist attacks, which in turn gave birth to the policy of preemption. A policy of preemption justifies attacking an enemy before the enemy attacks. Had the Bush administration carefully engaged in argumentative deliberation about WMD in Iraq, the evidence offered by the CIA and other intelligence agencies on the absence of WMD would have put pressure on decision makers to rebut. Absent argumentative dissent, Gerson then crafted a hybrid metaphor anchored in imperative thinking to justify a policy of preemption in Iraq, inviting my second question.

How Did Gerson's Hybrid Metaphor Implement Imperative Thinking and the Policy of Preemption?

Gerson's hybrid metaphor combines the two images, a smoking gun and a mushroom cloud, to create an imperative demanding action now. The images are powerful and highly emotive, short-circuiting and bypassing the prospects of argument and deliberation. Each image is formidable alone, but when they were joined, they became a remarkably potent force that helped persuade Congress and the American audience that imperative policy thinking was desirable. I explain here the force of the two images separately and then how they work in collaboration.

"The First Sign of a Smoking Gun"

The smoking gun image was introduced into popular use in 1972 by Congressman Barber Conable. He claimed that a taped conversation of wrongdoing by President Richard Nixon constituted an impeachable event that "looked like a smoking gun."[34] Conable's use of the smoking gun image is a simile, which is a loose analogy. The taped conversation of wrongdoing resembled ("looked like") but was not the same as a smoking gun. The smoking gun image, as used by Gerson, became a condensed analogy and a true metaphor when evidence of "yellowcake" and "aluminum tubes" was used as irrefutable proof that Saddam Hussein had WMD. It didn't just "look like" there was a smoking gun, there "was" a smoking gun.

The evidence supporting a "smoking gun" metaphor can be tested. Social psychologists suggest the use of "argument maps" to assess the evidence assembled by those who assert they have a "smoking gun" that proves a crime has been committed.[35] These maps describe the claims, the evidence in support of the claims, and the implications of the claims to determine their strength. Argument and argumentation are thus used to test claims derived from evidence. Hans Blix, who served as the chief United Nations weapons inspector in Iraq between November 27, 2002, and March 18, 2003, used his own version of an argument map to test Gerson's "smoking gun" metaphor in a press conference on January 9, 2003.[36] After Blix and the UN Monitoring, Verification and Inspection Commission had conducted seven hundred inspections of five hundred sites in Iraq, including those recommended by the United States, Blix reported that no "smoking guns" had been found.[37] The International Atomic Energy Agency, using these inspections, concluded that there "was also no indication that Iraq had attempted to import uranium since 1990 or that it had attempted to import aluminum tubes for use in centrifuge enrichment."[38]

Between November 27, 2002, and the launch of the US invasion of Iraq on March 19, 2003, the Bush administration did attempt to rebut Blix and his treatment of the "smoking gun" image as a tool designed to test the strength of the claim that Iraq had secured yellowcake uranium and aluminum tubes. In so doing, the Bush administration created and inflated any evidence it could find, using what Blix called "faith-based intelligence" to justify its intention to invade Iraq.[39] Again, the reports of the bipartisan

US Select Committee on Intelligence and US Army War College under-score the failure of the Bush administration to fairly judge Iraq's prewar WMD capacities and the prospects of a successful postwar occupation. The smoking gun metaphor may have invited argument, and it also functioned as an entryway to the mushroom cloud metaphor, which was designed to shut down argument.

"Might Be a Mushroom Cloud"

The image of a "mushroom cloud" is a powerful metaphorical imperative that inspires a deep primordial nuclear fear. Mushroom clouds and their association with a nuclear holocaust have "become etched in the public's memory and awareness."[40] Slovic, Lifton, Weart, and a host of other scholars have described the anxieties provoked by nuclear weapons.[41] The image of the atomic bomb mushroom, which represents the plumes that accompany the explosion of a nuclear bomb, captures and communicates nuclear fear. The second of the two metaphors in Gerson's hybrid fit the moment, crafted as it was less than a year, some 359 days, after the trauma of 9/11.

As James Carroll has noted:

> The reason 9/11 was so traumatizing for us, I believe, is that the vision we all had of the World Trade Center collapsing in a . . . horrible cloud is . . . that it was for us . . . the mushroom cloud that we had been dreading for a generation. We even designated the place Ground Zero. The only real ground zero exists in Hiroshima and Nagasaki. Now America has one, too. Nuclear dread is an inch below the surface of the entire military project that has unfolded since 9/11. We went to war in Iraq because we were afraid that Saddam Hussein could get a nuclear weapon.[42]

Gerson took rhetorical advantage of 9/11 by anchoring the hybrid met-aphor in a symbol that would remind the Bush administration's audience of its recent trauma. The pain and anguish of the attack on the World Trade Center, the deaths of over four thousand American citizens, and the evil of Osama Bin Laden were there to be exploited. Nuclear dread, unleashed and made sharp by 9/11, warped the decision-making capacities of Gerson and those of many of the Bush administration's political opponents, who sup-ported the Iraq invasion.

The mushroom cloud metaphor is particularly powerful because it is a symbol in Western culture of "decay and death."[43] The mushroom resides in the dark; it is a fungus that contributes to rot. As Weart has observed, wit-nesses of the first nuclear explosions might have used other symbols: "cauli-flower cloud," "great funnel," "raspberry," and so forth. Mushrooms, Weart continues, have "traditional associations with thunderbolts, witches, and fairies, or in short with magical powers."[44] Gerson's selection of the "mushroom cloud" metaphor allowed him to root his symbol in the experience and myths of his American audience.

This was an audience raised on movies, TV shows, and novels featuring the mushroom cloud as the sign of the apocalypse. In the 1950s and 1960s, directors and producers of movies about disasters and the end of time relied on "stock footage of . . . the mushroom cloud of the detonated atomic bomb," and "the same scenes were found in many different movies and soon became familiar referents to nuclear development."[45] When Gerson invented his hybrid metaphor in October 2002, he drew from a rhetorical situation in the early twenty-first century that harbored a

> fear of terrorists with nuclear bombs [that] stood on the shelf along with the other nuclear fears, but now it had moved to the front. Like fallout and reactor hazards in earlier decades, the threat satisfied the requirements for a risk whose likelihood people would tend to exaggerate by comparison with familiar risks like home accidents or fires. The image of a mushroom cloud rising over an American city was dreadful and memorable; the risk of harm was involuntary and unjust; the danger was novel and depended on unknowable secrets. Above all the idea was available in the mind, easily pictured by anyone raised on tales of nuclear weapons. Small wonder that the idea was popular with writers of thriller novels and television shows.[46]

Gerson was successful in drawing on nuclear fear and dread experienced by an audience that had suffered a recent trauma. However, the two metaphors in Gerson's hybrid were not equal.

Gerson's Hybrid Metaphor

The hybrid metaphor begins with the smoking gun, which leads to and ends with the atomic bomb mushroom. Indeed, the smoking gun metaphor, reflecting the influence of imperative thinking, is essentially eliminated in the hybrid as a vehicle for argument or testing. The "first" sign of the smoking gun, the metaphoric hybrid claims, "might" be a "mushroom cloud." The traumatized audience, faced with nuclear dread and fear, may not heed the qualifier "might" or detect how the "mushroom cloud" metaphor has absorbed the "smoking gun" into an unqualified claim that Iraq has and intends to use nuclear weapons.

The two metaphors work to move the audience to the highest level of fear and dread. Preventing Iraq from attacking the United States with nuclear weapons, the hybrid metaphor insists, is an imperative, and almost any possibility or risk of a mushroom cloud rising above the homeland is worth a preemptive attack. The standard the Bush administration set to justify an invasion of Iraq was strikingly low. That standard was based on Vice President Dick Cheney's "one percent" doctrine, which according to Ron

Suskind holds that "if there's just a one percent chance of the unimaginable coming due, act as if it is a certainty."[47] When evidence of a smoking gun must only reach a 1 percent level of probability, the threshold is easily met. And when this smoking gun is folded into the mushroom cloud metaphor, nuclear fear and dread become the dominant and unchecked emotional response. Gerson is responsible for capturing this doctrine in his hybrid metaphor, which invites an assessment of his ethical stance.

Conclusion: Judging the Presidential Speechwriter's Metaphors

How should we judge Gerson and his hybrid metaphor? Gerson served as the chief speechwriter and councilor for President Bush. He played an important role in promoting the Bush administration's AIDS relief program, which has and is saving millions of lives. He has emerged as a moral and eloquent critic of President Donald Trump. However, an evaluation of his body of work must include his contributions to the horrifically misguided war in Iraq. In this context, Gerson did not meet the ethical standards that he has set forth in his powerful critiques of the Trump administration or those general standards of decision making that should be in play when presidents consider going to war.

These standards are anchored in critical thinking, which is in turn dependent on the existence of the robust argumentation Loge has identified as essential to ethical political communication. Hans Blix asserts that the "common denominator" in the failure of the Bush administration to consider that it might be wrong about Iraq's possession of uranium yellowcake, high-strength aluminum tubes, and WMD was a *"deficit in critical thinking."*[48] Blix notes that in

> their efforts to get at reality, courts use cross-examination to force a critical consideration of evidence. In the academic world, use is often made of a peer-group review to ensure critical scrutiny of scientific works. The assertion about Iraqi weapons of mass destruction had been so oft repeated that it was taken for granted in much of the world. The intelligence communities themselves should have provided the critical thinking but, like others, they seem to have been somewhat carried away.[49]

To be fair, the intelligence community did alert Gerson and the administration, twice before President Bush's Cincinnati speech, that the evidence did not support the claim that Iraq had purchased uranium yellowcake. They were ignored.

To engage in critical thinking, assumptions must be challenged, evidence interrogated, alternatives considered, groupthink countered, conspiracy theories debunked, and metaphors questioned. A fair reading of Gerson's defense of his actions before the 2003 invasion of Iraq as recorded in his book *Heroic Conservatism* shows that they do not meet the standards he has applied in his critiques of the Trump administration, which have been developed in thoughtful essays published in the *Washington Post*.[50] Gerson has identified the problematic conspiracy theories and inappropriate metaphors used by the Trump administration. "Conspiracy theories can undermine a belief in truth itself" Gerson claims, "they elevate the arguments that serve your side, no matter how absurd or destructive they become. They honor what is useful above what is real and right." If someone is wrong about conspiracy theories, Gerson recommends that "we can try to persuade him or her" to reconsider.

Even in the face of evidence to the contrary, Gerson and the Bush administration elevated their belief in WMD out of the realm of empirical reality and made it immune to questioning. The Bush administration developed and then stayed within the umbrella of a conspiracy theory about Iraq's possession of WMD, which drew its persuasive power from Gerson's hybrid metaphor. There is no evidence that Gerson or others crafting the Bush administration's policy and rhetoric on the Iraq question seriously questioned their preexisting assumptions or took into account the efforts by the intelligence community on October 5 and 6, 2002, to undercut the uranium yellowcake claims.

Gerson has rightly criticized the Trump administration's use of apocalyptic language. Such language, Gerson contends, creates comparisons that don't "allow for limits." These comparisons are often "absurd" and "dangerous." They produce, according to Gerson, "inappropriate metaphors" that are "used by adults who should know better." Gerson then highlights the danger "that impressionable people might confuse vivid metaphors with reality" a "risk that should be named."[51] Gerson's hybrid metaphor, used as the battle cry of the Bush administration to sell the war in Iraq, confused two unfounded metaphors with a reality, with deadly consequences. He and other presidential speechwriters have an ethical responsibility to test their metaphors in the cauldron of critical thinking through argumentation. This test would better ensure that people do not confuse vivid hybrid metaphors with that promote war.

Notes

1 Chaïm Perelman and Lucie Olbrechts-Tyteca, *The New Rhetoric: A Treatise on Argumentation*, trans. John Wilkinson and Purcel Weaver (Notre Dame, IN: University of Notre Dame Press, 1969), 399.

2 Amber Boeynaems et al., "The Effects of Metaphorical Framing on Political Persuasion: A Systematic Literature Review," *Metaphor and Symbol* 32, no. 2 (2017): 118–134.

[3] Michael Isikoff and David Corn, *Hubris: The Inside Story of Spin, Scandal, and the Selling of the Iraq War*, 1st ed. (New York: Crown Publishers, 2006), 93–94.

[4] Russ Hoyle, *Going to War: How Misinformation, Disinformation, and Arrogance Led America into Iraq*, 1st ed. (New York: Thomas Dunne Books, 2008), 123.

[5] Dana Milbank and Pincus Walter, "Bush Aides Disclose Warnings from CIA," *Washington Post*, July 23, 2003, https://www.washingtonpost.com/archive/poli tics/2003/07/23/bush-aides-disclose-warnings-from-cia/d5b367e9-50b2-4dfd -9b0e-0bf3f1af0274/.

[6] Spencer R. Weart, *Nuclear Fear: A History of Images* (Cambridge, MA: Harvard University Press, 1988).

[7] Spencer Weart, "Nuclear Fear 1987–2007—Has Anything Changed? Has Everything Changed?" in *Filling the Hole in the Nuclear Future*, ed. Robert Jacobs (Lanham, MD: Lexington Books, 2010), 256.

[8] Jean Edward Smith, *Bush* (New York: Simon & Schuster, 2016), 316.

[9] Michael R. Gordon and Judith Miller, "Threats and Responses: The Iraqis; US Says Hussein Intensifies Quest for A-Bomb Parts," *New York Times*, October 8, 2002, 1.

[10] Select Comm. on Intelligence, Report on the US Intelligence Community's Prewar Intelligence Assessments on Iraq together with Additional Views, S. Rep. No. 108-301 (2004), https://fas.org/irp/congress/2004_rpt/ssci_concl.pdf.

[11] George W. Bush, Address to the Nation on Iraq from Cincinnati, Ohio, October 7, 2002, https://americanrhetoric.com/speeches/gwbushwariniraqcincinnati.htm.

[12] Smith, *Bush*, 316.

[13] Frank Rich, *The Greatest Story Ever Sold: The Decline and Fall of Truth from 9/11 to Katrina* (New York: Penguin Press, 2006), 231.

[14] Spencer R. Weart, *The Rise of Nuclear Fear* (Cambridge, MA: Harvard University Press, 2012), 278.

[15] Thomas E. Ricks, *Fiasco: The American Military Adventure in Iraq* (New York: Penguin Press, 2006).

[16] Joel Rayburn and Frank K. Sobchak, *The U.S. Army in the Iraq War* (Carlisle, PA: Strategic Studies Institute: US Army War College Press, 2019).

[17] Phillip Bump, "15 Years after the Iraq War Began, the Death Toll Is Still Murky," March 20, 2018, https://www.washingtonpost.com/news/politics/ wp/2018/03/20/15-years-after-it-began-the-death-toll-from-the-iraq-war-is -still-murky/.

[18] "Metaphor and War Again," https://escholarship.org/uc/item/32b962zb.

[19] Rich, *Greatest Story Ever Sold*.

[20] Select Comm. on Intelligence, Report on the US Intelligence Community's Prewar Intelligence Assessments on Iraq together with Additional Views.

[21] John C. Knapp and Azalea M. Hulbert, *Ghostwriting and the Ethics of Authenticity* (New York: Palgrave Macmillan, 2017).

[22] Lois Einhorn, "Ghostwriting: Two Famous Ghosts Speak on Its Nature and Its Ethical Implications," in *Ethical Dimensions of Political Communication*, ed. Robert E. Denton (New York: Praeger, 1991), 10.

[23] David A. Frank and WooSoo Park, "Syngman Rhee, Robert T. Oliver, and the Symbolic Construction of the Republic of Korea During the Global Cold War,"

Rhetoric Society Quarterly (2017): 207–226; and David A. Frank and WooSoo Park, "The Complicity of the Ghostwriter: Robert T. Oliver, Syngman Rhee, and the Rhetoric of a Dictator," *Rhetoric Review* 37, no. 1 (2018): 105–117.

24 George W. Bush, *Decision Points*, 1st ed. (New York: Crown Publishers, 2010), 340.

25 Michael J. Gerson, *Heroic Conservatism: Why Republicans Need to Embrace America's Ideals (and Why They Deserve to Fail If They Don't)*, 1st ed. (New York: HarperOne, 2007), 3.

26 Christine Evain, "How Is the United States's International HIV Prevention Programme Evolving?" *Advances in Social Sciences Research Journal* 5, no. 9 (2018): 78–94.

27 Peter Loge, "A Call to Return to the Study and Teaching of Political Communication Ethics," @Medium, November 2, 2018, https://medium.com/@Peter Loge/a-call-to-return-to-the-study-and-teaching-of-political-communication-ethics-80ea65f2b15c.

28 On the idea that argument and argumentation are central to ethical considerations, see Jonathan Glover, *Humanity: A Moral History of the Twentieth Century* (New Haven, CT: Yale University Press, 2000); Perelman and Olbrechts-Tyteca, *New Rhetoric*; Hugo Mercier and Dan Sperber, *The Enigma of Reason* (Cambridge, MA: Harvard University Press, 2017).

29 Gerson, *Heroic Conservatism*, 141–144.

30 Gerson, *Heroic Conservatism*, 141.

31 Michael J. Mazarr, *Rethinking Risk in National Security: Lessons of the Financial Crisis for Risk Management* (New York: Palgrave Macmillan, 2016).

32 Intelligence, Short Report on the US Intelligence Community's Prewar Intelligence Assessments on Iraq.

33 Milbank and Walter, "Bush Aides Disclose Warnings from CIA."

34 Michael Billig and Katie MacMillan, "Metaphor, Idiom and Ideology: The Search for 'No Smoking Guns' across Time," *Discourse & Society* 16, no. 4 (2005): 461.

35 Derek Beach and Rasmus Brun Pedersen, *Process-Tracing Methods: Foundations and Guidelines*, 2nd ed. (Ann Arbor: University of Michigan Press, 2019), 224–227.

36 Hans Blix, "Notes for Briefing the Security Council," January 9, 2003, http://www.un.org/Depts/unmovic/bx9jan.htm.

37 Hans Blix, "Weapons of Mass Destruction: The Challenges Ahead," *India International Centre Quarterly* 32, no. 1 (2005): 19.

38 United Nations, "United Nations Weapons Inspectors Report to Security Council on Progress in Disarmament of Iraq," March 7, 2003, https://www.un.org/press/en/2003/sc7682.doc.htm.

39 Blix, "Weapons of Mass Destruction," 19.

40 Luther J Carter, *Nuclear Imperatives and Public Trust: Dealing with Radioactive Waste* (New York: Routledge, 2015), 42.

41 Paul Slovic, "The Perception Gap: Radiation and Risk," *Bulletin of the Atomic Scientists* 68, no. 3 (2012): 67–75; Robert Jay Lifton, *The Broken Connection: On Death and the Continuity of Life* (New York: American Psychiatric Publishing, 1996), 386; and Weart, *Nuclear Fear*.

[42] James Carrol, "'House of War' Questions U.S. Reliance on Pentagon," interview by Steve Inskeep, *Morning Edition*, May 30, 2019, https://www.npr.org/tem plates/story/story.php?storyId=5438635.

[43] Valentina Pavlovna Wasson et al., *Mushrooms, Russia, and History*, 2 vols. (New York: Pantheon Books, 1957), 134.

[44] Weart, *Rise of Nuclear Fear*, 24.

[45] Joyce Evans, *Celluloid Mushroom Clouds: Hollywood and Atomic Bomb* (Boulder, CO: Routledge, 2018), 41.

[46] Weart, *Rise of Nuclear Fear*, 269–270.

[47] Ron Suskind, *The One Percent Doctrine: Deep inside America's Pursuit of Its Enemies since 9/11* (New York: Simon & Schuster, 2006), 62.

[48] Hans Blix, *Disarming Iraq*, 1st ed. (New York: Pantheon Books, 2004), 263. Emphasis in original.

[49] Blix, *Disarming Iraq*, 263.

[50] Michael Gerson, "Trump's Spread of Conspiracy Theories Undermines a Belief in Truth Itself," August 12, 2019, https://www.washingtonpost .com/opinions/trumps-spread-of-conspiracy-theories-undermines-a-belief-in -truth-itself/2019/08/12/b83a1668-bd22-11e9-b873-63ace636af08_story .html; Michael Gerson, "Trump's Ideology Isn't Populism: It's Catastrophism," February 25, 2019, https://www.washingtonpost.com/opinions/trumps -ideology-isnt-populism-its-catastrophism/2019/02/25/89a1fb2e-3940 -11e9-aaae-69364b2ed137_story.html; and Gerson, *Heroic Conservatism*.

[51] Gerson, "Trump's Ideology Isn't Populism."

8

Overview of Digital Political Communication and Marketing

Jennifer Lees-Marshment and Vincent Raynauld

Since the early 1990s, digital media channels have become integral components of established political elites' public outreach and engagement toolkit in the United States as well as several other countries (Johnson 2002; Kim, Heinrich, et al. 2018; Dimitrova and Matthes 2018). More recently, social media services—including YouTube, Facebook, Twitter, Instagram, Snapchat, and TikTok—have provided a wide range of political actors with a "dizzying and continually changing array of often subtly different ways [. . .] to display online advertisements to voters targeted on the basis of their geographic locations, demographics, likes and dislikes, and dispositions" during elections (Kreiss, Lawrence, and McGregor 2018, 9). Conversely, members of the public have also been turning more and more to digital media to seek out, acquire, and share political information, voice opinions, and be active politically through institutional as well as more informal channels of engagement (Bode 2016; Moeller, Kühne, and De Vreese 2018; Small et al. 2014). From a broader perspective, the emergence and popularization of digital communication platforms have profoundly impacted the ins and outs of political communication processes.

Political communication can be defined as a set of strategic activities "aimed at attaining or retaining power but also inextricably intertwined with many other elements of politics—such as the transmission of interests and demands of citizens, the symbolic legitimation of authority, and the clarification of alternative options in policy making" (Esser and Pfetsch 2017, 328; see also Blumler 2016). Over the last two decades, the accelerating growth, diversification, and specialization of the online mediascape have reshaped elite-led political communication in and out of elections. For example they have furthered the mediatization of politics. It can be viewed as "a long-term process through which the importance of the media and their spill-over effects on political processes, institutions, organizations and actors have increased" (Strömbäck and Esser 2014, 6; see also Blumler and Esser 2019). In other words, they have forced established political elites—including presidents, prime ministers, elected officials, political parties, and candidates during elections—to constantly rethink and retool their messaging, mobilization, and organizing tactics to better adapt to and leverage more efficiently the structural and functional properties of digital media platforms.

The aforementioned dynamics have also deepened the professionalization of politics. This process is characterized by several elements: (1) political communication being a mostly nonstop, permanent activity; (2) political communication becoming a centralized process (a small number of leadership entities coordinating political communication campaigns); and (3) experts playing an important role "in analyzing and reaching to member, target groups and stakeholders, in analyzing its own and the competitors' weakness and strengths and making use of that knowledge, and in news management" (Strömbäck 2007, 54; see also Bennett and Pfetsch 2018; Karlsen and Enjolras 2016). This chapter takes a deep dive into one aspect of this dynamic of professionalization: the role and effects of political marketers in digital politicking.

Political marketing is fundamental to political success. Established political elites rely increasingly on marketing to pursue their goals, whether it is winning elections or affecting policy change (Lees-Marshment 2019). Once a more hidden activity, marketing in politics has garnered more public attention in recent years, for various reasons. Among them is the impact of big data–driven market research on online advertising during the US 2016 presidential election and the 2016 Brexit referendum in the United Kingdom. At its core, "political marketing is about how political organizations and practitioners—including candidates, politicians, leaders, parties, governments and NGOs—use marketing tools and concepts to understand, develop products in response to, to involve as well as to communicate and interact with their political market in order to achieve their goals" (Lees-Marshment et al. 2019, 2). It involves strategy, market research, branding, communication, and delivery. Political marketing can play an important role in informing the design and rolling out of political communication campaigns:

- Market research, which includes polling, focus groups, and voter profiling, can help campaigns understand the political market (e.g., what voters want and think, and how they behave).
- Market segmentation can be used to break down the electorate into segments of varying sizes—also known as "target universes" (Schneider 2019)—based on various considerations, such as sociodemographic profile, preferences, interests, and objectives.

- Strategy can help identify and reach out to target political markets in efficient ways.

Politicians' increasingly diverse uses of digital media in their day-to-day outreach and engagement activities have helped reshape the dynamics of political marketing and how they contribute to political communication (Towner and Dulio 2012; Iosifidis and Wheeler 2018). Traditionally, direct marketing consisted of campaign leaflets distributed in mailboxes. But it has rapidly become more mobile, virtual, personalized, and instantaneous, first through emails followed by texting, then by ads on Web 1.0 media platforms and social media services such as Facebook and Instagram (e.g., Petre 2018; Kruikemeier, Sezgin, and Boerman 2016; Metz, Kruikemeier, and Lecheler 2019; Lalancette and Raynauld 2019). These changes have impacted the entire political communication cycle, from the ways in which politicians identify and gain insights into their target audience to how they build and adapt their public image, as well as how they conceive and deliver political and policy messages to the public. More important for this chapter, a large number of profound ethical issues have arisen that for the most part have received limited attention from the academic community. This chapter addresses this gap in the scholarly literature and offers a discussion of specific dimensions of the role of ethics in online political communication.

In the context of this chapter, ethics in political marketing communication is defined as "standards of conduct based on moral duties and virtues derived from principles of right and wrong" (Denton, Trent, and Friedenberg 2019, 142). In other words, they can be viewed as a rigid set of norms and practices guiding the behavior of individuals and organizations so they can be "right, good, appropriate" and ultimately make a positive contribution to society (Denton, Trent, and Friedenberg 2019, 142). This chapter zeros in on specific ethical issues related to digital political marketing communication. The first section focuses on how the rise of new practices in digital politicking has led to a lack of transparency in political communication. The second section addresses the growingly manipulative—and in some cases deceptive—nature of digital political communication. The third section discusses the negative effects of unethical forms of political marketing communication, while the last section introduces ethical principles that could help guide current and future dynamics of digital political communication.

Lack of Transparency in Digital Political Marketing Communication

Recent years have been marked by political elites' growing ability to gain granular insights into the preferences, interests, and objectives of members of the public through techniques leveraging the capabilities of newer technologies (Baldwin-Philippi 2017). Among these is big data market research, which can be defined as the use of technological tools, "computation power and algorithmic accuracy" (Boyd and Crawford 2012, 663) to acquire, archive, aggregate, and analyze large volumes of data from wide-ranging online and offline sources in order to acquire a better understanding of the preferences and goals of segments of the political market and—in many cases—specific individuals (Baldwin-Philippi 2017; Nickerson and Rogers 2014).

Market intelligence gained through big data–driven techniques can inform all aspects of political communication. For example, political ads can be developed and adapted based on which phrases would work best to sell policies and what slogans—such as Make America Great Again—would resonate with and more effectively mobilize narrow slices of the audience. Market intelligence can also be used to set the agenda, such as which policies should be discussed in order to address the demands of specific segments of the public. The content and format of political marketing appeals is carefully thought out. The images and words are chosen carefully, and direct marketing is sent directly to individuals based on their social, political, economic, or sociodemographic profiles (Raynauld and Lees-Marshment 2019). Before being released widely, political appeals can be tested to measure "how well messages perform against one another and using that information to drive content production and further targeting" (Baldwin-Philippi 2017, 628). It is questionable whether members of the public are aware of and understand how and to what degree data are influencing the production and circulation of political messages online (e.g., Tufekci 2014).

In the digital media space, political messages can be delivered quickly and at low cost to a specific audience through individualized ads on websites or through social media services (Kruikemeier, Sezgin, and Boerman 2016). Comparatively, offline-based forms of digital political marketing communication tend to be slower and more expensive and target a broader public (e.g., campaign flyers, billboards, TV ads) (see Raynauld and Lees-Marshment 2019). Digital political marketing communication is (1) highly direct and individualized in nature and (2) largely unseen by the broader public.

First, digital political marketing appeals are generally delivered to the receiver directly and are highly individualized in nature. Indeed, they are tailored to the preferences, interests, and goals of individual users, not just groups of people living in the same geographical area, as is the case with more traditional campaign flyers or posters. In the case of social networking platforms, political appeals can be "personalized and targeted based on users' available demographic profile information, stated interests, likes, and location that users shared voluntarily" (Kruikemeier, Sezgin, and Boerman 2016, 367; see also Papakyriakopoulos et al. 2018). They can also be based on information from other sources, including polls. Online direct political marketing is individualized to a significant degree. Online market research—especially with the help of big data research techniques—can help produce highly granulated psychological and political profiles of individuals. During the 2006 and 2008 federal elections in Canada, strategists for the Conservative Party of Canada generated fictional characters with the help of data in order to epitomize swing voters. Among them were (1) "Dougie," a single white man in his late twenties working at a well-known Canadian retail store ("Canadian Tire"), who agreed with the policies of the Conservative Party on crime and welfare abuse but was more interested in recreation than politics and might fail to turn out to vote; (2) "Rick and Brenda," a common-law couple with working-class jobs; and (3) "Mike and Theresa," who were better off financially and could become Conservative supporters except for their Catholic background (Turcotte 2012, 85). This understanding was then used to design highly persuasive political messages, both in the arguments featured and the visual appearance.

Second, unlike TV ads, billboards, posters, and speeches, which are mostly public in nature, digital political marketing communication can be unseen. Of particular interest are "dark" targeted political ads. They can be described as political advertisements that are not shared with the public at large but intended for specific individuals due their distinct format and content (Cadwalladr 2017). These ads can be circulated in different ways, including through a Facebook user's private timeline. Despite the archiving power of the contemporary internet, wherein every word politicians say and how they look can potentially be recorded and scrutinized with the help of smartphones and other media tools (e.g., Chadwick, Dennis, and Smith 2015), it can prove difficult to find targeted dark ads circulated on social media. It should also be noted that the practice of dark political ads remains largely unregulated in many national contexts.

When the content of political messages is not problematic, this does not by itself matter. It can simply mean sending details about a specific political or policy issue to someone who has shown interest or using positive images to address people's interests and desire to see change. However, when manipulation is at the core of the political appeal, the lack of transparency can raise fundamental ethical issues. From a broader perspective, it can represent a threat to the integrity and legitimacy of democratic processes.

The Potentially Manipulative Nature of Digital Political Marketing Communication

Digital political marketing appeals can give the sender of the communication more control over how the receiver decodes and understands it. Specifically, they can target receivers directly to avoid the filter of mass media organizations. In doing so, less "noise" can interfere with the transmission of a message, thus rendering it more potent and likely to achieve its goals. The design of the message can be encoded by those sending it out to make sure the message uses symbols or language likely to connect with the target audience (Entman 1993). As mentioned previously, political messages' data-driven design can help ensure that those receiving a message decode it as intended by communication professionals. In other words, there is more control over how individual users interpret and make sense of the message.

While this control represents a practical advantage, as it enables the broadcasting of strategic political appeals with limited outside interference, it can be the source of major ethical concerns. It can create room for misuse, including manipulation, that can negatively impact democratic processes. Unlike persuasion, which has been an important aspect of political communication, mobilization, and persuasion over several decades (Mutz, Sniderman, and Brody 1996), manipulation restricts, denies, distorts, and degrades the ability of those receiving political messages to think rationally and make informed choices (Beckman 2018, 24). This is because digital political marketing communication can lack (1) context and completeness, (2) prevent debate and discussion, (3) extend and bolster elite control, (4) bypass rational thinking, and (5) go largely unchecked.

First, because digital political marketing communication can be partial or incomplete due to strategic concerns, facts and figures can be taken out of context, without consideration for the complexity of a policy issue or political viewpoints. Moreover, rather than just providing information on a specific political or policy topic to a target audience, the messaging can be more nuanced through the selective use of data, thus manipulating people's preferences, interests, and dispositions as determined with the help of market research.

Second, digital political marketing communication can influence political cognition and behavior in ways that prevent the public from being rational when thinking through and making political decisions (Beckman 2018, 20). For example, the individualized nature of political appeals can lead to heightened levels of political fragmentation within the public. This can be defined as the "breakdown of broadly shared awareness, perception, and understanding of politics, which is acquired through common political knowledge, concerns, and goals, as well as the emergence of individual-based and ever-evolving micro-political realities—or enclaves—shaped by highly specific and wide-ranging interests and objectives" (Raynauld and Turcotte 2018, 14). This can in turn reduce levels of discussion, debate, and deliberation, as people who are exposed to narrow political messages have a different understanding of political reality (Metz, Kruikemeier, and Lecheler 2019). It can also prevent political socialization, which can drive public opinion formation processes within communities, families, professional environments, or other social settings (Beckman 2018, 31). From a broader perspective, digital political marketing communication can lead to deception, misinformation, and distortion of facts, as well as strategic omission of crucial information. This can ultimately reduce the intellectual autonomy of the targets of political appeals.

Third, digital political marketing communication can expand and—in many cases—reinforce political elites' control over political communication. For example, it can reduce the volume of information to be processed by the receiver. According to Beckman (2018, 31), this can enhance the ability of the sender to control all communication.

Fourth, digital political marketing communication can be designed in ways that appeal to the emotions in order to circumvent and manipulate "the rational thinking processes of voters" (Hacker 2014). Specifically, it can influence and—in many cases—alter cognitive processes, opinions, and behavior patterns (Beckman 2018, 40). As noted by Jones, Hoffman, and Young (2013, 1133):

> Feelings of anger prompt citizens to engage in greater electoral participation (Valentino et al., 2011), while feelings of anxiety lead to an increased interest in politics in general (Huddy et al., 2007), and positive feelings such as hope or enthusiasm increase awareness of one's environment and confidence that preferred outcomes will occur (Brader and Valentino, 2007; Just et al., 2007).

During the 2016 US presidential election cycle, Trump's digital media director, Brad Parscale, talked about wanting to "make [. . .] [voters] 'dance' by creating messages appealing to and resonating with specific segments of the electorate" (CBS 2018). Mark Thurnbull, the managing director of Cambridge Analytica, a company that worked for the Trump campaign, reinforced that point. He argued for the need to "drop the bucket further down the well than anybody else, to understand what are those really deep-seated underlying fears, concerns. It's no good fighting an election campaign on the facts because actually it's all about emotion, it's all about emotion" (Channel 4 2018).

Finally, digital political marketing communication can go largely unchecked. Because of the lack of transparency and relative invisibility of political communication, as discussed in the previous section, there is room for errors or problems. In many cases these issues cannot be singled out, investigated, and rebutted by experts, media organizations, or other politicians. This can lead to the further erosion of rational thinking due to emotive design. As argued by Beckman (2019), the lack of countervailing information can lead to the consumption of inaccurate or misleading information and prevent individuals from questioning or refuting communication themselves.

Disruptive Impact of Unethical Digital Political Marketing Communication

The consequences of problematic digital political communication have manifested themselves in the context of two consequential political events in recent years: (1) the 2016 UK Brexit referendum, in which citizens expressed themselves on whether the country should remain in or leave the European Union; and (2) the US 2016 presidential election. In both cases, the results were close and largely unexpected (Raynauld and Turcotte 2018; Virdee and McGeever 2018). In November 2016, Donald Trump was elected president with 304 electoral college votes, compared to 227 for Hillary Clinton, but nearly three million fewer voters and 46.1 percent of the popular vote compared to Clinton's 48.2 percent. In June 2016, people in Britain had voted in favor of leaving the European Union by a margin of just 4 percent (52 percent for leaving, 48 percent for remaining). These two political events have caused major disruptions in the political systems of both countries. They have also reshaped dynamics of power in the international political system, as the United States and the United Kingdom can be viewed as major economic, political, and diplomatic forces on the world stage.

As noted by Keaveney (2019), the outcome of the Brexit referendum has been the source of much democratic angst among elected officials, political parties, governmental agencies, and the public at large in the United Kingdom. Criticisms have included that claims made during the campaign were potentially inaccurate, oversimplified, or simply false. In many cases, this caused voters to make complex decisions while relying on inaccurate, faulty, or false political communication and ultimately feeling hoodwinked (Worcester et al. 2018). This is in line with the problems with digital political marketing communication outlined in previous sections of this chapter. For example, the Leave Campaign had a simple message on its campaign bus: "We sent the EU £350 million pounds a week. Let's fund the NHS instead. Vote Leave." Yet the reality of health funding was more complicated. First, the UK received funding back from the European Union (EU), and there was no promise that any future government would direct money saved from going to the EU to the NHS. Second, the message suggested that all the country's health problems could be solved with a simple vote on one day in 2016. The profound and huge implications of leaving the EU were never fully disclosed and discussed in online ads. Finally, the now-known hidden aspects of online ads, coupled with the breaches of privacy from the data utilized in the design of those ads, have led to suggestions that this type of communication caused substantial disruption to the operation of the UK government, with profound social and economic consequences.

Trump's campaign communication also drew on simplistic and negative messaging. As noted by Lalancette and Raynauld (2019, 889), he turned to Twitter and other social media services to "push out more unconventional political messages—which often consist[ed] of snarky responses to or attacks of his critics—to his millions of followers." While his attacks targeted specific social groups, such as immigrants, they also drew on the emotions of segments of society deeply dissatisfied with their living standards (Conley 2018). Cosgrove (2019) echoes that point. He notes that the digital messages were designed to be polarizing and forge an emotional bond with members of the US working class (Cosgrove 2019). This strategy was driven in part by data from Cambridge Analytica. This organization acquired through big data market research a granular understanding of the US political market and helped develop compelling political appeals focused on policy issues tapping into specific discontents: the economy and immigration. For example, thousands of versions of the same Facebook-based ads were specifically tailored to connect with specific slices of the market (Conley 2018; British Broadcasting Corporation 2017). According to Beckman (2019), the 2016 US presidential election can be seen as breaching ethical standards in political communication due to various elements. Chief among them was the widespread use of targeted communication that repeatedly delivered messages comprising false and misleading claims to select audiences identified on the basis of sociodemographics, preferences, and behavior.

Principles of Ethical Digital Political Marketing Communication

On the one hand, digital political marketing communication, which is increasingly driven by insights acquired through big data marketing research, can help established political elites better identify, understand, and respond to target audiences with specific preferences, interests, and objectives. This can have several positive outcomes, such as contributing to the inclusion of marginalized communities in the political process as well as the advancement of the public good (Lees-Marshment, Elder, and Raynauld 2019). On the other hand, and more important for this chapter, it can breach important ethical principles in political communication. Among these are transparency, impartiality, responsibility, inclusivity, fairness, and respect.

As Beckman (2018, 32) points out, digital political marketing communication can influence political cognition and behavior through "strategies driven by the systematic use of demographic, psychographic, and behavioral data." This has turned communication practitioners into "specialized data forensic scientists," constantly investigating, developing, and engaging in "new kinds of digital manipulation of public opinion" (see also Hargittai 2018). Building on that logic, Hacker (2014) argues that using data and digital communication in politics can be "ethically problematic," as it can have far-reaching consequences beyond a single election or campaign.

Highly targeted digital political communication also breaches the principle that political communication should be inclusive in nature, whether it is during or outside of elections. It should enable citizens to acquire information and be active politically. More important, it should help them be involved in formal and informal political processes in an informed way. Strategic political messages and mobilization initiatives that are rolled out online—especially in the social mediascape—are geared toward narrow segments of the population with usually narrow interests, preferences, and objectives (Walker and Nowlin 2018). For example, campaigns can include or exclude Facebook users from targeted political appeals based on various social, political, cultural, linguistic, economic, or technological (e.g., brand of smartphone) considerations (Singer 2018). Uses of big data exacerbate "exclusionary segmentation," wherein established political elites only target individuals and organizations that are useful to them (Marland 2012, 165–166). This can lead to the exclusion of a large number of individuals or other entities, such as those who have lower socioeconomic status or members of minority communities (Howard and Kreiss 2010).

As noted previously, communication can also lack transparency. Unlike more traditional approaches to political advertising, in which everyone is exposed to publicly visible messages, big data can help create highly targeted "dark" political appeals that can only be seen by individuals who may not be aware they are being targeted and may be less critical of the communication they absorb. It also involves intentional efforts to exclude voters, which breaches principles of transparency and inclusivity. During the 2016 US presidential election, the Trump campaign deployed significant efforts to intentionally discourage certain slices of the political market from voting. For example, it turned to digital political marketing communication to keep voting blocs likely to support the Clinton campaign (e.g., African Americans, young females, and idealistic white liberals) from feeling the need to vote on Election Day (Grassegger and Krogerus 2017). It should be noted that this approach has been used by a large number of political campaigns internationally over the past few decades (Bradshaw and Howard 2018).

Professional organizations engaging in more generic digital communication and, more specifically, digital political marketing, have adopted several codes of conduct and statements to guide their activities over recent decades. For example, the American Association of Political Consultants' (AAPC n.d.) code of professional ethics mentions that its members should adhere to specific standards of practice. Among them is impartiality: "I will use no appeal to voters which is based on racism, sexism, religious intolerance or any form of unlawful discrimination and will condemn those who use such practices." The Trump campaign's digital communication efforts breached this principle during the 2016 US presidential election. Bennett and Livingston (2018, 131) note that it emphasized forms of political appeal "blending nationalism, anti-globalism, racism, welfare nationalism, anti-immigrant and refugee themes, and the need for strong leadership and order" (see also Ott 2017).

Another professional organization of interest is the American Marketing Association (2019). Its statement of ethics states that marketers must "do no harm . . . consciously avoiding harmful actions or omissions by embodying high ethical standards"; "foster trust in the marketing system [. . .] avoiding deception in product design, pricing, communication, and delivery of distribution"; and "embrace ethical values" to uphold "consumer confidence in the integrity of marketing by affirming these core values." These core values include honesty, responsibility, fairness, respect, transparency, and citizenship. Many digital political marketing operations around the world have not always followed these principles. For example, they have failed to "acknowledge the social obligations to stakeholders that come with increased marketing and economic power" and to "recognize our special commitments to vulnerable market segments such as children, seniors, the economically impoverished, market illiterates and others who may be substantially disadvantaged." Gusterson (2017) notes that the Leave Campaign adopted a discourse focused on specific segments of the UK public while sidelining many others, such as immigrants.

As the conclusion of this chapter makes clear, the problematic use of digital marketing communication by a large number of media and political players—including journalistic organizations, elected officials, candidates during elections, and political parties—in recent years has raised several concerns. From a broader perspective, it has failed to upload certain standards of political communication and, by extension, has hurt democratic processes.

Moving Forward: The Case for Ethics in Digital Political Marketing Communication

As mentioned previously, digital political marketing communication is a highly direct form of marketing that can in some cases be unseen. It gives the sender of the communication more control over how the receiver encodes it. It can also be utilized in highly manipulative ways, thus damaging political communication processes in democratic contexts. It can lack context and completeness, prevent debate and discussion, extend and reinforce elite control, bypass rational thinking, and go largely unchecked.

It would be unrealistic to expect consultants to stop researching the market as well as using big data to identity and target specific segments of the public when designing communication. But as with many communication tools, it is important to reflect on how to best to use this approach to maximize the benefits and limit harmful effects. Doing so can be seen as part of broader efforts to adhere to certain professional standards in any field of activity.

Why Political Communication Professionals Are Responsible

Communications professionals should take responsibility for their work and the effects of it, whether intentional or not. Of particular interest is the ethical dilemma related to the impact of Facebook on recent elections in the United States. This social media platform was not designed to be a tool for political communication during election campaigns. It was not meant to be a tool for journalistic organizations and individual journalists to deliver content to the public. Its core mission was to help individuals and organizations connect with and communicate with each other. Despite this, following public and governmental pressure internationally, Facebook CEO Mark Zuckerberg took responsibility publicly for how the platform was used by different political forces to engage in unethical forms of digital outreach and engagement. He noted:

> Facebook is an idealistic and optimistic company. For most of our existence, we focused on all the good that connecting people can bring. As Facebook has grown, people everywhere have gotten a powerful new tool to stay connected to the people they love, make their voices heard, and build communities and businesses. . . . But it's clear now that we didn't do enough to prevent these tools from being used for harm as well. . . . We didn't take a broad enough view of our responsibility, and that was a big mistake. It was my mistake, and I'm sorry. I started Facebook, I run it, and I'm responsible for what happens here. So now we have to go through every part of our relationship with people and make sure we're taking a broad enough view of our responsibility.
>
> It's not enough to just connect people, we have to make sure those connections are positive. It's not enough to just give people a voice, we have to make sure people aren't using it to hurt people or spread misinformation. It's not enough to give people control of their information, we have to make sure developers they've given it to are protecting it too. Across the board, we have a responsibility to not just build tools, but to make sure those tools are used for good. (*Facebook, Social Media Privacy, and the Use and Abuse of Data* 2018)

It isn't enough for communication professionals to work just in the interests of their clients and not take responsibility for the impact of their actions. This is why the AAPC asks its members to sign and adhere to its code of ethics annually. It also asks them to live and work by the standards it sets, to "convey that they operate with integrity and adhere to standards of the profession, thus improving public confidence in the American political system" (American Association of Political Consultants n.d.).

Recommendations for Principles for Future Practice

Building on several authors' work (e.g., Denton, Trent, and Friedenberg 2019; Lees-Marshment, Elder and Raynauld 2019, 82), it can be argued that there need to be clear ethical principles guiding digital political marketing outreach and engagement. Following are some elements that should be considered when developing an ethical framework to guide practices of digital political marketing communication:

- *Inclusivity:* Targeted political appeals should not be used in ways that exclude specific segments of the public from the political process, especially if these segments can be defined as vulnerable.
- *Engagement:* Digital political communication should be designed in ways that maintain the intellectual autonomy of the public, while also being persuasive, not manipulative.
- *Transparency:* Political communication should be open and transparent so its structure and content can be scrutinized, discussed, and critiqued in informed ways.
- *Accountability:* Established political elites and communication professionals developing digital political messages should be held accountable for their effects.
- *Responsibility:* All aspects of political communication, including market research with the help of big data–driven research, should be used responsibly and accurately.
- *Professionalism:* Clear and broadly accepted standards should be put in place and upheld.
- *Common societal good:* Established political elites should consider the interests of society as a whole, not just individual candidates or campaigns. They should also avoid doing damage to society.

Incentives to Adhere to and Respect These Principles

It is possible to identify two main factors for professionals to adhere to and use these principles: (1) awareness of the potential impact of ethical breaches on society and (2) and professional self-interest. Ethically problematic practices negatively impact the public perception and credibility of those engaging in digital political communication as well as the political message itself. In short, they can harm in a significant way the integrity of digital political communication processes and can lead to reputational and monetary losses.

The impact of problematic political communication can also be practical. Several government inquiries into uses of big data and online communication have been launched following the 2016 US presidential election and the Brexit referendum. The CEO of Facebook and members of the Cambridge Analytica staff have also been called to testify before UK and US lawmakers, and their use of data has been the subject of documentaries and feature films (British Broadcasting Corporation 2017; Channel 4 2018; Horsford and Haynes 2019; *The Great Hack* 2019). When appearing before the UK Parliament and the US Congress, Facebook CEO Mark Zuckerberg conceded that Facebook did not do enough to prevent user data from being used in harmful ways by various organizations, including Cambridge Analytica (*Facebook, Social Media Privacy, and the Use and Abuse of Data* 2018). Facebook was fined UK £500,000—the maximum amount possible—for breaching the Data Protection Act (Hern and Pegg 2018). It also lost users concerned about privacy, which led to the decline of advertising revenue and stock value. Finally, there are calls in several countries for increased regulation of data-using companies, and the conditions under which communication professionals operate are now more restricted.

The ethics of digital political marketing communication are both desirable and necessary, especially in a context wherein there are more and more concerns about the integrity and validity of political communication processes in different national contexts. Establishing clear and specific ethical rules for political communication would bridge the gap and help some of the crises that are plaguing various facets of political communication (Bennett and Pfetsch 2018). Current and future practitioners in the fields of politics, communication, marketing, and public relations need to be aware of these issues, as they are expected to increase in importance over the next decades. By providing a preliminary discussion of ethics of digital political communication, this chapter lays the groundwork for researchers and practitioners to build expertise in this area. More important, it also provides insights that could lead to important discussions about the future of digital political communication.

References

American Association of Political Consultants. n.d. "Code of Ethics." https://theaapc.org/member-center/code-of-ethics/.

American Marketing Association. 2019. "Statement of Ethics." https://myama.force.com/s/article/Codes-of-Conduct.

Baldwin-Philippi, Jessica. 2017. "The Myths of Data-Driven Campaigning." *Political Communication* 34, no. 4: 627–633.

Beckman, Arthur. 2018. "Political Marketing and Intellectual Autonomy." *Journal of Political Philosophy* 26, no. 1: 24–46.

———. 2019. "Democratic Debate 9.2 Political Marketing and Unfair Competition in Politics." In *Political Marketing: Principles and Applications*, 3rd ed., by Jennifer Lees-Marshment, Brian Conley, Edward Elder, Robin Pettitt, Vincent Raynauld, and Andre Turcotte, 259–260. New York: Routledge.

Bennett, W. Lance, and Steven Livingston. 2018. "The Disinformation Order: Disruptive Communication and the Decline of Democratic Institutions." *European Journal of Communication* 33, no. 2: 122–139.

Bennett, W. Lance, and Barbara Pfetsch. 2018. "Rethinking Political Communication in a Time of Disrupted Public Spheres." *Journal of Communication* 68, no. 2: 243–253.

Blumler, Jay G. 2016. "Political Communication." In *The International Encyclopedia of Political Communication*, edited by Gianpietro Mazzoleni, Kevin Barnhurst, Ken'ichi Ikeda, Rousiley Maia, and Hartmut Wessler, 989–1005. London: Wiley-Blackwell.

Blumler, Jay G., and Frank F. Esser. 2019. "Mediatization as a Combination of Push and Pull Forces: Examples during the 2015 UK General Election Campaign." *Journalism* 20, no. 7: 855–872.

Bode, Leticia. 2016. "Political News in the News Feed: Learning Politics from Social Media." *Mass Communication and Society* 19, no. 1: 24–48.

Boyd, Danah, and Kate Crawford. 2012. "Critical Questions for Big Data: Provocations for a Cultural, Technological, and Scholarly Phenomenon." *Information, Communication & Society* 15, no. 5: 662–679.

Brader, Ted, and Nicholas A. Valentino. 2007. "Identities, Interests, and Emotions: Symbolic versus Material Wellsprings of Fear, Anger, and Enthusiasm." In *The Affect Effect: Dynamics of Emotion in Political Thinking and Behavior*, edited by W. Russell Newman et al., 180–201. Chicago: University of Chicago Press.

Bradshaw, Samantha, and Philip N. Howard. 2018. "Challenging Truth and Trust: A Global Inventory of Organized Social Media Manipulation." The Computational Propaganda Project. http://comprop.oii.ox.ac.uk/wp-content/uploads/sites/93/2018/07/ct2018.pdf.

British Broadcasting Corporation (BBC). 2017. "The Digital Guru Who Helped Donald Trump to the Presidency." August 13. http://www.bbc.com/news/av/magazine-40852227/the-digital-guru-who-helped-donald-trump-to-the-presidency.

Cadwalladr, C. 2017. "Revealed: Tory 'Dark' Ads Targeted Voters' Facebook Feeds in Welsh Marginal Seat." *Guardian*, May 27. https://www.theguardian.com/politics/2017/may/27/conservatives-facebook-dark-ads-data-protection-election.

CBS. 2018. "Trump Campaign Digital Media Director and 2020 Trump Campaign Manager Quoted in 'Who Is Brad Parscale.'" February 27. https://www.cbs.com/shows/60_minutes/video/eIHhrLFmOS2ZYFqRG68KQPAu0_aUK PKC/who-is-brad-parscale-/.

Chadwick, Andrew, James Dennis, and Amy P. Smith. 2015. "Politics in the Age of Hybrid Media: Power, Systems, and Media Logics." In *The Routledge Companion to Social Media and Politics*, edited by Axel Bruns et al., 7–22. New York: Routledge.

Channel 4. 2018. "Exposed: Undercover Secrets of Trump's Data firm." March 20. https://www.channel4.com/news/exposed-undercover-secrets-of-donald-trump-data-firm-cambridge-analytica.

Conley, Brian M. 2018. "Thinking What He Says: Market Research and the Making of Donald Trump's 2016 Presidential Election." In *Political Marketing in the 2016 U.S. Presidential Election*, edited by Jamie Gillies, 29–48. New York: Palgrave Macmillan.

Cosgrove, Kenneth M. 2019. "Democratic Debate 4.1: Trumps Political Branding; Expanding the Participation of an Underserved Market?" In *Political Marketing: Principles and Applications*, 3rd ed., by Jennifer Lees-Marshment, Brian Conley, Edward Elder, Robin Pettitt, Vincent Raynauld, and Andre Turcotte, 112–113. New York: Routledge.

Denton, Robert E., Jr., Judith S. Trent, and Robert V. Friedenberg. 2019. *Political Campaign Communication: Principles and Practices*, 9th ed. Lanham, MD: Rowman & Littlefield.

Dimitrova, Daniela V., and Jörg Matthes. 2018. "Social Media in Political Campaigning around the World: Theoretical and Methodological Challenges." *Journalism and Mass Communication Quarterly* 95, no. 2: 333–342.

Entman, Robert M. 1993. "Framing: Toward Clarification of a Fractured Paradigm." *Journal of Communication* 43, no. 4: 51–58.

Esser, Frank, and Barbara Pfetsch. 2017. "Comparing Political Communication: An Update." In *Comparative Politics*, edited by Daniele Caramani et al., 3–28. Oxford: Oxford University Press.

Facebook, Social Media Privacy, and the Use and Abuse of Data: Hearing Before the United States Senate Committee on the Judiciary. 2018. April 10. Statement of Mark Zuckerberg. https://www.judiciary.senate.gov/meetings/facebook-social-media-privacy-and-the-use-and-abuse-of-data.

Grassegger, Hannes, and Mikael Krogerus. 2017. "The Data That Turned the World Upside Down." *Motherboard*, January 28. https://motherboard.vice.com/en_us/article/mg9vvn/how-our-likes-helped-trump-win.

The Great Hack. 2019. Netflix, July 24. https://www.netflix.com/watch/80117542?source=35.

Gusterson, Hugh. 2017. "From Brexit to Trump: Anthropology and the Rise of Nationalist Populism." *American Ethnologist* 44, no. 2: 209–214.

Hacker, Kenneth L. 2014. "Ethical Dilemmas in the Use of Big Data Analytics (BDA) in Affecting Political Communication and Behavior." Working Paper. https://www.researchgate.net/publication/261176065_Ethical_Dilemmas_in_the_Use_of_Big_Data_Analytics_BDA_In_Affecting_Political_Communication_and_Behavior.

Hargittai, Eszter. 2018. "Potential Biases in Big Data: Omitted Voices on Social Media." *Social Science Computer Review* 38, no. 1: 10–24. doi:0894439318788322.

Hern, Alex, and David Pegg. 2018. "Facebook Fined for Data Breaches in Cambridge Analytica Scandal." *Guardian*, July 11. https://www.theguardian.com/technology/2018/jul/11/facebook-fined-for-data-breaches-in-cambridge-analytica-scandal.

Horsford, Lynn, and Toby Haynes. 2019. *Brexit: The Uncivil War*. London: House Productions. Film.

Howard Philip N., and Daniel Kreiss, 2010. "Political Parties and Voter Privacy: Australia, Canada, the United Kingdom and United States in Comparative Perspective." *First Monday* 15, no. 12, http://firstmonday.org/htbin/cgiwrap/bin/ojs/index.php/fm/article/view/2975/2627.

Huddy, Leonie, Stanley Feldman, and Erin Cassese. 2007. "On the Distinct Political Effects of Anxiety and Anger." In *The Affect Effect: Dynamics of Emotion in Political Thinking and Behavior*, edited by W. Russell Newman et al., 202–230. Chicago: University of Chicago Press.

Iosifidis, Petros, and Mark Wheeler. 2018. "Modern Political Communication and Web 2.0 in Representative Democracies." *Javnost—The Public* 25, nos. 1–2: 110–118.

Johnson, Dennis W. 2002. "Campaign Website: Another Tool, but No Killer App." *Journal of Political Marketing* 1, no. 1: 213–215.

Jones, Philip Edward, Lindsay H. Hoffman, and Danna G. Young. 2013. "Online Emotional Appeals and Political Participation: The Effect of Candidate Affect on Mass Behavior." *New Media & Society* 15, no. 7: 1132–1150.

Just, Marion R., Ann N. Crigler, and Todd L. Belt. 2007. "Don't Give up Hope: Emotions, Candidate Appraisals, and Votes." In *The Affect Effect: Dynamics of Emotion in Political Thinking and Behavior*, edited by W. Russell Newman et al., 231–260. Chicago: University of Chicago Press.

Karlsen, Rune, and Bernard Enjolras. 2016. "Styles of Social Media Campaigning and Influence in a Hybrid Political Communication System: Linking Candidate Survey Data with Twitter Data." *International Journal of Press/Politics* 21, no. 3: 338–357.

Keaveney, Paula. 2019. "Democratic Debate 9.1: The Brexit Referendum and the Limitations of Consumer Choice in Political Decisions." In *Political Marketing: Principles and Applications*, 3rd ed., by Jennifer Lees-Marshment, Brian Conley, Edward Elder, Robin Pettitt, Vincent Raynauld, and Andre Turcotte, 257–259. New York: Routledge.

Kim, Young Mie, Richard James Heinrich, et al. 2018. "Campaigns Go Social: Are Facebook, YouTube and Twitter Changing Elections?" In *New Directions in Media and Politics*, edited by Travis N. Ridout, 100–117. New York: Routledge.

Kreiss, Daniel, Regina G. Lawrence, and Shannon C. McGregor. 2018. "In Their Own Words: Political Practitioner Accounts of Candidates, Audiences, Affordances, Genres, and Timing in Strategic Social Media Use." *Political Communication* 35, no. 1: 8–31.

Kruikemeier, Sanne, Minem Sezgin, and Sophie C. Boerman. 2016. "Political Microtargeting: Relationship between Personalized Advertising on Facebook and Voters' Responses." *Cyberpsychology, Behavior, and Social Networking* 19, no. 6: 367–372.

Lalancette, Mireille, and Vincent Raynauld. 2019. "The Power of Political Image: Justin Trudeau, Instagram, and Celebrity Politics." *American Behavioral Scientist* 63, no. 7: 888–924.

Lees-Marshment, Jennifer. 2019. "Marketing Scholars and Political Marketing: The Pragmatic and Principled Reasons for Why Marketing Academics Should

Research the Use of Marketing in the Political Arena." *Customer Needs and Solutions* 6: 41–48.

Lees-Marshment, Jennifer, Brian Conley, Edward Elder, Robin Pettitt, Vincent Raynauld, and Andre Turcotte. 2019. *Political Marketing: Principles and Applications*, 3rd ed. New York: Routledge.

Lees-Marshment, Jennifer, Edward Elder, and Vincent Raynauld. 2019. "Democratic Debate 3.1: The Ethical Issues around Big Data in Politics." In *Political Marketing: Principles and Applications*, 3rd ed., by Jennifer Lees-Marshment, Brian Conley, Edward Elder, Robin Pettitt, Vincent Raynauld, and Andre Turcotte, 80–82. New York: Routledge.

Marland, Alex. 2012. "Yes We Can (Fundraise)." In *Routledge Handbook of Political Marketing*, edited by Jennifer Lees-Marshment, 164–176. New York: Routledge.

Metz, Manon, Sanne Kruikemeier, and Sophie Lecheler. 2019. "Personalization of Politics on Facebook: Examining the Content and Effects of Professional, Emotional and Private Self-Personalization." *Information, Communication & Society*, 1–18. https://doi.org/10.1080/1369118X.2019.1581244.

Moeller, Judith, Rinaldo Kühne, and Claes De Vreese. 2018. "Mobilizing Youth in the 21st Century: How Digital Media Use Fosters Civic Duty, Information Efficacy, and Political Participation." *Journal of Broadcasting & Electronic Media* 62, no. 3: 445–460.

Mutz, Diana Carole, Paul M. Sniderman, and Richard A. Brody, eds. 1996. *Political Persuasion and Attitude Change*. Ann Arbor: University of Michigan Press.

Nickerson, David W., and Todd Rogers. 2014. "Political Campaigns and Big Data." *Journal of Economic Perspectives* 28, no. 2: 51–74.

Ott, Brian L. 2017. "The Age of Twitter: Donald J. Trump and the Politics of Debasement." *Critical Studies in Media Communication* 34, no. 1: 59–68.

Papakyriakopoulos, Orestis, Simon Hegelich, Morteza Shahrezaye, and Juan Carlos Medina Serrano. 2018. "Social Media and Microtargeting: Political Data Processing and the Consequences for Germany." *Big Data & Society* 5, no. 2: doi:2053951718811844.

Petre, Elizabeth A. 2018. "Encouraging Identification with the Larger Campaign Narrative: Grassroots Organizing Texts in Barack Obama's 2008 Presidential Campaign." *Communication Quarterly* 66, no. 3: 283–307.

Raynauld, Vincent, and Jennifer Lees-Marshment. 2019. "Broadcast Political Marketing Communication." In *Political Marketing: Principles and Applications*, 3rd ed., by Jennifer Lees-Marshment, Brian Conley, Edward Elder, Robin Pettitt, Vincent Raynauld, and Andre Turcotte, 152–182. New York: Routledge.

Raynauld, Vincent, and André Turcotte. 2018. "'Different Strokes for Different Folks': Implications of Voter Micro-Targeting and Appeal in the age of Donald Trump." In *Political Marketing in the 2016 U.S. Presidential Election*, edited by Jamie Gillies, 29–48. New York: Palgrave Macmillan.

Schneider, Mike. 2019. "How to Break Through When Political Ads Have Never Been More Competitive." Campaigns & Elections, July 15. https://www.campaignsandelections.com/campaign-insider/how-to-break-through-when-political-ads-have-never-been-more-competitive.

Singer, N. 2018. "What You Don't Know About How Facebook Uses Your Data." *New York Times*, April 11. https://www.nytimes.com/2018/04/11/technol ogy/facebook-privacy-hearings.html.

Small, Tamara A., Harold Jansen, Frédérick Bastien, Thierry Giasson, and Royce Koop. 2014. "Online Political Activity in Canada: The Hype and the Facts." *Canadian Parliamentary Review* 37, no. 4: 9–16.

Strömbäck, Jesper. 2007. "Political Marketing and Professionalized Campaigning: A Conceptual Analysis." *Journal of Political Marketing* 6, nos. 2–3: 49–67.

Strömbäck, Jesper, and Frank Esser. 2014. "Mediatization of Politics: Towards a Theoretical Framework." In *Mediatization of Politics*, edited by Frank Esser et al., 3–28. London: Palgrave Macmillan.

Towner, Terri L., and David A. Dulio. 2012. "New Media and Political Marketing in the United States: 2012 and Beyond." *Journal of Political Marketing* 11, nos. 1–2: 95–119.

Tufekci, Zeynep. 2014. "Engineering the Public: Big Data, Surveillance and Computational Politics." *First Monday* 19, no. 7. https://firstmonday.org/ojs/index .php/fm/article/view/4901/4097%22%20%5Ct%20%22_new#author.

Turcotte, André. 2012. "Under New Management: Market Intelligence and the Conservative Resurrection." In *Political Marketing in Canada*, edited by Alex Marland et al., 76–80. Vancouver: University of British Columbia Press.

Valentino, Nicholas A., Ted Brader, Eric W. Groenendyk, Krysha Gregorowicz, and Vincent L. Hutchings. 2011. "Election Night's Alright for Fighting: The Role of Emotions in Political Participation." *Journal of Politics* 73, no. 1: 156–170.

Virdee, Satnam, and Brendan McGeever. 2018. "Racism, Crisis, Brexit." *Ethnic and Racial Studies* 41, no. 10: 1802–1819.

Walker, Doug, and Edward L. Nowlin. 2018. "Data-Driven Precision and Selectiveness in Political Campaign Fundraising." *Journal of Political Marketing.* doi:10.1 080/15377857.2018.1457590.

Worcester, Robert, Roger Mortimore, Paul Baines, and Mark Gill. 2018. "Brexit Britain, Two Years On." *Significance* 15, no. 3: 30–33.

PART II
Political Communication Ethics in Practice

9

Goalposts and Guardrails

A Mixed-Metaphor Guide to Ethics in Advocacy Campaigns

Elisa Massimino

An advocate's job is to cause change in the world. Much of this work is accomplished through focused, intensive issue campaigns built around a strategy to achieve a particular end. The struggle for marriage equality, ending the Central Intelligence Agency's (CIA's) post-9/11 torture program, scaling back use of the death penalty—none of these things happened by chance. Like all social or policy change, each of these victories was the result of numerous strategic decisions made by advocates, organizations, and coalitions, guided by grappling with questions like these:

- Which issues deserve our attention? Why this issue and not another one?
- What does victory look like? What—in particular—will we aim to accomplish?
- How will we frame the issue? What will our campaign be "about"?
- How will we fund the effort?
- Who will our allies be? Who do we see as our opponents?
- How do we know which compromises to make—and which will steer us off track?
- What happens when it's over?

Each of these questions has ethical dimensions. Sometimes the answer to one question will constrain the options for how you answer another. For example, funder interest may dictate a particular campaign focus. A decision to build a broad-based coalition or to team up with a particular ally may limit the kinds of compromises a campaign will be able to make down the road. A good advocate will think about these questions before launching a campaign and be clear about the goalposts (what winning looks like) and guardrails (what the scope of maneuverability is for strategy and compromise). While few advocacy campaigns go precisely as planned, the ones that produce change that sticks are those in which the players understand the ethical questions embedded in their advocacy and have a framework to grapple with them as new ones arise.

My Aim Is True: Setting the Agenda

The most precious commodities any of us have are time and attention. According to the nonprofit 80,000 Hours,[1] each of us has around that much working time (40 years × 50 weeks × 40 hours) in our careers—and that's before factoring in time to call your mom and check Instagram. What will you do with your 80,000 hours?

Keep in mind that even the most intellectually agile people can pay serious attention to only half a dozen or so things at any given time. Once we decide what to pay attention to, we have even less time to invest in doing the hard work that's needed to make change happen. Everything that gets on the agenda knocks something else off. The struggle for time and attention is truly a zero-sum game.

So, what will it be? Climate change or gun violence? Criminal justice reform or #MeToo? Nuclear proliferation or homelessness? Extreme poverty or voting rights? HIV/AIDS or campaign finance reform? The world is full of problems to be solved. How should you decide where to spend your most valuable commodities?

One approach might be to ask which effort will produce the greatest good for the most people.[2] Proponents of a concept called "effective altruism"[3] make the case that data can help people figure out where they can do the most good with their time and money by looking at a matrix of potential existential threats to life (like climate change, nuclear proliferation, or artificial intelligence run amok), where there is likely to be the highest return on investment of time and money (like fighting infectious diseases, where small inputs can save many lives), and which issues are not getting enough attention (like the suffering of animals).[4] The central idea is that decisions about how to spend your precious time should be based not on sympathy, emotion, or personal inclination but rather on data and analysis. In some cases, effective altruism suggests that the most effective way for a person to make change in the world is not to join an advocacy organization or participate directly in a campaign for change, but to devote his or her 80,000 hours to a career on Wall Street, make a boatload of money, and then give the bulk of those earnings to charities that are doing good work.[5] (Of course, that approach isn't universalizable; if everyone did it, there would be no charities or advocates doing good work, only people making lots of money.)

While a strict utilitarian approach like this might seem appealing—everyone wants to be effective, and no one wants to waste effort—anyone who has done the hard work of waging and winning an advocacy campaign knows that it is almost always a slog. Investing in social change is not the same kind of project as figuring out which health insurance plan or phone to buy,[6] particularly when we're talking about personal investment of your precious 80,000 hours (and not just investment of the money you earned at that fancy Wall Street job). Personal passion for an issue—something discounted, if not completely dismissed, by the effective altruists—can be hugely important to sustaining a difficult campaign effort that will undoubtedly have many ups and downs. To paraphrase Thomas Edison, success is 10 percent inspiration and 90 percent perspiration. You're going to need that 10 percent as fuel for the fight.

In some situations, choosing which issue to campaign on requires not only finding a worthy cause but prioritizing among competing goals. For example, in postconflict societies there is often a direct clash between the desire to hold perpetrators of rights violations accountable and the need to reconcile former combatants to rebuild community. Which is more worthy of a campaign? While there is no formulaic answer to such tensions, advocates can strengthen the legitimacy of these difficult choices by ensuring that community members whose lives have been directly affected by the conflict have agency and voice in determining priorities and that the campaign reflects their desires and needs.

Especially in situations like these, where two important goals seem to be in conflict, fear of violating the Hippocratic oath—first, do no harm—can also lead to paralysis.[7] The last thing a well-meaning advocate wants to do is unwittingly make things worse. But while it may be true that the road to hell is paved with good intentions, "turning a blind eye to the toughest problems in the world is a guaranteed shortcut to the same destination."[8]

So, while there's certainly some benefit in analyzing whether we're solving the "right" problems and trying to figure out where our limited resources can do the most good, spending too much time on analysis often leads to paralysis. As a society, we suffer less from too many people laboring inefficiently to right wrongs than from too few people laboring at all. The world is full of problems. Don't dither. Get out there and do something.

Once you decide which issue you want to tackle, it's time to get specific. You know what problem you're going to solve. Now, what does victory look like?

Define Winning

No campaign can succeed without a hard target. Unless you know and can clearly articulate what winning looks like, you will never be spiking the ball in the end zone (more on spiking the ball later).[9] In any issue area—gun violence, capital punishment, immigration, the rights of LGBTQ people, you name it—there are multiple possible objectives. Choosing a clear outcome—a change in the world that will be the direct result of your campaign—involves strategic choices that will help determine everything else about the effort. Each of these choices requires grappling with ethical questions.

Perhaps the biggest challenge for advocates when choosing a campaign outcome involves appetite: Do you go for the whole enchilada or just a nacho? Going for the big win may feel bold and inspiring at the outset but could turn out to be less effective if the campaign fails because it is overly ambitious. But bold and inspiring may be what you need to attract sufficient funding and public attention to get your campaign off the ground. Is there anything wrong with going for the big win even if you know at the outset you won't achieve it? If you decide that only a "comprehensive" solution is a worthy goal, you may find yourself grappling with the same ethical questions down the road when faced with a decision about which compromises you can accept in exchange for an incremental win (later in the chapter you'll find a discussion of guardrails to guide such compromises).

Is it wrong to aim at only part of a problem? Focusing on a narrower objective may secure incremental gains but feel unsatisfying, leaving you short of where you ultimately want to go and leaving behind some people you hope to protect. Advocates for prison reform knew they were settling for incremental change when they won passage of legislation in 2019 creating a pathway out of prison for tens of thousands incarcerated people, allowing them to serve the remainder of their sentences outside the prison walls and reducing prison time for people disadvantaged by the disparity in sentencing for crack and powder cocaine.[10] To underscore the incremental nature of the effort, the bill was dubbed by advocates "The First Step Act." The tens of thousands of prisoners it will help are a drop in the bucket for a criminal justice system in which seven million people are in jail, prison, or otherwise under judicial supervision. Was the effort worth it if the "first step" ends up being the last step? Congress is notoriously—and increasingly—slow to pass legislation, and no matter what the bill was called, many legislators with short attention spans and limited political capital may feel that passage of The First Step Act means "we've 'done' prison reform." If you set the bar too low or too narrow and win, does that risk moving the entire issue off the public radar, making further progress more difficult?

Many advocates at this stage of campaign planning argue that because of the powerful messaging component that campaigns can have (see the discussion about framing), there is a moral obligation to go for the big outcome, even if there's little chance of achieving it. This is particularly true when focusing on a narrower objective may be seen as signaling that some people's rights are more important than others. Surprisingly few advocates, however, ask the corollary question: Do I have a moral obligation to help some rather than none? Is it unethical to try to achieve only half your long-term goal? Half a loaf still feeds some hungry people. What about a quarter loaf? Or an eighth?

Deciding to confine your campaign to tackling a particular piece of a larger problem doesn't mean you get to escape from hard choices; you still have to decide which piece you will target. Do you campaign for marriage equality or ending workplace discrimination against LGBTQ people? An assault weapons ban or universal background checks for gun purchases? Relief for Dreamers or ending the separation of immigrant children from their parents?

Answering these questions—a mix of tactical, strategic, and ethical considerations—is one of the most complicated and difficult stages of any campaign. The answers are ultimately situation-specific and possibly unknowable. But they are nonetheless questions that you, as advocates, must answer.

Here are a few considerations that may help:

- *Paradigm shifts:* Sometimes seemingly unattainable goals seem unattainable because of a persistent status quo that both supporters and opponents of change have internalized. In these situations, you may need a broad, ambitious (even if immediately unattainable) goal to effectively shock the system and prompt a kind of paradigm shift that will open the possibility for radical change. This seems to be an ongoing challenge for advocates of stricter gun control. Preventing mass shootings, most of which are perpetrated with assault weapons, is a key priority for many gun control advocates. An assault weapons ban, which was once law and proved to be effective while in force, seems difficult enough to achieve. But even a winning campaign to reestablish the ban would leave an estimated tens of millions of assault weapons on the street. Fixing that would entail something like a mandatory buy-back program, a proposal that some gun control advocates think is so far beyond the possible that they fear even suggesting it makes incremental change less politically viable— that is, until someone actually does propose it,[11] changes the paradigm of what's "conceivable,"[12] and discovers that the proposal has the support of a majority of Americans.[13] That's called moving the goalposts (or expanding the "Overton Window"[14]). A bold, ambitious campaign can open up new avenues for change.
- *The arc of history:* Sometimes, timing is everything. One way to ground a decision about which objective to aim for is to ask not whether it's the right objective but whether it's the right moment. If something about the environment—a new political champion for your issue, an unexpected event that grabs public attention, an infusion of resources from a new donor—creates an opening for change on a particular outcome, that may be the best argument for moving ahead. Also, when considering whether

to campaign for a "first step" or a comprehensive solution, keep in mind that social change takes time. The arc of the moral universe, as Dr. Martin Luther King Jr. said, is long.[15] It may bend toward justice, but only when we make it bend. Sometimes the first step may be the only step for decades. But consider that some provisions of The First Step Act were included to remedy a prior reform bill that only went partway toward addressing the crack/powder cocaine sentencing disparities. Keep bending the arc.

- *The "Big Mo":* Particularly in today's polarized political environment, many social justice or public policy issues seem stuck in limbo. If they stay there long enough, people may begin to think they are insoluble. Situations like this need something to break the spell of paralysis. Even a small win can accomplish that, creating a sense of possibility that can lead to momentum. And momentum is magic for campaigns. Chip and Dan Heath, authors of *Switch* (one of my favorite books on how to make change), argue that big problems are rarely solved with commensurately big solutions but rather by a sequence of small individual steps.[16] They advocate "shrinking the change" to develop momentum and prove that a win is possible. Winning can bring in new allies and change facts on the ground, energizing an apathetic constituency, loosening up opposition, and seeding the ground for bigger wins down the road.

- *If all you have is a hammer:* The classic critique of applying the wrong solution to a problem says, "If all you have is a hammer, everything looks like a nail." It's a warning not to define a problem by the tools you have. But what if it's true that all you have is a hammer? Doesn't it make sense to look for nails that need hammering? One way to decide which problem to solve is to focus on what you can bring to the problem. Have the capacity to build a broad grassroots network? Focus on a campaign that needs mass mobilization to win. Have great contacts in the other political party? Pick a campaign in which bipartisan action is going to be essential. Have a great state-level network but nothing at the national level? Make sure your campaign plays to that strength.

Once you know what your goalposts look like, you'll need to figure out which plays you are going to need to run to get there. And that means deciding what your campaign is about.

What's It All About? Framing

Agenda setting identifies what matters: "Look at this! It's important!" Picking a target outcome tells people what you want and where you're headed. And framing says what kind of journey you're on, what a campaign is really "about."

"Definition is the heart of the political battle."[17] Deciding what to talk about—and what not to talk about—is a critical step in developing any advocacy campaign strategy. Defining what a debate is really "about" sets the boundaries for how that issue will be discussed and determines the debate's allies and opponents and, ultimately, what can be achieved. As such, it is fundamentally an ethical question.

For example, was the devastation from Hurricane Katrina "about" government failure, poverty, or race? Complex problems usually have more than one cause, so the real answer is probably "all of the above, and more." But to persuade someone to act, you need to pick one frame within which to orient your campaign.

If racism matters more than failure of the Army Corps of Engineers but is less likely to motivate action to make things better, is it ethical to focus on the latter and hope that fixing it helps address the former? What if that frame reinforces the deeper structural problem? By fixing levies and ignoring race, are we further entrenching racial divides? Do the endless bandages prevent us from dealing with the underlying wound? What if no one wants to deal with the wound, and in the meantime, people are suffering? As veteran pollster and political strategist Stanley Greenberg has said, "Those who figure out what the fight is actually about are able to set the agenda and motivate voters to get involved and pick a side."[18] As an advocacy campaign strategist, that's exactly what you want to do.

Making these choices can raise serious ethical questions. Typically, campaign strategists answer those questions with an eye to winning. Campaigns want to know all the angles and pick the one that is most likely to succeed. Here are some examples of real choices advocates have had to face when considering how to frame their campaigns. How would you come down on these questions?

Torture. The CIA's torture (euphemistically dubbed "enhanced interrogation") program was launched shortly after the 9/11 attacks and continued through most of President George W. Bush's second term. Human rights groups campaigned against the policy for a year using the frame that torture is a violation of international human rights standards and a federal crime. But the campaign did not make a dent in public opinion or persuade anyone who wasn't already convinced that the program should be shut down. Why? Because the message coming from proponents of the policy, including in the White House—that the program was producing vital intelligence that was saving American lives—was much more powerful. In other words, "torture works." At a time when fear was pervasive among the American public, stoked by color-coded threat levels and "unknown unknowns,"[19] a human rights (or even a law-and-order) frame for an anti-torture campaign didn't stand a chance.

That's why some advocates set out to learn whether the proponents' claims about torture's efficacy were true. If they learned that torture was effective in eliciting actionable intelligence, advocates would still oppose its use. But without meeting people where they were—in the grip of fear, believing that torture was keeping them safe—the campaign would remain stuck.

This was a risky gambit. Human rights advocates are not interrogation experts, so they needed to consult with people in the military, law enforcement, and intelligence communities to find out the truth. Fortunately, it turned out that those experts believed that torture and other such abuse of prisoners was not only not working, it was costing the United States valuable intelligence and fueling terrorist recruitment. Torture was undermining Americans' security.

The decision to make the antitorture campaign about security of Americans instead of the rights of suspected terrorists was pivotal. It led to the construction of a powerful coalition of military and intelligence leaders who became the tip of the spear in the public fight against torture. Over time, these well-respected figures helped change the terms of the debate, ensured passage of legislation reinforcing the ban on torture and other "official cruelty," and led to the end of the CIA program.

Making the campaign "about" torture's efficacy, while effective in ending the program, risked undermining the universality of the right to be free from torture. Should it matter whether torture is efficacious? What if some new torture techniques were developed down the road that produced reliable intelligence? Would the campaign be discredited? Importantly, the military and intelligence leaders at the forefront of the antitorture campaign themselves opposed torture on moral and legal grounds, not only because it was counterproductive from a security perspective. But Americans first needed a way to dismantle the opponents' frame about torture's efficacy in order to be able to hear the moral arguments against it.

Death penalty. Prior to the advent of forensic DNA evidence, debates about the death penalty tended to be grounded in moral or theological principles; either you believed the state has a right to take the life of someone convicted of certain serious crimes or you did not. Within that frame, a majority of Americans supported the death penalty.

DNA evidence has confirmed what many advocates suspected: that hundreds of people have been wrongly convicted for crimes they did not commit.[20] The availability of this evidence, and the steady exoneration of convicted people, including some on death row, opened up a new frame for anti-death-penalty campaigners: actual innocence. No matter what people think about the morality of the state taking human life, everyone agrees that it is immoral for the state to execute an innocent person. People are drawn to the drama of exoneration. Numerous movies and television shows built narratives around the vindication of innocent prisoners. Young lawyers sought jobs with new nonprofit firms dedicated to representing convicted prisoners, but only those who had strong claims of innocence. And support for the death penalty overall declined. [21]

Some death penalty abolitionists accused those making arguments based on innocence and fairness (rather than race or morality) of "cleaning the rope": making America safe for inflicting the death penalty on the guilty. Were the accusers right? Some of those same critics have now adopted the innocence and fairness frame. Are they right? By attacking effects of race and class, did we miss the opportunity to get at the underlying cause? Were the "innocence advocates" right to use a limited frame in order to draw in new opponents in the hopes of converting them to the broader abolitionist cause?

Finally, choosing a frame for your campaign can have consequences long after the campaign is over. Once an issue is effectively framed as being "about" one thing and not another, it can be very difficult to shift to a different frame. For example, if a campaign for the rights of LGBTQ people is framed around the idea that people are "born gay" or that there is a "gay gene," what happens if future scientific research suggests a more complicated picture in which environment plays a role? What if only some LGBTQ people have the gene? Will a focus on genetics encourage antigay activists to campaign for gene editing or embryo selection? If scientists discover that genetics play only a partial role in sexual identity, will that strengthen the argument from antigay activists that being gay is a lifestyle choice?[22] What might be the legacy for future campaigns of the frame you choose?

Show Me the Money: Funding Your Campaign

Changing the world is hard work and requires sustained effort, often over many years. That's why, for better or worse,[23] it is increasingly done by professionals, each of whom demands a professional response on the other side. Someone has to pay for this expertise. Does it matter who that is?

Decisions about who funds your campaign can have ethical implications for the campaign effort itself and the broader cause of which it is a part. Almost all social justice campaigns are wildly underfunded, and most organizations in this space spend a significant amount of time and energy raising the money it takes to challenge what are often well-funded and entrenched interests on the other side. Whose money do you take to level the playing field? If you lean left, can you take money from conservatives if they happen to agree with you on this one issue? If you lean right, can you take money from liberals? Consider George Soros, the billionaire financier who has funded innumerable progressive organizations and causes around the world, and the Koch brothers, conservative libertarian funders who co-own the second-largest privately held company in the United States. The Koch brothers have helped advance criminal justice reform and are increasingly funding civil society efforts. They also fund anti-climate-science efforts. So, fewer people will be unfairly imprisoned and our political discourse will be better, but we'll all die. Is it ethical to take their money? Does taking their money legitimize their other bad work? Climate change is driving global conflict. Yet Soros and Koch are teaming up to promote diplomacy and scale back US military intervention in foreign countries. Is Soros working with Koch to pull back from conflicts that Koch is fostering? Are you willing to be party to a project that may serve to redeem the reputation of someone whose views you generally abhor?

What about taking money from corporations? Is it ever ethical or wise for a climate activist to take money from a fossil fuel company? For a labor rights campaign to be funded by a company that operates sweatshops?

How about funding from wealthy individuals who have engaged in criminal or other despicable behavior? Think tanks and Ivy League schools are scrambling right now to explain why they accepted major donations from convicted sex offender the late Jeffrey Epstein, some of it solicited and accepted after his conviction. Would you take money from Epstein or others like him? Or is that money too tainted to use for good? Are there any guard-rails for navigating the ethics of these questions?

As a campaign strategist, even one whose campaign is struggling for resources, it's important when analyzing these questions to *look back* and *think ahead*.

First, look back. How did the donor obtain the money you're being offered? If you're concerned about unethical behavior of the donor, does it make a difference if the money in question is directly related to that behavior? Is it better or worse if you plan to use the funding to launch a campaign to support victims of people like Jeffrey Epstein?

Then, look ahead. Is the association with this funder ultimately going to undermine your cause? Does the fact that this funder underwrote your efforts impugn what you're doing? If you take money from a company that is involved in the issue area on which you're campaigning, will it damage your reputation for independence? One way to minimize this risk is to have a corporate donations policy that prohibits taking money from a company during the period in which it specifically or others in that industry are targets of your advocacy. Another is to set a percentage of total budget cap on donations from corporate funders.

The Company You Keep: Allies

While money is fungible, people are not. Because few campaigns are fought and won without allies, every campaign has to rumble with questions about who our allies will be. The strategic question is pretty clear:

Who do we need on our journey in order to get where we want to go? But embedded in that is an ethical question: Is it wrong to do the right thing with the wrong people?

Questions about who to team up with on a campaign are especially complicated when your strategy requires mobilizing a constituency whose members don't listen to you. No matter what the message is, the messenger matters. Liberals listen to liberals, conservatives to conservatives. To build a broad coalition for change, many campaigns look to team up with so-called strange bedfellows or unusual suspects. The logic is similar to questions about Koch and Soros and funding: Can you work with the bad guys on one good issue (however you define good or bad)? How bad does a person have to be to be beyond the pale? Is it a sliding scale? Does it depend on how much good could result from the alliance? Do the ends justify the means?

Concerned Women for America—a conservative group whose launch was inspired by hostility to the Equal Rights Amendment—and Human Rights First, whose mission is to encourage the United States to be a global leader on human rights, have little in common. The Venn diagram of their shared interests is comprised of precisely one issue: refugee protection. Facing impending new restrictions from the Ashcroft Justice Department that would have limited the rights of women fleeing severe gender-based violence to receive asylum in the United States, Human Rights First recruited Concerned Women for America to join forces and help build Republican support for a more protective policy. As a result of this effort, Senator Sam Brownback (R-KS) teamed up with Senator Hillary Clinton (D-NY) to press the Bush administration to protect women fleeing domestic violence.[24] Five years later, the woman whose case was at the center of the campaign was granted asylum, and gender-based violence was recognized as grounds for protection.[25]

A different set of considerations, with possible unintended consequences, arose when Human Rights First decided to partner with—and elevate the voices of—retired military leaders in the fight against the CIA torture policy. While this partnership was absolutely central in achieving a major campaign victory, it's possible that the strategy inadvertently furthered a trend about which there has been significant concern: that the voices of the military carry outsized weight in the marketplace of ideas.[26] According to Gallup, the military is by far the most trusted institution in the United States (74 percent of Americans trust the military "a great deal"; Congress is at the bottom of the list at 11 percent).[27] This is of course one of the reasons the partnership was so powerful; it's one thing for a human rights organization to campaign against torture and quite another for a former commandant of the Marine Corps to lead the charge. After the success of the antitorture campaign, many groups went looking for their own group of "generals" to attach to their issue so they could be taken more seriously. Was the victory on torture worth further entrenching a trend that can warp how Americans view public policy?

Taken together, these ethical questions add up to a larger question of what you are willing to sacrifice to win.

Savvy or Sellout: Compromising without Being Compromised

When a reporter asked Mike Tyson whether he was worried about Evander Holyfield's fight plan, Tyson famously responded, "Everybody has a plan until they get punched in the mouth." No matter how strategic and well-funded your campaign plan is, odds are—especially if your target outcome must go through a legislative process—you are going to be faced at some point with the need to bargain and compromise.

How do you approach decisions about which compromises to make—or if you should compromise at all? This can be particularly fraught in fields like human rights, which has been called "the new secular religion."[28] As such, many of the faithful would like to wall it up in a monastery and keep it—and themselves—free from the corruption of the corporeal world. As a funder once told me, "You guys are the angels; you don't want to get mixed up in politics and end up compromising your principles!"

But the corporeal world is where people live and where rights matter. Anybody who has tried to shape government policy to protect human rights knows that you can't win without compromise. Indeed, if you never wake up in the middle of the night in a cold sweat worrying that you're making the wrong trade-offs, it's a pretty good sign that you're not in the game. There are plenty of people who join the fight for human rights precisely because they want to be on the side of the angels. The problem is, if all you are is on a side, you're probably on the sidelines. And that's not where the fight is.

One reason people shy away from the fight is fear of selling out. How do you build guardrails for compromise to make sure you don't end up settling for an outcome that undermines your larger goals? There's no magic formula for this. But as the late General Jack Vessey, the legendary former chairman of the Joint Chiefs of Staff, once told me, when you head into a situation that you know has some moral hazard, you'd better set your "shove it" point—the point beyond which you say hell no and walk away—well in advance. Otherwise, the slope gets mighty slippery.

Sometimes the "shove it" point relates not to policy positions but to people. Are there people—because of their positions on other issues or their willingness to serve in an administration that's anathema to your cause—who should never be considered allies? How do you approach teaming up with actors whom you may go to war with on other issues down the road (see "The Company You Keep: Allies")? What about the risk of legitimizing or "normalizing" an abhorrent politician by facilitating a "win" that could be leveraged to his or her political benefit? One prominent donor in the field refuses to fund policy advocacy efforts directed at the Trump administration on the theory that persuading it to take positive action on human rights will only make it harder to defeat this president in the next election.

Is this the right approach? If it had prevailed, The First Step Act would never have been signed into law. How should you balance the short-term imperative for change—even incremental change—with your long-term vision for the way things should be?

In 2007, after decades of campaigning and struggle, the House was poised to pass the landmark Employment Non-Discrimination Act, the first bill that would protect LGBTQ people from workplace discrimination. But then came the punch in the mouth. Whip counts showed that the bill would pass only if protections for transgender people were stripped out. Representative Barney Frank, one of the bill's main sponsors and the founder of the congressional Equality Caucus, wanted to move ahead; LGBTQ groups excoriated him as a sellout, and worse. Frank was clear:

> The question facing us—the LGBT community and the tens of millions of others who are active supporters of our fight against prejudice—is whether we should pass up the chance to adopt a very good bill because it has one major gap. I believe that it would be a grave error to let this opportunity to pass a sexual orientation nondiscrimination bill go forward, not simply because it is one of the most important advances we'll have made in securing civil rights for Americans in decades, but because moving forward on this bill now will also better serve the ultimate goal of including people who are transgender than simply accepting total defeat today.[29]

In the end, LGBTQ groups withdrew their support, and the bill failed. Frank decried the irresponsible "ideological purity" of the Left. Today, a dozen years later, ENDA is not law, and LGBTQ Americans remain at risk of being fired from their jobs simply because of who they are. Who was right?

Victory Lap

Finally, win or lose, almost as important as the outcome is what happens when the fight is over. How do you describe it? Is a partial win a loss, or something to celebrate? What if your campaign failed completely? How do you treat your adversaries? Your allies? What about those who were on the winning team but may be your opponents in the next fight? Answering these questions requires threading a mix of ethical and strategic considerations, and an eye for the long game.

Advocacy campaigns are often decisive periods in broader movements for change. It's a tired metaphor that the struggle for justice is "a marathon, not a sprint" (as is the description of social justice advocates as "tireless." Not true. We tire!). In fact, these efforts are more like a relay. And everyone knows that in relays, a smooth handoff of the baton can make all the difference (just ask the 2016 Japanese Olympic relay team).[30] It's important to think carefully about these transition moments.

Accentuate the positive. Once a campaign is over, advocates have another opportunity to say what the campaign was "about" and to characterize the outcome. This is also a key moment to preview the unfinished business of the campaign and the battles that lie ahead. Advocates who've devoted more than their pro rata share of those 80,000 hours to a campaign that falls short are often tempted to highlight their disappointments. Indeed, humans seem hardwired to focus on the negative.[31] But for the sake of future campaigns, to establish a sense of momentum, and to rally the troops for another round, if the campaign produced tangible progress, lead with that. Don't let it be all about what you didn't get. Let a win be a win.[32]

Situational awareness. Campaigns are often intense experiences, and the drive to the goal line can make the rest of what's going on in the world seem like a blur. Before you spike the ball in the end zone, pause for a moment to make sure you understand how your victory dance will be seen by others. Consider the following example. On August 21, 2013, Syrian president Bashar al Assad ignored President Barack Obama's "red line" warning and launched a chemical weapons attack on the suburbs of Damascus, killing more than fourteen hundred people, four hundred of them children. As Obama prepared a retaliatory military strike, antiwar activists, led by MoveOn, mobilized to oppose it. Obama decided to seek congressional authorization for the strikes, and it soon became clear that he wouldn't get it. Public opinion was overwhelming against US military action, and a last-minute offer by Russia to negotiate removal of Syria's chemical weapons stockpile averted the need for a vote.

Those who had opposed the strikes were understandably jubilant. They had achieved their goal. They celebrated with blast email and a public rally framing the result of their campaign as "Peace wins."[33] But there was nothing about the campaign that brought peace to Syria, and characterizing a situation in which millions of Syrians were fleeing for their lives as "peace" was callous at best and dangerous at worst. It risked fostering American indifference to the suffering of Syrians and exacerbating the already insufficient political will in Washington to produce a response commensurate with the scale of the problem.[34] And it alienated those who might have shared the campaigners' broad goal of scaling back unauthorized military action but felt that this particular strike was needed to prevent further civilian deaths from Assad's chemical weapons. It's a big, complicated world out there. Sometimes your campaign is aiming at the lesser of two evils. Don't idealize your own cause.

It ain't over. You won your campaign, the whole enchilada. Woo-hoo! What a great feeling after a long slog to finally put something in the "win" column. Take your victory lap. But don't forget that the reason you had to launch a campaign in the first place was that there were folks on the other side who had a different idea about what winning looks like. To keep wins in the win column, you have to keep your eye on the prize. Antitorture activists learned this the hard way in the early 1990s. They had been campaigning for years to secure US ratification of the UN Convention Against Torture,[35] which had as a prerequisite making torture a crime in domestic law. But each time the bill criminalizing torture was introduced, some member of Congress succeeded in attaching an amendment that would impose the death penalty as punishment for violators. Most groups campaigning for ratification opposed the death penalty, so could not support the legislation. Finally, in 1994, Congress passed a clean bill—without the death penalty—allowing the United States to become a party to the treaty. Antitorture campaigners had a big party to celebrate the hard-won victory and moved on to the next challenge. Six months later, when no one was watching, the law was amended to add back the death penalty. It ain't over 'til it's over.

Learn to fail or fail to learn. Celebrating wins is important. But what about failure? Do we have any obligation to acknowledge when our campaigns fall short? No one likes to lose, and sometimes the fear of losing will lead advocates to think small or be too conventional. Winning is great, but failing is how we learn. Thomas Edison said he made a thousand attempts to invent the lightbulb. When a reporter asked him how it felt to fail a thousand times, Edison replied, "I didn't fail 1,000 times. The light bulb was an invention with 1,000 steps." Understanding why a campaign failed can be critical information for whoever is running the next leg of your relay. Analyze what happened and pay it forward.

Fear of failure can also inhibit ambition and the kind of big-idea goal setting that can be necessary to tackle social change. Sally Kohn, an author and television commentator with serious campaign strategy cred, argues that there should be a "fail lab" for activists that encourages outside-the-box thinking and expects—even celebrates, rather than fears—failure.[36] In a world of scarce resources, is there anything wrong with this approach? Can we justify funding failure if it opens a path to groundbreaking change?

Ways and means and ends. Perhaps the most important ethical consideration in the post-campaign period is how to treat your adversaries—and even your "unlikely allies"—once the campaign is over. Here, I think the answers are fairly straightforward. Treating people as ends, not means, is not only the right thing to do,[37] it's the smart thing to do. Today's allies may seem like strange bedfellows, but campaign relationships built on trust and respect can live longer than campaigns themselves, so your work together may lead to future collaborations. In an increasingly polarized political environment, these kinds of partnerships are difficult, rare, and necessary.

Do the hard work of making it easier for people on the other side of the political fence to do the right thing. Your post-victory message may frame the campaign in a way that will put your allies in a difficult position. Allow them to characterize the outcome too. Think about letting them take the post-victory lead on messaging. People take risks to ally themselves with those on the other side of a political divide. Don't make that harder.

Failed campaigns aren't the only ones that get a postmortem; successful campaigns are often analyzed as case examples for lessons learned. Don't let yours be a cautionary tale. Set the right kind of example. And don't forget to thank the people who did the right thing.

Fill the tank. Changing the world is a long—some say endless—road. Anybody on it is going to need a full tank for the journey. That 10 percent inspiration Edison talked about is your fuel. Make sure it's renewable. The great civil rights leader Representative John Lewis (D-GA) is an endless source. He urges us to take up the moral obligation to make change and to take joy in the fight: "Do not get lost in a sea of despair. Be hopeful, be optimistic. Our struggle is not the struggle of a day, a week, a month, or a year, it is the struggle of a lifetime. Never, ever be afraid to make some noise and get in good trouble, necessary trouble."[38]

Notes

[1] "80,000 Hours." n.d., https://80000hours.org/.

[2] See Julia Driver, "The History of Utilitarianism," in *The Stanford Encyclopedia of Philosophy*, ed. Edward N. Zalta (winter 2014 ed.), https://plato.stanford.edu/archives/win2014/entries/utilitarianism-history/.

[3] "Effective Altruism," n.d., https://www.effectivealtruism.org/.

[4] The views of moral philosopher Peter Singer, one of the founders of the animal rights movement, played a central role in developing the concept of effective altruism.

[5] Nicholas Kristof, "The Trader Who Donates Half His Pay," *New York Times*, April 4, https://www.nytimes.com/2015/04/05/opinion/sunday/nicholas-kristof-the-trader-who-donates-half-his-pay.html.

[6] "In most areas of life, we understand that it's important to base our decisions on evidence and reason rather than guesswork or gut instinct. When you buy a phone, you will read customer reviews to get the best deal. Certainly, you won't buy a phone which costs 1,000 times more than an identical model. Yet we are not always so discerning when we work on global problems." https://www.effectivealtruism.org/articles/introduction-to-effective-altruism/.

[7] Contrary to popular belief, the admonition to "first, do no harm" is not actually found in the Hippocratic Oath. See "The Hippocratic Oath," National Library

of Medicine, National Institutes of Health, n.d., https://www.nlm.nih.giv/hmd/greek/greek_oath.

8 Samantha Power, *The Education of an Idealist* (New York: Dey St., 2019), 487.

9 Advocates use a multitude of euphemisms—"fighting the good fight," "laboring in the vineyard," "speaking truth to power"—for what is, essentially, losing. These can soften the blow when a campaign falls short. But no matter what story you tell your funder, the constituents, or your mom, it's important not to believe your own spin. If you pick a clear outcome for your campaign ("speaking truth to power" and "fighting the good fight" don't count), you will know whether you won or lost. Don't kid yourself. Own up to where you end up. Losing is bad, but it's also how you learn.

10 Alan Pyke, "Bipartisan Coalition Bested Hardline Senators' Attempts to Sabotage Prison Reform Bill," Think Progress, December 19, 2018, https://thinkprogress.org/prison-reform-advocates-may-be-divided-but-senate-passage-of-first-step-act-shows-theyre-winning-d1aa5e801f45/.

11 Max Boot, "Thanks, Beto: We Need to Debate an Assault-Weapon Buyback," *Washington Post*, September 19, 2019, https://www.washingtonpost.com/opinions/thanks-beto-we-need-to-debate-an-assault-weapon-buyback/2019/09/17/864d09a4-d964-11e9-a688-303693fb4b0b_story.html.

12 "Princess Bride (Inconceivable [Montage])," video, March 4, 2007, https://www.youtube.com/watch?v=Z3sLhnDJJn0.

13 Tess Bonn, "Majority of Voters Support Assault Weapons Ban, Buybacks: Poll," *The Hill*, September 26, 2019, https://thehill.com/hilltv/rising/463256-majority-of-voters-support-assault-weapons-ban-mandatory-buybacks-poll.

14 Mackinac Center, "The Overton Window," n.d., https://www.mackinac.org/OvertonWindow.

15 Dr. Martin Luther King Jr., "Remaining Awake Through a Great Revolution" (speech presented at the National Cathedral, March 31, 1968).

16 Chip Heath and Dan Heath, *Switch: How to Change Things When Change Is Hard* (New York: Broadway, 2010), 44.

17 Frank Baumgarten and Bryan D. Jones, *Agendas and Instability in American Politics* (Chicago: University of Chicago Press, 2009), 29.

18 Stanley B. Greenberg, "The Republican Party Is Doomed," *New York Times*, September 10, 2019, https://www.nytimes.com/2019/09/10/opinion/republicans-democrats-2020-election.html.

19 Donald Rumsfeld, Department of Defense press briefing, February 12, 2002, https://archive.defense.gov/Transcripts/Transcript.aspx?TranscriptID=2636.

20 Innocence Project, "DNA Exonerations in the United States," n.d., https://www.innocenceproject.org/dna-exonerations-in-the-united-states/.

21 Frank R. Baumgartner, Suzanna De Boef, and Amber Boydstun, *The Decline of the Death Penalty and the Discovery of Innocence* (Cambridge, UK: Cambridge University Press, 2008).

22 Pam Belluck, "Many Genes Influence Same-Sex Sexuality, Not a Single 'Gay Gene,'" *New York Times*, August 29, 2019, https://www.nytimes.com/2019/08/29/science/gay-gene-sex.html.

23 "Would I Qualify to Be My Own Intern?" *Joy Olson's Blog*, January 29, 2018, https://joyolsonblog.com/2018/01/29/would-i-qualify-to-be-my-own-intern/.

24 Sam Brownback and Hillary Clinton, "Women's Human Rights and Asylum Policy," May 14, 2004, https://www.humanrightsfirst.org/wp-content/uploads/pdf/congress_let_rodi_051304.pdf.

25 This has all gone down the tubes under Trump.

26 See Rosa Brooks, *How Everything Became War and the Military Became Everything* (New York: Simon and Schuster, 2016).

27 The military has been the top-ranked institution or tied for the top-ranked institution each year since 1986. See Justin McCarthy, "U.S. Confidence in Organized Religion Remains Low," Gallup. July 8, 2019, https://news.gallup.com/poll/259964/confidence-organized-religion-remains-low.aspx.

28 Anthony Julius, "Human Rights: The New Secular Religion," *Guardian*, April 19, 2010, https://www.theguardian.com/commentisfree/2010/apr/19/human-rights-new-secular-religion.

29 Barney Frank, "Guest Post on ENDA from Congressman Barney Frank," The Bilerico Project. September 28, 2007, http://bilerico.lgbtqnation.com/2007/09/guest_post_on_enda_from_congressman_fran.php.

30 At the 2016 Olympic Games in Rio de Janeiro, none of the four members of Japan's 4 × 100 men's relay team had a personal best faster than ten seconds. But they beat some of the world's fastest sprinters—including the US and Jamaican teams—by focusing on perfecting the baton exchange. See Spikes, "The World's Best Exchange Rate," https://spikes.iaaf.org/post/japans-secret-to-relay-success.

31 Heath and Heath, *Switch*, 45–46. "[A] psychologist analyzed 558 emotion words—every one that he could find in the English language—and found that 62 percent of them were negative versus 38 percent positive. . . . According to an old urban legend, Eskimos have 100 different words for snow. Well, it turns out that negative emotions are our snow."

32 This is not the same thing as believing your own spin. See note 9.

33 Excerpts from email to MoveOn supporters: "Subject: How We Stopped a War": "the Senate is voting for peace?!" "Peace is winning." "We stood up for peace." "President Obama listened, and now peace may bloom." "Of course, we may still go to war—the war lobby is fierce and relentless. Even as we speak, warmongers in Congress are writing new war resolution language, thinking that if they tweak this word or that word, making it an itsy-bitsy, teensy-weensy war, it can pass. To that, we say, 'a big, fat NO.' We have shown that Peace can be more powerful than War." Email from MoveOn.org Political Action to author, September 12, 2013.

34 Elisa Massimino, "Don't Call It Peace and Don't Move On," *The Hill*, September 20, 2013, https://thehill.com/blogs/congress-blog/foreign-policy/323423-dont-call-it-peace-and-dont-move-on. (Note: this link omits the first paragraph of the original piece as it ran in *The Hill*, which read: "I recently received an email from Move On celebrating President Obama's decision to halt his request for Congressional authorization to strike Syria. Reading it, I cringed eight times. That's how many times the word 'peace' appears, as in: 'Peace is winning.' I doubt that many Members of Congress who opposed the President's request for an authorization to use force thought they would be achieving or keeping the peace by voting no. Regardless of one's view of U.S. military strikes on Syria—my organization, Human Rights First, has not endorsed them—their absence will not amount to peace for Syrians."

35 United Nations, "Convention against Torture and Other Cruel, Inhuman or Degrading Treatment or Punishment," December 10, 1984, https://www.ohchr .org/en/professionalinterest/pages/cat.aspx.

36 Sally Kohn, "The Need to Let People Fail," n.d., https://democracyjournal.org/ author/sally-kohn/.

37 Immanuel Kant, *Groundwork of the Metaphysics of Morals*, trans. Mary J. Gregor (Cambridge, UK: Cambridge University Press, 1998): "Act in such a way that you treat humanity, whether in your own person or in the person of any other, never merely as a means to an end, but always at the same time as an end."

38 John Lewis, "Do not get lost in a sea of despair. Be hopeful, be optimistic. Our struggle is not the struggle of a day, a week, a month, or a year, it is the struggle of a lifetime. Never, ever be afraid to make some noise and get in good trouble, necessary trouble. #goodtrouble," Twitter, June 27, 2018, 10:15 a.m., repjohnlewis.

10

Yes, We Must Do Better (But It's Not as Bad as You Think)

Edward Brookover

Let me say this from the outset—as a society, as a country, as a people—we must do better with political communication. It's how we speak to each other, how we listen to what is said. It's how our candidates talk about themselves, their platforms, their opponents. It's how the media portray today's happenings. It's how campaigns are run and the tools used to communicate with voters. It's part of our social media platforms. Yes, political communication is everywhere.

Let me repeat myself so there is no confusion as we discuss ethics and political communications: yes, we must do better. We must do better because the times in which we live are as bad as they have ever been in American politics, right?

For example, Congress has an approval rating of 18 percent.[1] Our forefathers imagined these public servants would be a direct link to our citizenry. Now confidence in these elected officials is at a historic low, and few trust them to plot a course for our country.

News audiences for all types of television networks are dwindling.[2] Earlier generations had fewer electronic news choices, leading to newscasters often becoming the arbiters of what constituted news, what was right and wrong with America at any given time. Today Americans search news sources that often fit their personal, political, or moral views.

Anonymous postings on social media sites attack our views, our values, our families, and ourselves. Friendships can be lost and relationships strained on these venues. It seems we are constantly bombarded with unwanted opinions and statements. Even talk show host Ellen DeGeneres was vilified on Twitter after sitting with former president George Bush at a football game. Vitriol replaces courtesy and fanaticism replaces logic, leading us to seek shelter by only communicating with those who agree with us.

Facebook, Twitter, Instagram, YouTube, and other social media companies are viewed by many as content creators instead of as platforms for individuals to communicate with their families, their friends, and even the general public. The result is a growing level of distrust among users of these tools. As these entities have attempted to control content, frustration has grown to the point that some politicians are calling for the dissolution of the larger of these organizations.[3]

Negative campaigning seems to be at an all-time high. Every election year the number of negative ads increases. Voters claim to be tired of these ads. We hear our friends and neighbors saying they won't watch these ads anymore and certainly don't plan on voting for any candidate who runs a negative campaign.

This list of our beefs with our political system and the underlying ethics behind our political communication seems endless. The list must be worse today than at any other time in American history, right? We have more people involved with more communications systems with more money to spend on politics than ever before. It's only logical that our system is almost hopelessly broken, and certainly our ancestors would be appalled at our behavior today. Today is the worst it has ever been until we reach a new low tomorrow. Or so it seems.

Yes, we must do better. But it's not as bad as you think.

Our history is filled with political venom, horrific ad hominem attacks on candidates, and dirty tricks. Our political past does not make any of today's behavior right, but today's environment is not new.

Take former president Richard Nixon. His name is synonymous with Watergate, one of the great constitutional crises in our history. Nixon was directly involved in a series of campaign dirty tricks and criminal activities aimed at defaming his political opposition and winning reelection to the presidency in 1972. But this was not the first of Nixon's elections involving breaking and entering, dirty politics, and virtual truckloads of illicit campaign money.

In his 1960 campaign for president, Nixon cut a secret deal for his family members to receive hundreds of thousands of dollars from billionaire recluse and government contractor Howard Hughes. The campaign of soon to be president John Kennedy caught wind of this plan and wanted to publicize it. Lacking any evidence, the Kennedy campaign arranged for a robbery to obtain the necessary documents so members of the media friendly to Kennedy could print this story.[4]

In the middle of this operation was brother of the president and future attorney general of the United States Robert Kennedy. The news became public just before the election, and Kennedy won in a squeaker. Nixon was furious, believing the election had been stolen from him—setting the stage for Nixon to never let himself be outmaneuvered again.

Wild accusations about our presidential candidates have been almost commonplace in our system. In the election of 1884, future president Grover Cleveland, a bachelor, was accused of fathering an unwed child and forcing the mother into a mental facility. The supporters of his Republican opponent, James Blaine, were more than happy to spread this story far and wide. The Blaine team used the campaign ditty "Ma, Ma, Where's my Pa. Sitting in the White House, Ha, Ha, Ha."[5] Cleveland ultimately won, but the damage was done to his reputation and followed him through his two terms as president.

American heroes have been used to spread campaign rumors and innuendo. In the election of 1836, Martin Van Buren was accused of wearing a woman's corset. The accusations were based on a supposed letter from Davy Crockett, a well-known American frontiersman and hero of the Battle of the Alamo in the fight for the independence of Texas.[6]

Our forefathers were not immune from vicious and questionable political attacks. The presidential election of 1800 between John Adams and Thomas Jefferson was conducted by supporters of each candidate via newspaper articles and pamphlets distributed to the voting public. Jefferson's supporters implied that Adams wanted our young country to return to a closer friendship with England, potentially starting a war with France to secure closer relations with Britain. The Jefferson supporters also spread the rumor that Adams wanted his daughter to marry a member of the British nobility, thereby establishing a royal bloodline in America.

The Adams contingent was not to be outdone. They accused Jefferson of being a "half breed" and supporting killing members of the upper class. They disseminated stories about Jefferson as a Francophile who would go to great ends to subjugate America to the wishes of the French.[7]

What does this rather brief review[8] of political shenanigans have to do with ethics and political communication? Well, everything, frankly. We need to do better, but it's not as bad as you think!

Our founding fathers devised a system of government built to sustain all types of disagreements, arguments, controversy, and scandals. Their distrust of government also led to ensuring the inevitable tensions arising between government and the governed would be adjudicated in favor of the people, except in specific instances outlined in our Constitution. While they could not possibly have foreseen Facebook and Twitter, they did understand the nature of human discord, that people will ultimately act in their own self-interest.

Our republican form of government is designed for big changes to be brought about slowly, hopefully when a general consensus can be established among the electorate. When this happens, good programs and policies are enacted. In the ultimate governmental failure, our country will enter into a civil war. The middle ground—often meaning no or little government action on the problems of the day—leads to voter consternation, bickering, and increasingly hostile political proclamations.

We should not immediately launch into a series of ill-designed laws and regulations hoping to control the press, the politicians/officeholders, the political consultants, and even the American public. Instead we should first examine the basic underlying causes of conflict in designing, producing, and distributing political communication that seem to be of concern to our country.

The most obvious source of questionable political communication for politicians and political consultants is the pressure to win the election. Even the most honest, dedicated, and principled of politicians/candidates for public office cannot enact their policies without serving in public office. Their commitment to putting their principles into action in government can lead to the temptation to stretch the truth or to mislead the public during an election.

Candidates are also public figures whose names are on the ballot. Whatever is said and done during the campaign is associated with them, and rightfully so. Since many of the candidates are already public figures in their own right—business leaders, community organizers, and so forth—they are the voice in a campaign most often concerned with consequences other than winning and losing.

But the campaign also becomes most personal for them. Any attack or comparison from the opposition becomes an affront to their principles, their values, their careers, and even their families. As these attacks mount during the heat of the battle, candidates will begin to believe it is time for them to retaliate in the same way their opponent is attacking them. This belief of being "wronged" during a campaign can lead to a candidate adopting a scorched earth policy in dealing with the opposition. The pressure from supporters mounts, and calls for candidates to hit back at their opponents grow. Few candidates can withstand this internal pressure. The voting public will ultimately make the final judgment on whether or not a candidate reacted properly to his or her opponent. How a candidate reacts to this pressure can be very predictive of how that person will react when serving in public office.[9]

The candidate/politician often feels the most pressure in providing policy answers to the community's problems. Rightly or wrongly, politicians believe their victory depends on whether or not the voting public agrees or disagrees with the solutions they describe during their campaigns. The temptation to overpromise what they can produce in office is the greatest temptation for candidates to violate the public's ill-defined standards for political communication.

The candidate is ultimately responsible for everything said and done inside the campaign. Our system of voting for individual members of Congress, state legislatures, and city councils means there is no one to hide behind when it comes to the performance of a campaign. In countries with a parliamentary form of government (which includes almost all elected forms of government in the world), candidates can blame their party or their party leader for their performance, their public policies, and their contrasts with their opponents.

In the United States, you are responsible for your own campaign. The good news is that this means as a candidate you can take a stance different from those of your political party colleagues if you see fit. You have the ability to chart your own course if you choose. But it also means the entire public, as well as members of your own party, independents, and members of the opposition party, will judge you on an individual basis.

The pressures on a political consultant are very focused. As a political professional, I'm not judged on whether I ran the best campaign, the coolest campaign, the prettiest campaign, or even the most honest campaign. In the long run, I'm judged on whether my candidate wins or loses. Winning makes me smart, quotable, and successful. Losing means I am supposed to reconsider my thinking, tactics, and efforts. Losing too many races will lead to a career change for even the most charismatic, creative, principled consultants.

So what governs how a consultant behaves? What keeps consultants from simply ignoring all precepts of honest campaigns and, say, asking the campaign to say anything just to get elected?

Most political consultants I know came to this business because they hold a set of principles about the direction of the country. Consultants want to make a contribution to their values and their cause and choose to work behind the scenes rather than run for public office and put their names on the ballot.

This commitment to values and principles also means virtually all consultants also believe in our country, our system, and our electoral process. We want to win. We make plans. We spend our lives thinking about campaigns, about how the voters react to our campaigns and our candidates. We learn about marketing, advertising, mass psychology, and moving public opinion in our direction.

Consultants and campaign staff take these rather unique skills from campaign to campaign, from one part of the country to another. It is a very nomadic business. Often it is not clear where their next job will be or where they will be living during the next election cycle.

The tough nature of this business separates those who just win from those who win with the type of campaign that makes a candidate want to hire them again and again. Balancing the candidate's need to be seen in a positive light by the public with the consultant's need to win usually makes for a symbiotic relationship, leading to political communication that is within the public's acceptable limits.

How they view the election can also serve as a guide for the type of political communication political consultants will employ in a campaign. I viewed my fellow Republicans running against my candidate in a primary as competitors. The Democratic candidates we faced in the general election were the opposition. My enemies wanted to destroy my family, my country, my way of life. They may even have wanted to kill me. Keeping the difference between competitors, opponents, and enemies in mind can serve to temper the type of language a campaign will use in attacking or drawing contrasts.

For members of the media, pressure is felt to produce content that gains viewers on TV, engagement, or subscriptions on social media.[10] Of course what this leads to is more money and more profits for the media companies. There is nothing wrong with earning a profit in our capitalistic system. In fact, earning a profit should be celebrated.

But to gain attention with all the competing forms of media today often requires more strident, more forceful, outspoken headlines. The content of the stories often follows these guidelines. The media, in searching for the balance between profits and reporting, react to what works for them. As our public looks more for confirmation of their views from news sources rather than "hard" news, we cannot place all the onus on the media to produce a more balanced view of the news of the day.

The media would likely do better to self-admit that many if not most information outlets are representing a particular point of view. For most of our nation's history, the news media were seen as advocates for one point of view or another, and our citizenry was able to discern right from wrong, good from bad as the media presented partisan points of view. It wasn't until the 1920s that the news media began to define themselves as objective observers of the events of the day.[11] This goal of objectivity was pursued and possibly maintained during a time of few news sources for the public to consume and when our country had common and easily identifiable enemies to rally against.

Today's world has seen an exponential growth of information sources, leading to more points of view to be accommodated. A more complicated world means there are more possibilities for what people might see as best for our country, their communities, or themselves.

This multitude of choices makes presenting a truly objective point of view all but impossible providing analyses of public events. If analysis is not seen as objective, the viewing public begins to look for a source that comports with their beliefs. To gain more viewers, the media react by providing content sympathetic with the most loyal viewers, all while trying to maintain the cloak of objectivity. The public then begins to question the media's claims to be objective, because news sources are not providing them with information they see as credible. The news media become part of the political discussion, part of the community making judgments of our government and our officeholders.

The public also deserves scrutiny when determining causes for the decline in our political communication. The advent of social media has provided a new communications loop for the public to give feedback to our elected officials, campaigns, and the news media. It is also much easier now to find others who agree with your own point of view, your own method of expressing your values. The downside of this collective nature of social media is that it often leads to a herd mentality. Inside the herd, some are encouraged to make more and more outlandish claims, with no outside verification. And from there it becomes easy to attack those who disagree with you in a very personal manner. With no direct in-person interaction with political opponents, some see no reason to consider other points of view or to couch their views in a way to attract new people to their side of a political discussion.

This type of upheaval is to be expected during the massive, fast changes taking place in virtually every aspect of our lives. But it does not and should not replace the respect owed to our fellow citizens who disagree with our points of view.

Yes, we can do better. But it's still not as bad as you think.

Our system is designed to withstand this type of upheaval. We have made it through a civil war, world wars, and threats both internal and external. We don't need new laws to control our politics or our citizens. We can make changes in our behavior that will contribute to a better political discussion and to better government.

We can start with having each of our major players in political discussions—politicians, political consultants, the press, and the public—committing to doing one simple thing better.

For our candidates and officeholders, commit to policy positions you can keep while in office. Regaining the trust of the public in your keeping your word would be a major step in restoring the confidence in our government. Restoring trust would enable the public to feel comfortable engaging in a true discussion of the issues rather than resorting to ad hominem attacks because they do not believe your positions or proposals are realistic or authentic.

For our political consultants, commit to attacking or contrasting with your opponents in a manner in which their response will be to engage you on the issue or the values you are discussing rather than simply responding with the accusation that you are not telling the truth. This is not to seek an end to negative campaigns. Nor is it to say you cannot attack the character of your opponents if they have behaved in a manner the public may find distasteful. Letting the public know the differences between candidates is important for voters in making decisions about who to elect. The public will decide if your attacks have crossed a line by not voting for your candidate.

But our system would be better served if campaigns engaged in political communication that will interest and engage the public in learning more about their candidates and campaigns.

For the news media, commit to running stories that return to four of the basic questions of news gathering: who, what, when, and where. There is plenty of time and space for commentary and analysis. Reporters and analysts have the experience and background to contribute to the public and political discussions. Make a distinction between the news stories that report what happened, who said what, and the contents of a proposal or new law. Separate those hard news stories from the analysis. Making a commitment to report the hard news will attract an audience and rebuild the public's confidence in the media. As trust is regained, the analysis provided by a news organization will gain more traction and hopefully more consideration by those with opposing points of view.

For the public, make a commitment to be better consumers of information. Commit to listening to the statements and points of view of politicians you may not support or news organizations you may not agree with. Just because a statement comes from someone or someplace you do not necessarily follow or know does not make that information automatically invalid or untrue.

There is much angst in our society today. Our divisions are strong; the country seems split. This is nothing new or surprising. We are in a period of upheaval in how we learn, work, and receive and transmit information. These times lead to uncertainty. But that's OK. Our system is strong and built to survive times like this.

Yes, we can do better. But it's not as bad as you think.

Notes

1   "Congressional Performance," Rasmussen Reports, October 3–6, 2019, http://www.rasmussenreports.com/public_content/politics/top_stories/rate_congress_oct08.

2   "Network News Fact Sheet," Pew Research Center, June 25, 2019, https://www.journalism.org/fact-sheet/network-news/.

3   Soo Rin Kim, "The Love-Hate Relationship between 2020 Presidential Candidates and Tech Giants: A Delicate Dance of Money, Online Influence and Populist Anger," *ABC News*, July 27, 2019, https://abcnews.go.com/Politics/love-hate-relationship-2020-presidential-candidates-tech-giants/story?id=64490545.

4   Mark Feldstein, "Mark Feldstein: JFK's Own Dirty Trick on Nixon," *Twin Cities Pioneer Press*, January 14, 2011, https://www.twincities.com/2011/01/14/mark-feldstein-jfks-own-dirty-trick-on-nixon/.

5   Angela Serratore, "President Cleveland's Problem Child," *Smithsonian Magazine*, September 26, 2013, https://www.smithsonianmag.com/history/president-clevelands-problem-child-100800/.

6 "Martin Van Buren, 8th Vice President (1833–1837)," United States Senate, https://www.senate.gov/artandhistory/history/common/generic/VP_Martin_VanBuren.htm.

7 Matt Weeks, "The Dirtiest Presidential Campaigns in the History of United States Politics," Owlcation, June 11, 2016, https://owlcation.com/humanities/The-Dirtiest-Presidential-Campaigns-in-the-History-of-United-States-Politics.

8 For more on political dirty tricks, see "Anything for a Vote: Joseph Cummins," in *Anything for a Vote: Dirty Tricks, Cheap Shots, and October Surprises in U.S. Presidential Campaigns* (Philadelphia: Quirk Books, 2012); and Melissa Lafsky, "The Complete History of Dirty Politics: A Q&A on Anything for a Vote," Freakonomics, November 6, 2007, http://freakonomics.com/2007/11/06/the-complete-history-of-dirty-politics-a-qa-on-anything-for-a-vote/.

9 For an in-depth look at the inside of a presidential campaign, see Theodore White, *The Making of the President 1960* (New York: Atheneum Books, 1961); Richard Ben Cramer, *What It Takes: The Way to the White House* (New York: Random House, 1992); and Mark Halperin and John Heilemann, *Game Change* (New York: HarperCollins, 2010).

10 For an in-depth look at how the media cover a presidential campaign, see Timothy Crouse, *The Boys on the Bus* (New York: Random House, 1973).

11 "The Lost Meaning of 'Objectivity,'" American Press Institute, n.d., https://www.americanpressinstitute.org/journalism-essentials/bias-objectivity/lost-meaning-objectivity/.

11

Instructions Not Included

The Limited Function of Laws, Norms, and Political Incentives in Political Communication Ethics

Kip F. Wainscott

Back in 2000, on an otherwise ordinary September day, the afterglow of Labor Day was making way for autumn in Washington, DC, and the presidential election contest between Governor George W. Bush and Vice President Al Gore was beginning to move into high gear. The first debate between the candidates was approaching, and an aide to Gore was preparing for a mock debate with the candidate the following day—during which the aide would portray Governor Bush—when a mysterious package arrived in the mail containing briefing materials and an enclosed video.[1]

As the aide and his assistant began reviewing the parcel's contents, they were astonished when they realized what they were looking at: this was a treasure trove of the Bush campaign's debate prep materials, complete with a recording of the governor's private practice session.[2] Immediately recognizing the moral and ethical implications of accepting such information, the aide collected the items, contacted his lawyer, and instructed the attorney to deliver the materials to the Federal Bureau of Investigation. Within ninety minutes of receiving the package, its contents had been reported to authorities and were out of the aide's possession.[3]

This episode illustrates a highly specific ethical dilemma encountered in perhaps the highest-stakes realm of political communication strategy: presidential debates. Perhaps unsurprisingly, the aide's response to this scenario is widely acknowledged to have been ethical and appropriate; years later, at a foreign summit at which the aide was present, then-president Bush would personally commend him for doing the right thing.

There are many ethical models and philosophies discussed throughout this text that will validate the aide's actions; ethics can and should play a guiding role in shaping behavior and communication strategies in the public sphere. But for those professionals who haven't known the joy of studying ethical principles, are there any rules or other guideposts in US politics that may function as a proxy for the ethical approach? Ethics aside, are there any laws that might have encouraged Al Gore's aide to alert investigators to the mysterious package, rather than use the information to develop a cutting debate strategy against Bush? What other considerations might come into play to guide behavior in these cases?

This chapter examines at a high level the extent to which laws, unwritten rules, and other externalities may intersect with and inform ethical responsibilities in political communication. By and large, and for reasons I touch upon in greater detail later in the chapter, the ethics of political communication are mostly left to the discretion of the practitioner and not formally regulated. Nonetheless, there are *some* outer limits to the law's hands-off approach to political communication, as well as some noteworthy principles that have at times been regarded as load-bearing guideposts in American democracy.

To better understand their place in political communication—and perhaps more important, their limitations—I look at three categories of guideposts. First, I review the role of the law in political communication, which mostly involves a narrow category of regulations to prevent corruption and promote transparency. Second, I examine democratic norms and the ways that these unwritten rules may or may not help inform political communication behaviors. And third, I consider whether political incentives themselves may play a part in incentivizing ethical (or unethical) behavior. After examining these external considerations and reviewing their significant limitations, I conclude by contemplating voluntary steps that practitioners may undertake to create their own helpful guideposts.

The Limited Reach of the Law

In the United States, political communication falls into a category of speech that enjoys the highest level of protection under the Constitution's First Amendment.[4] The Supreme Court has long held that speech concerning "politics, nationalism, religion, or other matters of opinion" is at the heart of the First Amendment, such that any laws or regulations that may implicate political communication are subject to "strict scrutiny" in the courts (the highest standard of judicial review, under which the government must be able to show that the law is narrowly tailored to achieve a compelling government interest).[5] Put simply, it is very difficult—by design—to set any legal parameters on the practice of political communication.

The general inability of the law to provide ethical boundaries in the realm of political communication helps to protect and preserve a fundamental tenet of democracy: freedom of expression. And while the First Amendment generally protects nearly all forms of speech—and political speech especially—it is worth noting that communication practitioners in the political realm may occasionally come into contact with certain laws and regulations of political activity that can withstand constitutional scrutiny—rules that have perhaps been "narrowly tailored to achieve a compelling government interest," such as preventing corruption or the abuse of government power. Interpreting the rules and regulations that may be involved in political communication is naturally a job for lawyers, rather than, say, digital directors or press secretaries. However, as you develop communication strategies and advice in different political (and potentially governmental) contexts, the following legal considerations may be relevant to your work:

- *Political advertising rules:* The laws and legal opinions related to campaign advertising are myriad and complex, to the point where even the definition of political advertising depends on where and how you're communicating your message. But in a highly general and elemental sense (which is never how lawyers like to describe things), you can think of it this way: campaign advertisements are typically paid political speech. As a shorthand illustration, if you voluntarily submit your argument for electing a particular candidate to a newspaper op-ed page, it's not an ad; if you pay money to feature that same argument in the newspaper, it's an ad. The implications of shifting from a mere communication to an advertisement depend on a lot of variables, but most constitutionally allowable political advertising laws can be described as transparency measures—typically, you can expect that paid political messages may require the inclusion of a "paid for by" disclaimer (though even this requirement may depend on what medium you're using)[6] and also may require you to make certain registrations or disclosures with federal, state, or local election authorities.[7] These requirements help to enable citizens to understand who is ultimately promoting the communication and also to distinguish organic speech (or what may be considered independent commentary) from paid political advertising.
- *Grassroots lobbying restrictions:* As part of your career as a political communications practitioner, you may find it helpful in some instances to deploy a grassroots organizing strategy in support of a particular issue or cause. Such strategies typically include a rousing call to action, such as "contact your representative today, and tell them to oppose long reading assignments in ethics class!" Even if you or your organization does not lobby elected officials directly, calling on others to assert legislative pressure can sometimes implicate rules and regulations designed to promote transparency in the context of issue advocacy.[8] In certain contexts (particularly at the state level), these calls to action may involve laws that require the filing of certain disclosures with an ethics or campaign finance office,

and grassroots lobbying can also have tax and reporting implications for nonprofit organizations.[9]

- *Conflicts of interest:* If your career leads you into government, you could encounter a collection of ethical rules meant to guard against conflicts of interest, particularly if you move between the private sector and government. For example, political appointees in the executive branch are prohibited from advising directly on matters that are "directly and substantially related to [their] former employer or former clients" for the first two years of government service.[10] Upon leaving government, you may likewise be subject to rules limiting your ability to lobby former colleagues in government on behalf of a new employer or clients for a limited period of time.[11] Federal ethics rules may also require you to report certain financial holdings and nongovernment earnings[12] to advance accountability and transparency in public works.

In considering these examples, note that these laws provide very little real ethical instruction. Mostly they create conditions in which voters, citizens, and journalists can evaluate information and perhaps draw conclusions about the ethics or propriety of certain actions; only the postemployment rules and conflicts of interest examples truly place any restrictions on behavior, and political communication practitioners will encounter those rules only in highly specific circumstances.[13]

While lawmakers have made regulatory efforts to promote ethics in government and political campaigns, such laws are intentionally designed not to infringe on the essential right to political expression—and while this is very much an important and necessary limitation on the law's reach, it mostly means that professional political communicators cannot conveniently substitute a statutory framework for an ethical one. While a law may require that a communication's funding be disclosed, regulations are generally agnostic as to whether that same communication is perhaps manipulative or vengeful or misleading. In the context of political communications, the law can provide only very limited ethical guidance.

The Fragile Support of Democratic Norms

In the United States, our political system has often functioned with assistance from a somewhat dynamic set of unwritten rules and practices, and the importance of such norms in American democracy has been long acknowledged among political observers and scholars.[14] At various points in the nation's history, democratic norms have helped provide certain behavioral guardrails for our politics, based in part on wide acknowledgment among practitioners that a departure from these rules could damage our system of government.

There are two norms in particular that Harvard professors Steven Levitsky and Daniel Ziblatt characterize as the "soft guardrails" of democracy.[15] These are mutual toleration and forbearance, and each is relevant to the work of a modern political communication practitioner.

Mutual Toleration

Mutual toleration is essentially the concept of accepting your political opponents in a democracy as legitimate, acknowledging their right to advance their own ideas, win popular elections, and govern according to the framework established by the Constitution.[16] In political communication, this norm can be thought of as the practice of resisting the impulse to vilify your opponents or question their patriotism; it allows for drawing contrasts and exploiting weaknesses on policy or political grounds but requires recognition on some level that your opponents are rightful actors in our system, rather than enemies. As Levitsky and Ziblatt summarize it, "mutual toleration is politicians' collective willingness to agree to disagree."[17]

In this century, one high-profile example of mutual toleration especially stands out from the 2008 presidential campaign. The Republican nominee, Senator John McCain, was confronted by a supporter during a televised town hall, who expressed fearfulness about the Democratic nominee, then-senator Barack Obama, implying that McCain's opponent might not be a citizen and could not be trusted.[18] McCain interrupted the questioner and defended his opponent, "No Ma'am. [Obama] is a decent family man [and] citizen that I just happen to have disagreements with on fundamental issues, and that's what the campaign's all about."[19] According to accounts at the time, the assembled crowd of McCain supporters reacted negatively, responding with a chorus of boos.[20] Still, when another questioner expressed fear at the notion of an Obama presidency, McCain stood fast. "I have to tell you. Sen. Obama is a decent person and a person you don't have to be scared of as president of the United States."[21]

Despite real-time, vocal urging from his supporters, Senator McCain declined to attack his opponent in existential terms. Instead, McCain used his platform to affirm the legitimacy of his political rival, in what can be characterized rightly as a noble gesture to an important American norm.

Forbearance

Forbearance is the notion of political actors exercising restraint with respect to their governing authority and institutional prerogatives.[22] Perhaps the great early exemplar of forbearance in American politics is George Washington, who, upon declining to seek a third term as president, cautioned officials to embrace restraint in the use of power.[23] In his celebrated farewell address, he advised that "a free country should inspire caution in those entrusted with its administration, to confine themselves within their respective constitutional spheres, avoiding in the exercise of the powers of one department to encroach upon another," warning that such encroachment could lead to consolidation of power and "a real despotism."[24]

In one illustration of the practice of forbearance across the branches of government, Levitsky and Ziblatt highlight the voluntary nature of cooperation between the legislative and executive branches to fill Supreme Court vacancies. They note that although the Senate has always reserved the right to reject presidential appointments to the court, in the one-hundred-year span from 1880 to 1980, the Senate approved more than 90 percent of appointees, and only three presidents had nominees rejected. In a particularly compelling example, "[t]he ultraconservative Antonin Scalia, a Reagan appointee, was approved in 1986 by a vote of 98 to 0, despite the fact that Democrats had more than enough votes (47) to filibuster."[25]

Having worked in both government and politics, I can say with some confidence that the term "forbearance" won't often appear on your team's strategic communications roadmap. That said, scholars are right to point out that our democracy could scarcely function without it: presidents could undermine the rule of law by granting pardons freely; Congress could shut down the government perennially by refusing to fund it.[26] In your career, forbearance may mean resisting the full use of leverage or political power available, instead allowing the government and our political system to work.

Norms as Soft—and Inconsistent—Guardrails in Political Communication Ethics

Armed with a bit more understanding of two prominent norms in American democracy, perhaps you can envision observing these rules in the context of a political communication strategy. In a nod to mutual toleration, perhaps you encourage your boss to praise her opponent's commitment to public service before attacking the opponent's legislative record on a debate stage. In an exercise of forbearance, perhaps you advise the senator to pick fights over presidential appointees only very judiciously. But can these principles function as ethical guideposts? Probably not.

There are at least two reasons norms are ill-suited to inform your ethical approach to political communication. First, their applicability across the growing field of political communication is somewhat limited. Although these unwritten rules have played an essential role in the functioning of our political system, they operate generally in service of a functioning democracy rather than in promoting ethical behavior and simply aren't applicable to many of the wide-ranging ethical questions that you're likely to encounter in the complex arena of political communication. While tolerance and forbearance may be relevant considerations, particularly in the context of partisan elections and governance, you won't find the concepts particularly useful as you contemplate, for example, your responsibility to correct disinformation that may be circulating in support of your issue campaign on environmental protection.

The second reason norms are perhaps a poor proxy for ethics is that even where these rules may intersect with your work, they are unreliably observed; they are merely practices, not enforceable rules, and their meaning tends to change and evolve. While mutual toleration in 2008 meant that Republican John McCain was quick to defend his Democratic opponent Barack Obama as a legitimate rival and decent man, the 2016 Republican nominee persistently and publicly questioned President Obama's legitimacy[27] and suggested during the campaign that his 2016 Democratic opponent should be imprisoned.[28] Forbearance, too, has endured shaky periods throughout American history; while the Civil War is perhaps the most glaring example, the recent spike in filibuster use in the Senate would be unrecognizable to nearly every previous generation of politicos who served in the chamber.[29] During political periods in which norms may not be respected or practiced, their historical relevance is of little practical use to the staffer trying to navigate the ethics of the contemporary moment.

Rather than thinking of norms as providing ethical instruction, perhaps it's more useful to hold them as a reminder that our political system is not invincible or necessarily permanent. Recent scholarship regarding norms in the United States and elsewhere tends to show that democracies rely heavily on beliefs and practices that are vulnerable to decline and erosion.[30] Levitsky and Ziblatt note that democracy is "a game that we want to keep playing indefinitely," and it's appropriate to think of norms as modes of helping us to avoid a final score.[31]

Unreliable Political Incentives

I opened this chapter with an anecdote about the aide to Vice President Gore who received an anonymous package containing the Bush campaign's strategy materials. The aide in that scenario—the Gore team adviser who was best positioned to prepare the candidate to square off against Bush in the high-stakes presidential debates—didn't just take the step of reporting the incident and turning over the materials to federal investigators; he also recused himself from the Gore campaign for the duration of the election season. And while engaging with law enforcement may have been incentivized by federal law, the latter step was a wholly voluntary response, with potentially consequential implications for Al Gore's presidential aspirations (in the end, the debates did not go well for Gore, Bush appeared to gain an advantage, and perhaps the late-game recusal of a key aide played some part in Gore's underwhelming performance).

Nearly two decades later, in a reflective interview with a political reporter, Gore's aide described his motivations for the recusal as a combination of wanting to act honorably and recognizing that his continued involvement in the campaign could be used against the candidate politically. There were political incentives to do the right thing, at least in the aide's assessment of the politics.

Throughout your career in political communication, you will be expected to regularly contemplate the optics of decisions and actions; such political acumen will perhaps be the central feature of your skill set. Could the politics of doing the right thing provide an ethical compass to guide your decision making? Does politics incentivize or reward ethical communication practices?

Political winds are notoriously fickle, and it should perhaps come as no surprise that the incentives that drive compelling communication strategies are occasionally crosswise with principles of ethics. While there are examples, like the one I have described, in which ethical behavior and smart politics seem to dictate the same response, as a communication professional you are likely to encounter scenarios in which the incentives raise difficult ethical dilemmas (and many such scenarios will be far more mundane).

One prevalent illustration of this tension is seen in the prolific use of micro-targeting to drive bespoke political messaging to hyper-specific audiences.[32] The political advantage of these techniques is straightforward: communication can be personalized to align with individual preferences and priorities that are most likely to elicit the desired action or engagement. Notwithstanding the improvements in message precision and efficiency, this practice is often enabled by data collection processes that are less than transparent and may therefore involve important ethical questions.[33]

Another example is the proliferation of political disinformation and polarizing content to drive engagement online. Disinformation campaigns can be highly effective at exploiting fear and societal cleavages, and studies have shown that false narratives are both memorable and have a high probability of effectively fooling audiences into believing them.[34] Disinformation also drives engagement—a common metric of success in digital campaign communication—with studies showing fabricated partisan content in some cases outpacing interactions with credible mainstream news organizations.[35] In the high-stakes world of electoral campaigns, there are certainly incentives that reward communication strategies that efficiently and reliably persuade voters to share or remember helpful narratives; however, I hope you can easily recognize the ethical degradation involved in strategies that pollute the political information environment and deceive voters with misleading or false information. Whatever political incentives may motivate the tactical spread of disinformation, they are clearly at odds with ethical political communication practice.

As noted previously, another reason that political incentives provide poor ethical guidance is that political assessments change frequently; the politics around even what may be characterized as "ethics-related policies" can shift rapidly. In 2008, when Barack Obama declined to accept public financing in support of his presidential campaign, it was covered as a political risk—the public financing system had been an enduring feature of the post-Watergate era political ethics reform movement, and then-senator Obama had been a prominent proponent of campaign finance reform, including public financing, to promote ethics in politics.[36] In the election cycles since then, the political expectations surrounding public financing have changed significantly; no major party nominee has accepted public financing, and it's widely accepted that even the most vocal critics of money's role in politics will forego participation in the public system.[37]

In sum, while political considerations may occasionally weigh in favor of ethical behavior, they will not reliably do so. Mostly, politics incentivizes winning (or at least some form of competitive advantage or negotiating leverage) and does so without privileging ethical considerations in any consistent way. For these reasons, political incentives contribute little value to informing a practitioner's ethical roadmap.

Concluding Note: The Unmet Need

My goal for this chapter is, in part, to provide some context for the reasons you might find yourself without reliable ethical guardrails as you enter the professional world of political communication. As the topics covered here illustrate, our political system largely leaves ethical judgments to the electorate and to practitioners themselves. However, while you will not find an off-the-shelf ethical guidebook in the form of laws, norms, or political incentives, it's possible that knowledge of these themes can help to inform the development of your own ethical framework in the context of political communication.

Based on the few legal parameters touched on here, we can see, for example, that combating corruption (or the appearance thereof) is a "compelling government interest" and an issue of which to be cognizant in politics. Our knowledge of key democratic norms cautions us that our political system is vulnerable to overzealous partisanship and factionalism and requires some level of tolerance and restraint in order to function properly. We know that political objectives can at times incentivize ethically murky (or wrong) behaviors, and that political attitudes are themselves variable. How can political communication practitioners use this information to inform ethical decision making? And how might the limitations of these guideposts encourage practitioners to be mindful of their own responsibilities?

One suggestion is for practitioners to develop a personal framework, one that can be operationalized to help evaluate decisions in a way that's consistent with your ethical code as well as the objectives of our laws and political system. Based on some of the topics outlined in this chapter, such a code of conduct could include tenets such as the following:

- *Safeguard democracy:* Be intentional about whether your tactics will inflict damage on the integrity of our institutions or our elections.
- *Promote political pluralism:* Accepting that political ideas are diverse and that opponents are legitimate participants in democracy strengthens tolerance and may help mitigate harmful polarization.
- *Respect the integrity of political information:* Misinformation distorts the information upon which voters and citizens rely; elections are neither free nor fair if the public is deprived of the ability to reasonably ascertain what's true and what is not.
- *Default to transparency and operate with concern for conflicts of interest:* Taking care to promote trust and avoid the appearance of corruption can help promote ethical behavior, advance confidence in our system, and position your default practices in line with legal compliance obligations.
- *Protect the confidentiality of sensitive information:* We know that the collection and use of data—including voter and constituent information—can involve difficult ethical considerations, particularly in the realm of digital political communication. Take care to ensure that all data are collected lawfully, stored responsibly, and utilized ethically.

These ideas are offered for illustrative purposes, of course. And while each is meant to be responsive to some of the topics explored in this chapter, practitioners should be thoughtful about what tenets may apply to their work more specifically. As a student thinking about a preferred career in political communication, what might be some tenets to inform your own decision making in that role?

As I have shown, much of the responsibility here will be yours. The next generation of campaign managers, digital strategists, communication directors, and press secretaries will play a part in both breaking new political barriers and safeguarding our democratic system. But all of these also share an abundance of responsibility for the role that ethics and integrity play in this important work. I hope that you will embrace that responsibility in your work, perhaps with attention to the limited ability of our legal and political systems to provide stronger safeguards on their own.

Notes

1 Russell Berman, "Uh-Oh, We Shouldn't Have This," *Atlantic*, June 14, 2019, accessed August 25, 2019, https://www.theatlantic.com/politics/archive/2019/ 06/trump-fbi-foreign-election-interference-gore-downey/591748/.

2 Berman, "Uh-Oh, We Shouldn't Have This."
3 Berman, "Uh-Oh, We Shouldn't Have This."
4 Victoria L. Killion, "The First Amendment: Categories of Speech," *Congressional Research Service*, January 16, 2019, accessed September 1, 2019, https://fas.org/sgp/crs/misc/IF11072.pdf.
5 Killion, "The First Amendment."
6 See, for example, 11 C.F.R. § 110.11(c)(1).
7 See 52 U.S.C. § 30103(a); 11 C.F.R. §§ 102.1, 104.1-18; see also, for example, Colo. Rev. Stat. § 1-45-108; Wash. Rev. Code §§ 42.17A.200-270.
8 See, for example, 3 Maine Rev. Stat. §§ 312-A(7-B), 316.
9 Kip F. Wainscott, "Laws Governing Interactions with the Executive Branch," in *The Lobbying Manual*, ed. Rebecca H. Gordon et al., 142–145 (Washington: The American Bar Association, 2016).
10 "Executive Order: Ethics Commitments by Executive Branch Appointees," Exec. Order 13770, January 28, 2017.
11 Christopher DeLacy and Andrew H. Emerson, "Updated Post-Employment Rules and Restrictions for Former Federal Government Officials," *Holland & Knight Political Law Blog*, March 20, 2017, accessed September 28, 2019, https://www.hklaw.com/en/insights/publications/2017/03/updated-postemployment-rules-and-restrictions-for.
12 5 U.S.C. § 109 (a)(8).
13 There are other types of laws aimed at curbing corruption in politics—for example, restrictions on accepting gifts in public office and limitations on campaign contributions—but they are even less directly relevant to the practice of communications.
14 See, for example, James Bryce, *The American Commonwealth* (New York, Macmillan, 1896), 1: 393–394; and Steven Levitsky and Daniel Ziblatt, *How Democracies Die* (New York, Broadway Books, 2018), 127.
15 Steven Levitsky and Daniel Ziblatt, *How Democracies Die* (New York, Broadway Books, 2018), 9.
16 Steven Levitsky and Daniel Ziblatt, "How a Democracy Dies," *New Republic*, December 7, 2017, accessed September 23, 2019, https://newrepublic.com/article/145916/democracy-dies-donald-trump-contempt-for-american-political-institutions.
17 Levitsky and Ziblatt, *How Democracies Die*, 102.
18 Emily Stewart, "Watch John McCain Defend Barack Obama Against a Racist Voter in 2008," Vox, September 1, 2018, accessed Sept. 23, 2019, https://www.vox.com/policy-and-politics/2018/8/25/17782572/john-mccain-barack-obama-statement-2008-video.
19 Stewart, "Watch John McCain Defend Barack Obama."
20 Jonathan Martin and Amie Parnes, "McCain: Obama Not an Arab, Crowd Boos," Politico, October 10, 2008, accessed Sept. 23, 2019, https://www.politico.com/story/2008/10/mccain-obama-not-an-arab-crowd-boos-014479.
21 Martin and Parnes, "McCain."
22 Levitsky and Ziblatt, "How a Democracy Dies."
23 Thomas R. Pickering and James Stoutenberg, "Did George Washington Predict Donald Trump?" *New York Times*, February 18, 2018, accessed September 23, 2019,

https://www.nytimes.com/2018/02/18/opinion/george-washington-don ald-trump.html.

[24] Pickering and Stoutenberg, "Did George Washington Predict Donald Trump?" quoting *Washington's Farewell Address to the People of the United States* (Hartford, CT: Hudson and Goodwin, 1813).

[25] Levitsky and Ziblatt, *How Democracies Die*, 136.

[26] Steven Levitsky and Daniel Ziblatt, "How Wobbly Is Our Democracy?" *New York Times*, January 27, 2018, accessed September 23, 2019, https://www.nytimes .com/2018/01/27/opinion/sunday/democracy-polarization.html.

[27] Chris Megerian, "What Donald Trump Has Said Through the Years About Where President Obama Was Born," *Los Angeles Times*, September 16, 2016, accessed September 23, 2019, https://www.latimes.com/politics/la-na-pol-trump-birther -timeline-20160916-snap-htmlstory.html.

[28] Jeremy Diamond, "Trump on 'Lock Her Up' Chant: 'I'm Starting to Agree,'" CNN, July 29, 2016, accessed September 23, 2019, https://www.cnn .com/2016/07/29/politics/donald-trump-lock-her-up/index.html.

[29] Levitsky and Ziblatt, *How Democracies Die*, 163.

[30] Didi Kuo, "Comparing America: Reflections on Democracy Across Subfields," *Perspectives on Politics* 17: 778–800, accessed Sept. 23, 2019, doi:10.1017/ S1537592719001014.

[31] Alan Z. Rozenshtein, "A Whimper, Not a Bang," *LawFare Book Review*, September 13, 2018, accessed September 23, 2019, https://www.lawfareblog.com/ whimper-not-bang.

[32] "Digital Microtargeting," in *Political Party Innovation Primer*, vol. 1 (Stockholm: International Institute for Democracy and Electoral Assistance, 2018), 1:6–7, accessed September 19, 2019, https://www.idea.int/sites/default/files/publica tions/digital-microtargeting.pdf.

[33] "Digital Microtargeting," 19–20.

[34] Darrell M. West, "Research Report: How to Combat Fake News and Disinformation," The Brookings Institution, December 18, 2017, accessed September 23, 2019, https://www.brookings.edu/research/how-to-combat-fake-news-and-dis information/.

[35] Dean Jackson, "Issue Brief: Distinguishing Disinformation from Propaganda, Misinformation, and 'Fake News,'" National Endowment for Democracy, June 2018, accessed September 23, 2019, https://www.ned.org/wp-content/ uploads/2018/06/Distinguishing-Disinformation-from-Propaganda.pdf.

[36] Adam Nagourney and Jeff Zeleny, "Obama Forgoes Public Funds in First for Major Candidate," *New York Times*, June 20, 2008, accessed September 23, 2019, https://www.nytimes.com/2008/06/20/us/politics/20obamacnd.html; and Don Gonyea, "Obama Rejects Public Financing," *All Things Considered*, National Public Radio, June 19, 2008, accessed September 23, 2019, https://www.npr .org/templates/story/story.php?storyId=91703936.

[37] Kathy Kiely, "Public Campaign Funding Is So Broken That Candidates Turned Down $292 Million in Free Money," *Washington Post*, February 9, 2016, accessed September 23, 2019, https://www.washingtonpost.com/postevery thing/wp/2016/02/09/public-campaign-funding-is-so-broken-that-candidates -turned-down-292-million-in-free-money/.

12

Defense of the Dark Arts

A Primer on the Ethics of "Oppo"

Andrew Lautz

D o a quick Google search for the term "opposition research." You will get a diverse set of results. Unsurprisingly, the top hits are Google's dictionary definition of the term and the Wikipedia entry on the topic. Then there are some articles from sources such as FiveThirtyEight,[1] NPR,[2] and Bloomberg.[3] The *Huffington Post* even has a page for stories tagged "Opposition Research." But one description of opposition research—"oppo" for short—pops up a number of times in the Google search: "dark art."

As someone who spent nearly four years in the world of oppo, less than some of my colleagues but long enough to understand the ins and outs of the field, I find the term "dark art" funny. It reminds me of *Harry Potter* and the infamously unfortunate series of Hogwarts professors who taught Defense Against the Dark Arts. Maybe this moniker for oppo is intentionally related to the famous set of books about "The Boy Who Lived," used by people who wish to conjure up an unsavory image of oppo. But much like Severus Snape, the quasi-antagonist, deeply tortured soul of a professor who taught Defense Against the Dark Arts in the sixth *Potter* book, these political "dark arts" are deeply misunderstood.[4]

There is a good reason people do not understand oppo. Misperceptions abound from prominent figures on both sides of the aisle. Hillary Clinton's former press secretary told the *Washington Post* in 2017 that he would have gladly passed along the salacious "Steele dossier," on Donald Trump's alleged relationships with Russian officials, because "[o]pposition research happens on every campaign."[5] President Trump defended his son's 2016 meeting with a Russian lawyer tied to the Kremlin by saying, "[i]t's called opposition research."[6] Comments from a top Clinton official and the president of the United States himself have contributed to a warped understanding of what oppo is—and what it is not.

I saw and heard these misperceptions at work firsthand. My previous line of work has been called "dumpster diving," "digging for dirt," "slinging mud," and worse. Often the people who speak out most strongly against oppo are those who at the moment are the subject of it. I am here to argue fiercely that contrary to perceptions, the field of opposition research can be ethical. Like any other political activity—fund-raising, polling, advertising—there are both ethical and unethical ways to practice the "dark arts." Of course the field is fraught with ethical land mines, some of which I hope to illustrate with examples later in the chapter. Campaigns are fast-paced beasts, and it is easy to make split-second decisions that sacrifice ethics for expediency.

Oppo is also necessary, however. Voters deserve to make informed decisions, and the research that my colleagues and I delivered to our bosses, clients, and media gave voters important information about the men and women who sought to represent them in government. What follows is my best attempt at a road map for navigating the many ethical questions you will confront if you dip into the world of diving in dumpsters, digging for dirt, or slinging mud at your political adversaries. I hope that if you understand the opposition research process and the competing interests who read and use oppo, you will be better equipped to follow your moral compass while working in the field. It is not always an easy task, but I promise it is easier than having a long tenure as a Defense Against the Dark Arts professor at Hogwarts.

A Brief History of Oppo

While "opposition research" is a relatively new term in the centuries-long history of American politics, the practice has been around for as long as there have been contested races for office. One famous example reaches back to the eighteenth century and has been popularized recently by the smash Broadway hit *Hamilton*.

Alexander Hamilton—an author of the *Federalist* papers, signer of the US Constitution, and treasury secretary of the United States[7]—was an early victim of American opposition research, thanks to an angry, imprisoned man whose wife Hamilton was having an affair with at the time.[8] The man, James Reynolds, upset that Hamilton would not assist him after Reynolds was imprisoned for committing forgery, "got word to Hamilton's Republican rivals that he had information of a sort that could bring down the Federalist hero."[9] The rest is, quite literally, history:

> [In 1792] James Monroe, accompanied by fellow Congressmen Frederick Muhlenberg and Abraham Venable, visited Reynolds in jail and his wife at their home and heard the tale of Alexander Hamilton, seducer and home-

wrecker, a cad who had practically ordered Reynolds to share his wife's favors. What's more, Reynolds claimed, the speculation scheme in which he'd been implicated also involved the treasury secretary.[10]

The story gets complicated from there: Monroe and Muhlenberg approached Hamilton with the information and agreed to keep it a secret, but Monroe made copies of the letter that Hamilton's mistress had written to Hamilton and sent them to Thomas Jefferson. After Hamilton "impugned Jefferson's private life," rumors of Hamilton's own misdeeds made their way into a Republican document published in 1797.

How the rumors impacted Alexander Hamilton is a subject for historians to debate, but *Hamilton* musical creator Lin-Manuel Miranda makes his own view of the impact clear: Thomas Jefferson, James Madison, and Aaron Burr dance around Hamilton following the publicizing of his affair, singing that he is "never gon' be president now."[11]

If it is fair to say that opposition research has prevented political stars from ever running for president, it's more than fair to acknowledge that oppo has also been deployed with a heavy hand on the campaign trail. Perhaps the most famous example, and one that no doubt has been displayed and discussed in political science classrooms around the nation, is the 1988 "Willie Horton" ad from the Bush-Dukakis presidential campaign. CNN's Doug Criss explains in a 2018 article why the ad was so controversial:

> The "Willie Horton" campaign ad was produced by supporters of George H.W. Bush for his 1988 presidential campaign against Michael Dukakis. Horton, an African-American man, was a convicted murderer who raped a white woman and stabbed her partner while furloughed from prison under a Massachusetts program in place when Dukakis, the Democratic nominee, was governor. The TV ad is now considered one of the most racially divisive in modern political history because it played into white fear and African-American stereotypes.[12]

Discussed less often than the ad itself is the role opposition research played in turning the Willie Horton ordeal from a tragic local story to a national, racially divisive symbol of Michael Dukakis's record as governor. Roger Simon of the *Baltimore Sun* discusses the oppo process in a 1990 piece on Willie Horton:

> "The only group that I was very interested in having report to m[e] directly," [famous Republican strategist Lee] Atwater said after the election, "was opposition research." Opposition research was headed by Jim Pinkerton, 30, who had worked in the 1980 Reagan campaign, at the White House and at the Republican National Committee. "He had about 35 excellent nerds who were in the research division," Atwater said. "They came back with enough data to fill up this room."

Pinkerton, too, claimed he first heard about the furloug[h] issue from the Democratic debate in New York. A light went off in his head. And he called one of his best Massachusetts sources, Andy Card, a former Republican legislator now working at the White House. Pinkerton asked Card about furloughs. Card filled him in on Willie Horton. So Pinkerton told Atwater about Willie Horton and a light went of[f] in Atwater's head, too. "It's the single biggest negative Dukakis has got," Atwater said.[13]

What strikes me about this profile is how many technical similarities there are between the Atwater operation of the 1980s and the professional operations of both parties in the twenty-first century. There are research nerds, they are young, and they pull "ever[y] controversial thing [candidates have] ever said, every controversial position they [have] ever taken or policy they [have] carried out."[14] The nerds produce thousands of quotes from hundreds of sources, all available in digital form for "instant recall." Of note, some of the oppo used in the general election actually comes from the primary stage of the campaign. This is useful for when a victim of oppo cries foul and the attacker can claim: "Your party raised it first!" Often the best opposition research hits come from existing news stories that are given new life by campaign strategists, ad-makers, and candidates.

The Horton story, despite being an ugly example of racial politics and stereotypes, reveals enough about the technical oppo process that I don't need to spend too much time on what day-to-day operations at an "oppo shop" are like. You can find opposition researchers in many places. National party organizations (the Republican National Committee, the Democratic Senatorial Campaign Committee, etc.) have them. Most federal or gubernatorial campaigns will have a person or a team dedicated to opposition research. And then there are the oppo-only shops. The major ones as of this writing are American Bridge on the Democratic side and America Rising, my former employer, on the Republican side. These organizations are usually businesses, rather than political action committees or nonprofits. They have clients in campaigns across the nation. Some opposition research shops now even offer their services to the corporate world. Though the private nature of these businesses makes it impossible to pinpoint just how much revenue they bring in, a quick Federal Elections Commission search would tell you that it is a multi-million-dollar business—and it is growing.[15]

So What Does Oppo Actually *Mean*?

Oppo is *not* compromising information passed along from foreign governments, and it's not rumors or innuendo whispered on the street by anonymous sources. To help clear up any misunderstandings, a brief review of what opposition research actually entails is worthwhile. Though every researcher has different methods and processes, here I take you through my former research process as an example. I started every research book I wrote with a time line of the candidate's life (from birth to the present). Time lines are useful in part because they inform researchers where they need to look next (such as a candidate's business records or voting history), and in part because they inform the researcher where gaps exist in the candidate's record. I followed this time line with a look into the candidate's personal history: family, education, residence, and more. This section of research books can lead to some tension. Before I worked in opposition research, I worked for a congressional candidate whose campaign manager was very upset that the candidate's religion was included in a leaked version of the research book on him. I only came to realize once I was working for an opposition research firm that all of this personal information is part of a basic fact-finding process. It is simple due diligence, rather than a narrative that an opponent will use to attack someone.

If the candidate has ever owned a business, then the researcher needs to add a whole new set of searches to the agenda: business entity records, labor complaints, court cases, tax filings, and so forth. The same goes for a candidate who has started or run a nonprofit. Candidates with political histories involve even more work. From their time(s) as a candidate for other positions, the researcher needs to look at old campaign websites, articles about those races, any video or audio that may have cropped up online from the prior campaign(s), and campaign contribution and disbursement records. Candidates who made it to elected office require a significant, additional set of work: voting records, official expenses, newsletters or other correspondence issued by their offices, committee attendance records, and so forth. Voting records and committee attendance records, in particular, can be hard to come by in some states. For one campaign I had to travel hundreds of miles to review roll call votes for the state legislature. Most good research books will also consider how the policy positions a candidate has taken will impact the community. For example, one research book I completed included a study of the impact that Waxman-Markey cap-and-trade legislation would have on a particular state and region of the country.

Wealthy candidates—and there are many running for federal or statewide office—present a unique set of challenges. Some hire accountants to help them identify tax breaks that citizens of more modest means do not typically take advantage of. Some are prominent investors in start-up businesses, which can lead the researcher down whole new rabbit holes. Financial records themselves are a time-consuming part of any researcher's checklist. Any candidate for Congress has to file personal financial disclosures with a list of income, assets, and liabilities, both as a candidate and as a member of Congress. Some wealthier members have disclosures that are dozens of pages long, with hundreds of assets, and each asset needs to be scrutinized as if it could contain a hidden hit. And every candidate for federal or statewide office, of any means, has to file at least some campaign finance information. Researchers often comb through the list of donors for any questionable actors or for signs of outsized influence on a candidate's campaign. They will also look through the list of expenditures for any signs of waste, abuse, or luxury.[16]

The Truth, What Is Convenient, and What Helps You Win: Pick Two

The victims of opposition research can often make a pretty good case for why the field is slimy, wretched, misguided, and all sorts of other terrible things. One example comes from a campaign I was involved in, a bitter primary race between a sitting member of Congress and a more conservative businessman. I spent months diving into a court case involving the businessman, poring over thousands of pages of documents. Though the case had closed years before, I discovered a new angle that the media had missed when they covered the proceedings. We had good reason to believe the businessman had at best mismanaged his family's finances and at worst used them for selfish purposes. As was always the procedure at a professional opposition research company, I carefully did my research, wrote down my findings, provided evidence, and had it checked and double-checked by colleagues and my boss. Our communications team pitched the story to top reporters at a statewide news outlet. The reporters, too, did their due diligence and gave the businessman an opportunity to tell his side of the story, and we successfully had our research placed at the outlet within a week or so. While our research was solid, and I believe to this day that our assessments of the case were correct, the businessman's response was emotional. He accused his opponents and the reporters of not knowing the full story and noted that one of his parents was close to death at that point in his life. He claimed that he had always played an outsized role in managing the family's finances, and that he had always done so with care and with his parents' best interests in mind. It certainly was one of several gut-check moments for me as a researcher: had I caused a family half a country away some kind of harm, concern, or dismay, all over a relatively meaningless primary campaign? The candidate ended up dropping out of the race early—not over these allegations, I believe, but because a different political opportunity came up.

Part of the reason opposition research ethics is difficult is that there is a central tension inherent in the work: truth versus convenience versus what helps you win. Picture this as a triangle, and imagine that most of the time you only get to pick two of the three sides. What happens most often in campaigns is that operatives pick the latter two: convenient arguments that help their candidates win. Some examples are claiming your opponent is just a puppet for some larger, more divisive political figure (as of this writing,

President Donald Trump, House Speaker Nancy Pelosi, Senators Chuck Schumer and Mitch McConnell); claiming your opponent wholeheartedly supports certain policies because *other* members of that person's party support those policies (e.g., repealing Obamacare, the Green New Deal); and claiming your opponent is beholden to someone else because of campaign donations or votes with someone X percent of the time.[17] Of course the inherent downside of this approach is that it often leaves out at least part of the truth. While facts matter to most campaign operatives, and airtight accuracy is a rule in the opposition research business, building an easy narrative that helps your candidate win always requires some suspension of disbelief. Will this senator really do anything and everything the president asks him to do, regardless of the consequences for his state and constituents? Probably not. Does that representative's uncomfortable silence on the Green New Deal mean she is an enthusiastic supporter of the proposal (and, for that matter, all of its alleged consequences: destroying the American economy, culture, and all ways of life as we know it)? Again, probably not.

The answer then is simple, right? Pick truthful arguments that help your candidate win. The obvious problem, if you are following along with my metaphorical triangle, is that these arguments are not convenient. They require hours upon hours of research, edits, and double- and triple-checking. They require technology, access to reams of data, and resources that only professional operations can usually afford. That is where companies like American Bridge and America Rising step in. If you are a campaign manager, you can have access to literally hundreds of pages of information about your candidate's opponents at your fingertips in just a few months. It is going to cost you, of course, and campaigns are perpetually short on money, time, and staff.

That is one reason professional research shops are such an important resource today. The research on the court case involving the businessman who was staging a primary challenge to a sitting member of Congress took up a solid month of my life, forty to fifty hours a week, reading page after page of dry legalese. If I was one of five or ten staffers on the campaign, I would have had to split those research duties with events on the campaign trail, volunteer management, and of course, other research requests. Because I worked at an organization with dozens of people, I had the time and space to dive deep into a court case and come out with some meaningful new research. Two other weeks of my life at America Rising were spent "in the field," doing research far away from home. I spent time on floors at a law library, read through two-thousand-page books on every 1970s roll call vote in a state legislature, and learned how to use a microfilm reader. Again, this time at libraries and reading microfilm (and eating cheap fast food) was spent to build truthful arguments to help our candidates win.

If you are still with me on this metaphorical triangle, you may have a simple question: Why not choose all three points? What is the need for opposition research if a campaign can find arguments that are truthful, convenient, and help the candidate win? Such opposition research hits do exist, and they are often the most effective narratives in campaigns. Scores of Republican members lost their US House seats in the 2018 midterm elections because they voted in favor of repealing Obamacare. Their repeal vote is a fact. It is convenient—I found the official roll call vote from the clerk of the House in about thirty seconds. And in swing districts around the country where voters identified access to health care as a top concern, this one vote helped a whole bunch of Democrats win elections.[18] However, campaigns are long, dynamic beasts. Many federal campaigns will put out several ads, issue dozens and dozens of news releases, and participate in several debates over the course of a campaign. While the truthful and convenient arguments that help candidates win will often be repeated over and over again on the campaign trail, few campaigns can get by on those arguments alone. It is up to the opposition researcher to build truthful but inconvenient arguments. The challenge for researchers is how to do so ethically, especially with the pressure of bosses, clients, and other research needs.

How to Approach Opposition Research with Ethics in Mind

It may disappoint you to discover that I have no silver-bullet answer to the question "How do I conduct and deploy opposition research ethically?" In almost four years doing oppo, I came across candidates from across the ideological spectrum and with a variety of backgrounds. Ethical considerations differ in primary elections and general elections, between businesspeople and nonprofit leaders and public servants, and of course, in the widely divergent interests and preferences of coworkers, principals, and clients.

If you are writing your first opposition research book, as I once was, you have to think about three audiences as you approach ethical questions. These three audiences happen to dovetail nicely with the three stages every opposition research book goes through:

1. *Doing the research:* The audience in this first stage is you. Even as an entry-level researcher, you have significant questions to consider. Assembling an opposition research book is not a simple matter of checking boxes, but instead involves building narratives. What kind of narratives would you be proud to see deployed by your preferred candidate in a debate or in a television ad? What narratives would make you cringe or turn away? The examples later in this section provide some more food for thought as you chew on these questions.

2. *Presenting the research:* The audience in this second stage is your bosses and your clients. Once you have assembled reams and reams of data, it's your job to organize the research book in a coherent way and present that information to decision makers higher up in the food chain. One of the most difficult considerations at this stage is ensuring you have approached an opposition research "hit" from multiple angles. If you are criticizing a candidate for changing positions on an issue, for example, do you have the full story? If you are presenting evidence that the candidate is behind on property taxes this year, are you sure the data are accurate? Again, examples are provided later in this section.

3. *Deploying the research:* The audience in this third stage is, well, everyone, or at least the universe of voters your bosses and clients are seeking to influence. Though I spent less time in oppo than some of my colleagues, I was around long enough to see my research deployed in ads, at debates, on statewide cable news channels, in YouTube videos that reached millions of viewers, and in posts and tweets that were shared by thousands of people. I do not suggest for a moment that my experience was unique; in the age of digital media, all opposition researchers will see their work deployed far and wide if they work in the field long enough. One concern in this stage is that communicators and ad-makers on a campaign can take liberties with your research. You may see an ad on television that takes a careful point you made in your research book and turns it into an extreme assumption about your opponent. (I have seen this happen to my research more than once.) Once more, I provide some examples to illustrate the difficult ethical considerations that come up in this final stage.

If you work at a smaller firm or campaign, or if you have principals who are generous about including you in the research process, you may have a chance to make an impact at each stage I have mentioned. As a junior-level employee, though, you may have the research taken out of your hands at some point, with directives to move on to some other candidate or project. What follows are some examples, drawn from my real-life experience in oppo but generalized to protect the identities and work of those involved. I identify the stage of the research and provide some ethical questions to consider, but I don't provide answers. Everyone's ethical road map is different, and I believe providing my answers to these challenges would be a disservice to folks who are trying to chart their own course. However, I close this chapter with some thoughts on opposition research, why it's necessary, and what questions practitioners need to ask themselves in order to "do oppo" while following their moral compasses.

1. *The guilt-by-association line of attack:* You are doing opposition research in a general election, working for a Republican congressman who's

seeking to unseat a Democratic governor running for a second term. The campaign knows that illegal immigration has become a major issue on the trail, so the Republican's campaign manager makes a research request on the subject. She wants you to look up cases in the last four years in which undocumented immigrants committed violent crimes. It does not matter if the governor was directly involved, the campaign manager says; they want to tie the governor to any crimes committed on the governor's watch. The request makes you a bit queasy, for two reasons: (1) in many of these cases the governor may not be at any fault for the crime that occurred, and (2) the research would also feed into a false narrative that undocumented immigrants are dangerous and should be feared. Do you do the research, but share with the campaign manager your concerns? Do you refuse to do the research? Do you offer an alternative line of attack, perhaps with research that the governor's immigration policies have been ineffective, inadequate, and/or expensive? Or do you conduct the research, figuring that violent crime on a public servant's watch is, after all, fair game in elections?

2. *The mysterious divorce:* You are doing opposition research in a primary election, working for a Democratic businesswoman up against the party establishment's choice, a city councilor. As you are conducting public records searches on the councilor, you notice something strange: in 1995, the councilor divorced a man, even though she's talked about meeting and dating her current husband in 1993 (before they were married in 1996). Do you include these records in your research book? Is it possible that the data on Nexis are inaccurate, and that there was no such divorce? If you do include the records, do you offer any kind of note urging caution with the data? Do you explore further? If you do, could you be going down a rabbit hole that is actually a point of pain for the city councilor? Even if it is a straightforward case of an extramarital affair, is that a valid point of attack in a political campaign?

3. *The missing congresswoman:* You're presenting opposition research to your clients, who are the consultants and managers for a Democratic state senator looking to unseat a ten-term Republican congresswoman. One major checklist item for the consultants is getting a sense of the congresswoman's attendance record at her committee hearings; rumor has it her attendance has dropped off in recent years as she attends more ritzy DC gatherings. You have combed through every source you could, including the Government Publishing Office (GPO) and committee websites. You even took a trip over to the Library of Congress for some missing records. However, you could only find about 75 percent of the committee hearings. From what you could find, the congresswoman's attendance rate is 80 percent—not terrible, but "Congresswoman X misses one in five hearings" could be potent in an ad. However, you are worried

about the missing 25 percent of hearings. If she has a 100 percent attendance rate at those missing hearings, her attendance rate would actually
be 85 percent, not 80 percent. This may sound like splitting hairs, but
the congresswoman's campaign will certainly press you on accuracy if
you're wrong. Do you present your existing attendance rate, knowing it's
based on a thorough scrub of all available hearings? Do you present the
attendance rate as incomplete and warn the consultants against using the
figure in media? What if the consultants are upset, thinking that it should
be easy to find attendance records for a member of Congress? What if the
congresswoman's team has a more complete sense of her attendance and
can easily rebut your 80 percent figure?

4. *The former National Rifle Association (NRA) member:* You are presenting opposition research to your clients, a team at the Democratic Senatorial Campaign Committee (DSCC). You wrote a research book on a
moderate Republican congressman who's running against an incumbent
Democratic senator in a purple state. After a mass shooting in this state
two years ago, the Republican congressman, an NRA member, initially
stuck to the party line: "thoughts and prayers," mental health resources,
and a crackdown on violent video games, but no measures that would
make it harder for someone to get a gun. Around a year ago, though, the
congressman suddenly had a change of heart. He came out in support
of background checks, "red flag" laws, and an assault weapons ban. He
even canceled his NRA membership. The DSCC is suspicious, and rightfully so: the congressman, who comes from a red district, changed his
positions three months before announcing his campaign for US Senate.
What they do not know, but you do, is a small nugget of information
buried carefully in an interview the congressman gave a local blogger:
he changed his views on gun violence after the daughter of a close family friend was a victim of a shooting that didn't quite make headlines. Is
the congressman still an opportunist? Why didn't he change his positions
on guns after the mass shooting, which had more than just one victim?
Do his new positions erase his years as an NRA member and supporter?
Does attacking his change of heart bring up painful memories for him, or
worse, for his close friend who lost a daughter? The DSCC wants to go
on the attack, but you are not so sure. How do you present this section of
the research book to them?

5. *The solution in search of a problem:* Your client is a political action committee (PAC) hoping to get a Republican mayor (who is running against a
Democratic mayor) elected to a US Senate seat. They come to you with
a request to deploy your opposition research in a television ad that will
blanket the state through October. The only problem is that they are not
using your existing research. They have already written and filmed the
ad, comparing crime in the Republican mayor's city with crime in the

Democratic mayor's city. The ad is full of generalities, "more drugs, more crime, more violence," with nothing to back them up. Your job? Back up the ad with statistics. You are not even sure if the right data exist. You are also not sure if the data back up some, all, or none of these claims. The PAC has already purchased the air time, and they have already spent $250,000 producing and fine-tuning the ad. It would have been nice if they had approached you for a fact-check before doing all this, but they did not. Do you try as hard as you can to make the statistics work? Do you ask what kind of changes can be made to the ad's script for cheap? Do you urge the PAC to *avoid* doing this kind of backwards fact-finding in future ads? Or does that escalation of the conflict make you risk losing business with these people down the road?[19]

6. *The case of the candidate who loves ISIS:* You are in the midst of a Republican primary for governor, working for a businessman candidate, and your boss sends you a message with a YouTube link to an ad using your research. Your opponent is a Republican congresswoman. You had done research on the congresswoman's votes to cancel the 2001 and 2002 Authorizations for Use of Military Force (AUMFs), which give the US military the authority to operate in Afghanistan, Iraq, and other areas of the world to fight the war on terror. The congresswoman had voted to cancel the AUMFs three times, not because she wants to end the wars but because she didn't trust President Obama to manage the wars. She wanted Congress to rewrite the AUMFs, and she was clear about why. It is dismaying to you, then, that the ad claims the congresswoman "sided with ISIS terrorists over our troops." The ad even superimposes a smiling image of the congresswoman next to an image of jihadists with guns held high. This is a gross misinterpretation of your research, and you are sure the fact-checkers and the congresswoman's campaign will be blowing the whistle on it. Do you approach your boss and your candidate, telling them this ad is wrong? Do you go even further and insist they take the ad down? Do you ask to be involved in the ad-making process going forward?

Conclusion

Each of these examples is rooted in my real experiences. When it came to my involvement, I cannot say I made the most ethical decision every time. In fact, most of the time I took an active approach to ethics in the first stage (doing the research) but a more passive approach to ethics in the second and third stages (presenting the research and deploying it). I wanted to please my bosses and our clients, and I wanted to help us win races. I was in the first stage of my career, too, and I was worried about being seen as weak, compromising, or not up to the task of doing oppo. That is why when I have the chance, I share this one piece of advice with college students: as you draw your ethical road map, do not only consider how you *make* choices in this space; consider how you'll *respond* to decisions imposed on you by someone else. My toughest dilemmas have come from bosses or clients asking me to do something that makes me uncomfortable. On the one hand, I had an obligation to complete tasks handed to me. On the other, I had an obligation to maintain my personal standards—my ethical road map. I cannot say I always made the right choice, but I would have done so more often if I had spent time thinking about how to work with my superiors on moral quandaries.

That thought process is particularly important for opposition research. I stand by my original thesis: opposition research can be done ethically, just like any aspect of political campaigns. Given oppo is focused on the real and perceived flaws of your opponent, though—and not the strengths of your candidate—the waters get muddier by design. New practitioners in this field would do well to

- know what oppo is and what oppo is not;
- understand that many campaigns rely on the most convenient narratives, sometimes sacrificing the truth in the process, and that opposition researchers can and should do better;
- understand that oppo is about pursuing a higher plane of research and about creating narratives that are truthful, rigorously fact-checked, and difficult to find;
- know that research is actually a three-part process (*doing* the research, *presenting* it, and *deploying* it to voters and media), and that the opposition researcher must consider ethics at each and every stage; and
- accept that no one in this field is going to make the most ethical decision all of the time, and that political communication ethics is a living, breathing process (and not a static set of easily definable rules and processes).

I have attempted to help get you one step closer to each of the stated objectives in this chapter. A lot, however, depends on your ethical road map, your moral compass. Mine has not failed me, despite moments when I thought it would. I am confident that with careful thought, a good group of mentors and contemporaries, and a good sense of your boundaries and limits, you too can practice the dark arts ethically—and longer than Severus Snape served as a Defense Against the Dark Arts professor.

Notes

[1] Hilary Krieger, "An Introduction to the Dark Arts of Opposition Research," FiveThirtyEight, October 31, 2017, accessed January 26, 2019, https://fivethirty eight.com/features/an-introduction-to-the-dark-arts-of-opposition-research/.

2 "What Is and Isn't Permissible in the World of Campaign Opposition Research," NPR, August 7, 2018, accessed January 26, 2019, https://www.npr.org/2018/08/07/636423580/what-is-and-isnt-permissible-in-the-world-of-campaign-opposition-research.

3 Joshua Green, "A Former Obama Operative Built a New Anti-Republican Attack Machine," Bloomberg, October 4, 2018, accessed January 26, 2019, https://www.bloomberg.com/news/features/2018-10-04/a-former-obama-operative-built-a-new-anti-republican-attack-machine.

4 "Ranked: The Defence Against the Dark Arts Teachers," Pottermore, n.d., accessed January 26, 2019, https://www.pottermore.com/features/ranked-the-defence-against-the-dark-arts-teachers.

5 Adam Entous, Devlin Barrett, and Rosalind S. Helderman, "Clinton Campaign, DNC Paid for Research That Led to Russia Dossier," *Washington Post*, October 24, 2017, accessed January 26, 2019, https://www.washingtonpost.com/world/national-security/clinton-campaign-dnc-paid-for-research-that-led-to-russia-dossier/2017/10/24/226fabf0-b8e4-11e7-a908-a3470754bbb9_story.html?utm_term=.2863bff353f9.

6 David Jackson and Fredreka Schouten, "Trump Calls Donald Trump Jr.'s Meeting with Russian Lawyer 'Opposition Research,'" *USA Today*, July 13, 2017, accessed January 26, 2019, https://www.usatoday.com/story/news/politics/2017/07/13/donald-trump/475459001/.

7 "Alexander Hamilton," in *Encyclopedia Britannica*, n.d., accessed February 2, 2019, https://www.britannica.com/biography/Alexander-Hamilton-United-States-statesman.

8 Angela Serratore, "Alexander Hamilton's Adultery and Apology," *Smithsonian Magazine*, July 25, 2013, accessed February 2, 2019, https://www.smithsonianmag.com/history/alexander-hamiltons-adultery-and-apology-18021947/.

9 Serratore, "Alexander Hamilton's Adultery and Apology."

10 Serratore, "Alexander Hamilton's Adultery and Apology."

11 "The Reynolds Pamphlet," Genius, n.d., accessed February 9, 2019, https://genius.com/7909996.

12 Doug Criss, "This Is the 30-Year-Old Willie Horton Ad Everybody Is Talking about Today," CNN, November 1, 2018, accessed February 9, 2019, https://www.cnn.com/2018/11/01/politics/willie-horton-ad-1988-explainer-trnd/index.html.

13 Roger Simon, "How a Murderer and Rapist Became the Bush Campaign's Most Valuable Player," *Baltimore Sun*, November 11, 1990, accessed February 9, 2019, https://www.baltimoresun.com/news/bs-xpm-1990-11-11-1990315149-story.html.

14 Simon, "How a Murderer and Rapist Became the Bush Campaign's Most Valuable Player."

15 "Disbursements," Federal Election Commission, n.d., accessed February 9, 2019, https://www.fec.gov/data/disbursements/?two_year_transaction_period=2018&data_type=processed&recipient_name=america+rising&recipient_name=american+bridge&min_date=01%2F01%2F2017&max_date=12%2F31%2F2018.

[16] The use of private jet services is always a big find and typically a good hook for most reporters to write about.

[17] A quick note on this: in most statewide or federal campaigns, a $2,000 donation really doesn't matter in the scheme of things. So, if you see an ad claiming that some Democrat kneels at the feet of Nancy Pelosi because her leadership PAC donated to that candidate, check the FEC records. Pelosi and her PAC donate to dozens of candidates per cycle (same with Schumer, and McConnell, and other members of Republican and Democratic leadership). Vote percentages are also a bit of a fickle statistic. It can sound bad that a moderate Republican "votes with Mitch McConnell" 97 percent of the time, but keep in mind that a significant proportion of roll call votes in both the House and the Senate are slam-dunk bipartisan votes. See Laurel Harbridge-Yong, "Congress Is More Bipartisan Than You Think," *Monkey Cage* (blog), *Washington Post*, May 4, 2015, accessed August 24, 2019, https://www.washingtonpost.com/news/monkey-cage/wp/2015/05/04/congress-is-more-bipartisan-than-you-think/.

[18] Bob Bryan, "The Midterm Elections Cemented Obamacare's Legacy and Showed Democrats Can Actually Win on Healthcare," *Business Insider*, November 7, 2018, accessed August 24, 2019, https://www.businessinsider.com/2018-midterm-election-results-obamacare-healthcare-big-winner-2018-11.

[19] This may seem like a strange example, but like the others outlined in this chapter, it is based on real events. I trust any opposition researcher will share my pain in acknowledging that communicators and consultants often make the ads and then find the facts for them (rather than the other way around).

Bibliography

"Alexander Hamilton." In *Encyclopedia Britannica*. n.d. Accessed February 2, 2019. https://www.britannica.com/biography/Alexander-Hamilton-United-States-statesman.

Bryan, Bob. "The Midterm Elections Cemented Obamacare's Legacy and Showed Democrats Can Actually Win on Healthcare." *Business Insider*, November 7, 2018. Accessed August 24, 2019. https://www.businessinsider.com/2018-midterm-election-results-obamacare-healthcare-big-winner-2018-11.

Criss, Doug. "This Is the 30-Year-Old Willie Horton Ad Everybody Is Talking about Today." CNN, November 1, 2018. Accessed February 9, 2019. https://www.cnn.com/2018/11/01/politics/willie-horton-ad-1988-explainer-trnd/index.html.

Entous, Adam, Devlin Barrett, and Rosalind S. Helderman. "Clinton Campaign, DNC Paid for Research That Led to Russia Dossier." *Washington Post*, October 24, 2017. Accessed January 26, 2019. https://www.washingtonpost.com/world/national-security/clinton-campaign-dnc-paid-for-research-that-led-to-russia-dossier/2017/10/24/226fabf0-b8e4-11e7-a908-a3470754bbb9_story.html?utm_term=.2863bff353f9.

Green, Joshua. "A Former Obama Operative Built a New Anti-Republican Attack Machine." Bloomberg, October 4, 2018. Accessed January 26, 2019. https://

www.bloomberg.com/news/features/2018-10-04/a-former-obama-operative-built-a-new-anti-republican-attack-machine.

Harbridge-Yong, Laurel. "Congress Is More Bipartisan Than You Think." *Monkey Cage* (blog), *Washington Post*, May 4, 2015. Accessed August 24, 2019. https://www.washingtonpost.com/news/monkey-cage/wp/2015/05/04/congress-is-more-bipartisan-than-you-think/.

Jackson, David, and Fredreka Schouten. "Trump Calls Donald Trump Jr.'s Meeting with Russian Lawyer 'Opposition Research.'" *USA Today*, July 13, 2017. Accessed January 26, 2019. https://www.usatoday.com/story/news/politics/2017/07/13/donald-trump/475459001/.

Krieger, Hilary. "An Introduction to the Dark Arts of Opposition Research." FiveThirtyEight, October 31, 2017. Accessed January 26, 2019. https://fivethirtyeight.com/features/an-introduction-to-the-dark-arts-of-opposition-research/.

"Ranked: The Defence Against the Dark Arts Teachers." Pottermore, n.d. Accessed January 26, 2019. https://www.pottermore.com/features/ranked-the-defence-against-the-dark-arts-teachers.

"The Reynolds Pamphlet." Genius, n.d. Accessed February 9, 2019. https://genius.com/7909996.

Serratore, Angela. "Alexander Hamilton's Adultery and Apology." *Smithsonian Magazine*, July 25, 2013. Accessed February 2, 2019, https://www.smithsonianmag.com/history/alexander-hamiltons-adultery-and-apology-18021947/.

Simon, Roger. "How a Murderer and Rapist Became the Bush Campaign's Most Valuable Player." *Baltimore Sun*, November 11, 1990. Accessed February 9, 2019. https://www.baltimoresun.com/news/bs-xpm-1990-11-11-1990315149-story.html.

"What Is and Isn't Permissible in the World of Campaign Opposition Research." NPR, August 7, 2018. Accessed January 26, 2019. https://www.npr.org/2018/08/07/636423580/what-is-and-isnt-permissible-in-the-world-of-campaign-opposition-research.

13

How Political Fact-Checkers Obscure Larger Truths in the Pursuit of Small Ones

Anson Kaye

In January 2013, the *New Republic* ran an article about then-president Barack Obama.[1] In its four thousand or so words, it covered a variety of topics that other journalists might have found interesting: how the president was approaching his second term, or the calamity then unfolding in Syria, or whether there was any hope of the administration being able to work with Republicans in Congress on the significant issues of the day. Important stuff that had an impact on not only Americans but people across the globe.

But none of that caught the attention of the *Washington Post*'s Glenn Kessler. Instead, Kessler honed in on an exchange located midway through the article in which one of the reporters asked the president if he'd ever fired a gun. The president's answer was: "Yes, in fact, up at Camp David, we do skeet shooting all the time." Simple enough. (And really, in the context of everything that was going on in the world, who cares?) But when Kessler read those words, he smelled a rat.[2]

Now Kessler wasn't just any reporter. He was a political fact-checker. One of the originals in fact, a standard-bearer for the genre. So before I go any further, let me address that. What does it mean to be a "fact-checker," at least in the journalistic context?

In a certain sense, every reputable reporter is a fact-checker. If you are a reporter and you are authentically interested in helping the public understand what is going on in their world, you will seek to be accurate, honest, and factual in your reporting. That means that if a source tells you something, you double or triple check it with other source materials. If you discover something on your own, you'll seek out others to validate your discovery. You are checking the facts as you understand them, to make sure your understanding is correct. You are fact-checking.

There are well-known examples of reporters failing to adequately check the facts they are reporting and getting burned, such as Dan Rather and President George W. Bush's military record and Judy Miller and the Iraq war. No doubt there are other, less familiar examples. When this happens, the journalist has betrayed the compact he or she has with consumers. Instead of providing a reliable venue for people to grow their understanding of the world around them, journalists become almost the perfect vessel to inject falsity deep within the public consciousness.

So there are good reasons for news outlets to want to check the facts that others, particularly those in power, are sharing with them. It's part of their duty. And sometimes that tenacity leads to remarkable results. If Bob Woodward and Carl Bernstein had taken the Nixon administration at face value, for example, no one might have ever discovered the behind-the-scenes malfeasance being engaged in by the then-president and his aides. Luckily, they kept digging, and a corrupt presidency was brought down.

In fact, how and whether journalism is doing a good enough job separating fact from fiction has long been a point of controversy in our public debates. During the civil rights movement, for example, one way America was forced to come to terms with what it was like to be African American in the South was via the pictures that publications like the *New York Times* ran in their pages and the film that ran on the evening news of local authorities setting police dogs and fire hoses on marchers. Some of those who were invested in segregation endeavored to undermine the power of those images by saying they were misleading or untrue. Fortunately, media outlets continued to run them, and they helped a nation change.

At around the same time, journalists found themselves ensnarled in other stories that were at once deeply complex and urgently important to get right. But in some of these cases, the government actors best positioned to provide the public with the information they needed to know about, say, Vietnam or Watergate, were intentionally deceiving the reporters whose job it was to publicize the facts. News outlets started forming investigative units. A tonal shift in reporter/government relations accelerated. The press was becoming more aggressive and skeptical.[3]

While all of these factors are important, a president who took office in 1980 may have done most to fuel the rise of the political fact-checker. The prevalence of misstatements and inaccuracies in President Ronald Reagan's various pronouncements—both on the campaign trail and once in office—led news outlets to pay special attention to the efficacy of what he, and his administration, said. And while the media's devotion to this task may have waxed and waned over the Reagan years, a template was created, one that gathered steam in the ensuing decades.[4]

Now, of course, we have a president who has unleashed an unprecedented assault on the status of journalists as agents of truth. President Donald Trump's loud proclamations of "fake news" whenever the media report something he doesn't like, combined with the internet-fueled rise of alternative "news" sources that parrot his party line, have done more to undermine the idea of truth or fact in the public square than anything in recent memory.

Doesn't this mean that now more than ever we should be encouraging news outlets to invest more deeply in political fact-checking? If the marketplace is to be believed, perhaps the answer is yes. According to the Duke Reporters' Lab, there are now more than 185 news organizations around the globe publishing political fact checks.[5] And reporters like Kessler get countless page views for the fact checks they write.

So what's the problem? It's the job of reporters to check facts, and consumers appear to have an appetite for fact checks. And if politicians don't like it, well, maybe they shouldn't play so fast and loose with the facts all the time. Everybody wins, right?

Maybe not. I think there is something deeply unethical about the kinds of conclusions fact-checkers sometimes draw about what is, and is not, factual, and that their checks often do more to undermine truth than help consumers see it for what it is. Why? Let's head back to 2013.

The *New Republic* article that referenced President Obama's skeet shooting ran on a Sunday. The next day, the White House press briefing lasted around forty-five minutes, during which spokesperson Jay Carney was asked around fifty questions. Lots of them were about immigration reform; that made sense, as it was a hot topic in the Senate at the time. Some were about unrest in Egypt, others about the economy and the federal budget. Still others referenced the *New Republic* piece, specifically the president's comments about brain injuries in football and the conflict in Syria. These were all eminently worthy lines of inquiry.

And then, in the middle, there was one brief exchange about skeet shooting. Here's the verbatim transcript from the briefing, as posted by the White House:[6]

Q: On a different topic, how often does the President go skeet shooting? (Laughter.) And are there photographs of him doing so?

MR. CARNEY: I would refer you simply to his comments. I don't know how often. He does go to Camp David with some regularity, but I'm not sure how often he's done that.

Q: Is there a photograph of him doing it?

MR. CARNEY: There may be, but I haven't seen it.

Q: Why haven't we heard about it before?

MR. CARNEY: Because when he goes to Camp David, he goes to spend time with his family and friends and relax, not to produce photographs.

OK, that sounds simple enough. And it seems to have basically answered the questions the White House press corps had about the subject, save for one query, two days later, about a House Republican backbencher challenging the then-president to a skeet shooting contest[7] (here, again, is the verbatim transcript):[8]

Q: On another matter, Jay?

MR. CARNEY: Yes.

Q: Marsha Blackburn has challenged the President's comments about skeet shooting at Camp David. She's skeptical of them and she says she's a better skeet shooter than he is and wants to be invited to Camp David for a contest. Your reaction?

MR. CARNEY: I have none. (Laughter.)

Now, in my view, you would be within your rights to ask whether it was ethical for reporters to even be asking questions about skeet shooting. Only a handful of reporters in the world get to sit in the White House briefing room. It's a prestigious gig. The briefings are televised. They last less than an hour. And they are a rare opportunity to ask questions of the spokesperson for the most powerful leader in the world.

All of this means the questions asked there necessarily take on an outsized importance. Asking a question in the White House press briefing elevates the issue and sanctions it as something worthy of serious attention. *This must be a big deal, they're asking about it at the White House!* There is nothing wrong with that, assuming the issue really is of national import.

But what happens when a story that isn't noteworthy gets cloaked in significance by virtue of the attention it is paid by the press? Does elevating an unimportant "story" into something "newsworthy" benefit news consumers? Or does it instead necessarily warp their understanding of what's going on in the world, what they need to care about and pay attention to? To be clear, news platforms aren't portals into which an endless array of information can be dropped and served. News outlets have to decide what to publish and what not to. Simply choosing to report something makes it significant, no matter what is said about it. And of course what journalists say can ratchet up or down public perception of its importance relative to all the other important things in the world (and the countless other things that aren't deemed so).

So if that's true—if it's true to say that simply reporting something can confer significance—then one must ask: What ethics should guide the kinds of questions reporters ask, given that everything they report is necessarily lifted out of the vast soup of information in the world and joined with the relatively infinitesimal bites of information that massive numbers of people are exposed to every day and thereby can shift public attention, form opinions, and shape worldviews? In that environment, if you as a journalist are insufficiently rigorous in your own vetting of the kinds of questions you ask, have you stepped over an ethical line?

A similar debate has been playing out in journalistic and political circles in recent years about something called "false equivalence." False equivalence happens when reporters insist on telling "both sides" of a story, even when by any rational analysis one side's position has less merit than the other.

For example, think about the long-standing insistence of media outlets on including the voices of climate change skeptics in stories about climate change. This continued to happen after there was nearly universal scientific consensus that climate change was happening and that human conduct was a factor in it. Nonetheless, media outlets felt bound to tell "both sides" of the story.

Both sides of the story? There are people who contend that the earth is flat (I know this because I've seen their videos on YouTube). However, none of those people get paragraph inches in stories in which understanding the shape of the earth might prove significant, such as stories about transportation and urban planning, or about how gravity works, or bungee jumping. That's good, because if by virtue of the media flat earthers had gained broader purchase in the public square, inevitably we'd have to start factoring their theories into our thinking about how to implement things big and small. (Some experts say the Space Needle is the best place for bungee jumping, though flat earthers are quick to point out that when they finally find the edge of the world it is likely to provide a bungee jump experience of unrivaled excitement. . . .) That would be imbecilic.

So then what about the press insisting on providing a platform for climate deniers long after scientific consensus had made it clear they didn't know what they were talking about? Among the experts, there was no debate: climate change was real. It was the media (who themselves are not experts) who chose to keep elevating the notion that it wasn't—and it really was just the media. If the media had refused to cover skeptics and those who parroted their views (as they do flat earthers), that line of argument would have exited the public square. But the media kept it alive, and in so doing enabled and gave cover to those who opposed taking the steps required to ameliorate a crisis now in full bloom. Was that responsible? Was that ethical? Or was it a shortsighted way to stop people who don't like the idea of climate change from being mad at the media?

Another example is the media's coverage of the 2016 presidential general election. (This seems like a good time to mention that I worked for both President Obama and Secretary of State Hillary Clinton's presidential campaigns.) I remember exactly where I was when I first saw the *Washington Post*'s coverage of the *Access Hollywood* tape on which Donald Trump bragged about sexually assaulting women.[9] I watched it. Then I watched it again. Then a third time. It was that hard to fathom. I remember Trump's rushed video apology that came out later that night, then his put-upon defiance that grew as one allegation after another of sexual assault came rolling in.

You might expect that a candidate for president caught on tape talking about how he sexually assaults women, combined with what would eventually become seventeen women alleging that he indeed sexually assaulted them, would be treated by the press as a more newsworthy development than just about anything else on the campaign trail. That's unprecedented stuff, which, by any estimation, calls into deep question the character and fitness of the candidate to serve. And to be sure, the media gave the story heavy coverage. So: nothing to see here, right? Well . . . look a little closer.

In December 2016, the Harvard Kennedy School's Shorenstein Center on Media, Politics and Public Policy released the fourth of its series of studies into how the media covered Secretary of State Clinton and Donald Trump in the presidential run-up.[10] This fourth installment focused on media coverage from August 2016 through Election Day. During that time frame just 13 percent of the news coverage that Donald Trump received relating to his fitness for office was positive; 87 percent was negative. Pretty damn bad. For Secretary Clinton, the percentages were exactly the same: 13 percent of the stories about her fitness were positive, 87 percent negative.

How could that be? The *Access Hollywood* tape broke in October 2016 and was followed by a torrent of sexual assault allegations from various women. And yet even as Trump was in the heart of that maelstrom, the media found some way of reporting news just as negative about his opponent.

Emails, you say? Yes, the press had long been fixated on the fact that Secretary Clinton had merged her personal and official email accounts. The Federal Bureau of Investigation (FBI) looked into it and closed its investigation in July 2016, with no charges. Then nine days before the election, FBI director James Comey sent a letter to Congress saying that the agency had "learned of" more emails that appeared to be "pertinent" to the investigation, only to send a second letter on November 6 reporting that nothing about the new emails changed the FBI's decision to close the investigation in July. To be sure, much of this led to negative coverage. Maybe that explains it.

Or maybe it's better explained by a Tweet like this one authored by ABC News chief political analyst Mathew Dowd seven days before the election: "Either you care both about Trump being sexual predator & Clinton emails, or u care about neither. But don't talk about one without the other."[11] Because God forbid you exercise some journalistic judgment and conclude that verifiable evidence that one candidate for president is a sexual predator is actually more newsworthy than whether the other had merged email servers, much in the same fashion, it should be added, that other similarly situated officials had done.

Regardless of what you may make of my analysis, the Shorenstein Center concluded that "political reporters made no serious effort" to determine whether "the allegations surrounding Clinton" were "of the same order of magnitude as those surrounding" Trump.[12] Perhaps that helps explain how "Clinton's alleged scandals" racked up four times the media attention that Trump received for his "treatment of women."[13] Imagine the impact that had on an electorate that for the most part learns what they need to know about the candidates from the media. As the *Washington Post* characterized the study's findings, the 2016 media coverage was nothing less than a "feast of false equivalency."[14] And it's one reason Donald Trump became president.

Kessler wasn't exactly engaged in false equivalency when he took his deep dive into skeet shooting, but what he was doing was pretty similar. Think of the ways Republicans and other conservatives tried to frame the president in their messaging. He was Barack *Hussein* Obama. The guy with the terrorist name, who palled around with terrorists. Who was all teleprompter, celebrity artifice. Who had faked his birth certificate: the foreigner, secret Muslim, illegally occupying the White House. It was a line of attack at once deeply personal and aimed at portraying him not just as the other, but also as a fraud right down to his very core. If he was literally a "fake American," what wouldn't he lie about?

I'm not sure skeet shooting would have caught Kessler's attention without that surrounding conservative noise. But I am sure that once he had posted his piece, just the very fact of Kessler's question became part of the larger picture conservatives wanted people to have about President Obama. On issues no matter how big or small, he was a fraud through and through. Someone who might go through the motions of being an American, but who was always hiding something darker underneath.

Should that context matter to reporters? The answer to me is: of course. How can it not be part of the calculus you use to determine whether to follow a story? It need not be the only calculus, but behaving as if what you choose to report should only be judged on the four corners of the story itself is at best attempting to shield yourself with a standard that applies to no other industry in the world and at worst a breathtaking kind of arrogance. Stories don't operate in a vacuum. They feed off of and feed everything else that's happening in the public square at the time they are published. Consumers' understanding of what is reported has something to do with what's actually in the story and a lot more to do with how they understand that broader landscape.

So what did Kessler actually say? Underneath the headline: "The White House's Curious Silence about Obama's Claim of Skeet Shooting," he wrote that "the White House" had been "oddly silent" about the president's claim in the *New Republic* article of having gone skeet shooting. Referring to White House spokesperson Jay Carney's assertion that when President Obama goes to Camp David it's to "relax, not produce photographs" (and that he therefore hadn't seen any of the president shooting skeet), Kessler was quick to point out that that explanation "did not stop the White House from releasing" other photos of the president at Camp David from time to time. And in a reference to the second Carney exchange detailed earlier in this chapter, Kessler reported that "Carney tersely said he had no response to a challenge from Rep. Marsha Blackburn (R-Tenn) for a skeet shooting contest with the president." Finally, Kessler let his readership know that the *Washington Post* had emailed the White House three times for the name of another guest who could confirm the "president's account" but that "we received no response all three times."[15] Egad, Kessler's done it again! Unless . . . let's ask some questions about his questions.

First of all, that headline. "Curious Silence"? Curious? Really?

Now I know Kessler didn't write the headline. But he did write the words "oddly silent" to describe the failure of the White House to jump at his demands.[16] Is it "odd" or "curious" for the nerve center of the most powerful country in the world to not immediately set in motion its internal fact-finding team to try to track down how much the president skeet shoots? Or would the reverse in fact be the curious thing? I mean, the White House spokesperson had actually answered questions about skeet shooting in the briefing. The answers may not have been satisfying to Kessler, but neither is it accurate to suggest that the White House had gone phone silent. In fact, if you want the White House to track down something as trivial as whether the president has gone skeet shooting before, you may have to work for it. But maybe you can't see that if you've already convinced yourself that you've caught the president doing that bad thing you assume he is up to.[17] Maybe . . . but that doesn't sound a lot like what fact-checking is supposed to be about.

Second, how about Kessler's characterization of Carney being "terse." That's what you might expect from a spokesperson trying to shut down a line of inquiry he doesn't like, I suppose. And neither I, nor, as I understand it, Kessler, was in the briefing room. But we do have those transcripts. Go back and look at them. The answer Kessler characterizes as terse elicited laughter from the reporters who were actually there. Does that sound like the reaction they would have to someone who was being terse? Or is it instead a bemused spokesperson getting sympathetic laughter from reporters who know how silly their own line of questioning is. That's what it sounds like to me. Kessler calls it "terse."

Now I'll continue on through Kessler's reporting and see what other evidence he brings to bear. First, he notes that he has "searched high and low" but has been unable to find any public coverage of Obama skeet shooting either before becoming president or after. He did uncover audio of Obama congratulating a US Olympian for winning gold in skeet shooting but then tells us that when Obama had some other Olympians over to the White House he "made no reference to having attempted skeet shooting" himself, touching instead on other sports that had inspired him (like running, weight lifting, and swimming—which also, perhaps unsurprisingly, appear to be the sports that the Olympians in attendance had excelled at).[18]

If that isn't enough to convince you that something's amiss, Kessler notes that despite the diversity of recreational activities available at Camp David, Obama is an "infrequent" visitor there, and that people "close to him" note he is an "urban guy" who prefers "basketball" or "golf." "Again," Kessler says, "no mention of skeet shooting." Kessler also finds reason to arch an eyebrow when he digs into Obama's personal history with firearms—evidently he doesn't talk much about having handled firearms, either in casual or policy circumstances. "Generally," Kessler concludes, "a politician who has handled firearms will advertise that fact to gun owners."[19]

So, to sum up, the additional trove uncovered by Kessler consists of (1) the absence of evidence of Obama skeet shooting; (2) his failure to mention skeet shooting when in the presence of Olympians or to talk about guns very much at all; (3) that he doesn't go to Camp David frequently (I guess despite the fact that he could skeet shoot there?); and (4) that others characterize him as "urban," a guy far more interested in sports like "basketball" and that sport you can find on just about any city street corner: "golf."

Well.

What are the rules that apply when journalists are communicating in the political space, anyway? If the idea is always to win the argument with enough people or to get as many clicks as possible for your article, or shares of your tweets, or likes for your post, then maybe anything goes. In an increasingly democratized media landscape—in which the entities that used to be our trusted sources for "truth" have seen their influence diminish (the *New York Times*, academia, the judiciary, science, etc.) while organically partisan platforms have seen theirs grow—maybe the only thing to do is run as fast as everyone else, throw anything you can against the wall, see what sticks, and then move on to the next thing. Because chances are that everyone will have forgotten what you were talking about twelve hours later, and the only ones who will get a chance to speak at all are those who can demand and hold an audience, by whatever means.

That's a pretty grim view. And it is one that holds hardly any room for ethics.

Was Kessler's reporting on President Obama's skeet shooting the worst example of journalistic excess in the past decade? Of course not. But if we are to have any hope of rebuilding some kind of infrastructure that actually helps citizens distinguish between fact and fiction, truth and rhetoric, then it is going to have to come from outlets like the *Washington Post*. When they fall for the clickbait or get swept up into the ugly political winds, there's no one standing behind them to get them back on track. They are the line of last defense. They need to do better. That may seem unfair to individual reporters or outlets, but if you don't want that mantle, don't adopt a slogan like "Democracy Dies in Darkness." If you want to shine a light, shine it on the stuff we need to know, the stuff that actually matters. Otherwise, you are part of the problem.

And that goes for political professionals, too. We have a choice to make about how much to leverage the current political climate for our short-term gain, knowing that in so doing we may be creating long-term pain, not just for our candidates but for our country and democracy itself. How we make those choices will determine how the new ethics that guide this new age of political communication are formed and hardened. They aren't in place yet.

Maybe one place to start is that nether region that operates between candidates and journalists, where statements are offered and facts are checked. For candidates, it may be that we have entered an age in which being straightforward, honest, and accurate about what you believe and what your proposals can actually do is not just good ethics, but good politics, too. Voters have heard the big promises that never deliver too many times before. Their antennae are up, and their skepticism is high. That's a good thing. Maybe we should try to meet them where they are a little more often and see how people feel about a democracy that does a better job of meeting a slate of real, albeit more modest, goals than one that seems to constantly promise but rarely deliver on bigger ones.

But journalists, and specifically fact-checkers, have a role to play here, too. One of the big promises government actually has delivered on gives us our last example of why.

Since its inception in 1963, Medicare has been about one thing: guaranteeing that seniors, who presumably are no longer in the workforce, can get the health care they need. It's had some tweaks and expansions over the years, and it's not perfect, but it's one of the most popular programs in the federal government for a reason: it delivers, basically, on that big promise.

Then, in 2010, former congressman Paul Ryan got a budget passed through the House that would have fundamentally changed the very nature of Medicare. Instead of providing a primarily government health-care program for seniors, it would have turned it into a voucher system that would have let seniors purchase private insurance, though because the voucher wasn't pegged to inflation, its value, over time, would have gone down and down and down. Democrats looked at the program for what it did and said that voting for the Ryan plan was a vote to end Medicare. Fact-checkers called that claim the "Lie of the Year."[20]

The lie of the year? Say what you will about the Ryan plan, a program that puts seniors back into the private health-care market armed with a voucher the value of which diminishes over time and saying "OK, there's your health-care coverage" is not the same thing as Medicare. It may be a program you prefer. It may be one you hate. But the thing that was essential to Medicare was to be changed at a cellular level, as were the values and trade-offs that informed the creation of Medicare in the first place. Yes, it was true that the program was still called Medicare. But Medicare it wasn't.

What happens when fact-checkers step into highly charged political debates, pick and choose the "facts" they deem worthy of consideration, and then draw hard and fast conclusions such as that something is the "lie of the year"? Well in this case the fact-checkers' perhaps well-meaning effort to bring clarity to a complicated area of policy ended up pushing a small truth (no, no one actually pulled the plug on the entire Medicare program) that obscured a much larger one (had the bill passed, Medicare would have been in significant respects unrecognizable). And in so doing the fact-checker handed a terrific fig leaf to those who were deeply invested in no one finding out how huge a Medicare change they had in mind.

This is another example of fact-checkers getting so lost in the detail—whether it's the scribbles on the side of a much larger bill or the recreational aside buried in a much more important policy conversation—that they obscure the larger, more important truths, the ones people really do need to understand to navigate through the political world. That's outrageous. And it's unethical, too.

Oh, and what about skeet shooting, anyway? Had President Obama lied about it in that *New Republic* article? In a word: no. A week after Kessler started his "reporting," the White House released a photo of Obama—yes—skeet shooting at Camp David.

Wow. Thank goodness we got to the bottom of that.

Notes

1 Franklin Foer and Chris Hughes, "Barack Obama Is Not Pleased," *New Republic*, January 27, 2013, https://newrepublic.com/article/112190/obama-interview -2013-sit-down-president.

2 Glenn Kessler, "The White House's Curious Silence about Obama's Claim of Skeet Shooting," *Washington Post*, January 31, 2013, https://www.wash ingtonpost.com/blogs/fact-checker/post/the-white-houses-curious-silence -about-obamas-claim-of-skeet-shooting/2013/01/30/be78bb10-6b35-11e2 -95b3-272d604a10a3_blog.html.

3 Michael Schudson, "When the Media Had Enough: Watergate, Vietnam and the Birth of the Adversarial Press," excerpted from *The Rise of the Right to Know: Politics and the Culture of Transparency, 1945–1975*, *Slate Magazine*, October 10,

2015, https://www.salon.com/2015/10/10/when_the_media_had_enough_wa tergate_vietnam_and_the_birth_of_the_adversarial_press/.

4 Michael Dobbs, *The Rise of Political Fact-checking* (Washington, DC: New America Foundation, 2012), 4–5.

5 The Duke Reporters' Lab was founded by Duke University journalism professor Bill Adair, who also created the political fact-checking website PolitiFact. The Lab "maintains a database of global fact-checking sites" that is accessible through its homepage, https://reporterslab.org/.

6 The White House, Office of the Press Secretary, press briefing by Press Secretary Jay Carney, January 28, 2013, https://obamawhitehouse.archives.gov/the-press -office/2013/01/28/press-briefing-press-secretary-jay-carney-1282013.

7 "Skeptical Congresswoman Challenges Obama to Skeet Shooting Match," CNN. com, January 28, 2013, https://politicalticker.blogs.cnn.com/2013/01/28/ dubious-congresswoman-challenges-obama-to-skeet-shooting-match/.

8 The White House, Office of the Press Secretary, press briefing by Press Secretary Jay Carney, January 30, 2013, https://obamawhitehouse.archives.gov/the-press -office/2013/01/28/press-briefing-press-secretary-jay-carney-1282013.

9 David Fahrenthold, "Trump Recorded Having Extremely Lewd Conversation about Women in 2005," *Washington Post*, October 7, 2016.

10 Thomas Patterson, "News Coverage of the 2016 General Election: How the Press Failed the Voters" (Harvard Kennedy School's Shorenstein Center on Media, Politics, and Public Policy, December 6, 2016).

11 Erik Wemple, "Study: Clinton-Trump Coverage Was a Feast of False Equivalency," *Washington Post*, December 7, 2016.

12 Patterson, "News Coverage of the 2016 General Election," 19.

13 Patterson, "News Coverage of the 2016 General Election," 15.

14 Wemple, "Study: Clinton-Trump Coverage."

15 Kessler, "White House's Curious Silence."

16 Kessler, "White House's Curious Silence."

17 I particularly enjoy the reference to the three emails not replied to over a less than forty-eight-hour period as more evidence of nefarious stonewalling. As the former spokesperson for a number of elected officials, I can assure the reader that it does in fact take more than forty-eight hours to respond to press inquiries sometimes, no matter how many times the reporter repeats them, something that I imagine is especially true when someone is in a gig that requires prioritizing among the thousands of questions one is receiving about whatever the nine hundred leading world crises are that day.

18 Kessler, "White House's Curious Silence."

19 Kessler, "White House's Curious Silence."

20 Bill Adair and Angie Drobnic Holan, "Lie of the Year 2011: 'Republicans Voted to End Medicare,'" Politifact.com, December 20, 2011, https://www.politifact.com/ article/2011/dec/20/lie-year-democrats-claims-republicans-voted-end-me/.

14

Ethics in Political Speechwriting

Rachel Wallace

Political rhetoric can feel like an abstract concept; an idea debated by Aristotle and Socrates; or a useful lens for academics and pundits to analyze campaign slogans—"Yes We Can," "Morning in America," "Make America Great Again"—and famous speeches, like President Abraham Lincoln's Gettysburg Address or President Ronald Reagan's Berlin Wall speech. For speechwriters, however, political rhetoric is a profession, a way to make a living and, often, to make a difference.

There are few writing jobs outside of speechwriting that offer good pay, steady employment, and the chance to shape public perception and public policy. But the opportunities that come with speechwriting also present unique ethical questions, and not all of them can be answered simply by following basic ethical practices for writing. Put simply, a political speechwriter's ethical guidebook must be different from that of the average writer.

When I first started ghostwriting, I would proudly send an op-ed to my parents or my family, who often replied not with praise but with bewilderment about why my name was not on the byline.[1] I was paid to write something that I would not receive credit for, at least not publicly.

The very act of ghostwriting can raise ethical questions. The speaker gives a speech that is arguably not his: he did not draft it and may not have edited it or even thought much about the ideas contained in the speech. How is that ethical?

This quandary goes both ways: What ethical considerations exist for a writer who will not be held to the same level of accountability as the person who gives the speech? What does she owe to her principal? What kinds of control is she permitted to have over her own work, when it is inherently written for another person to own?

This chapter explores these questions by examining the ethical responsibilities a speechwriter has to her audience, her principal (DC shorthand for someone's boss), and herself, building on an overview of what speechwriters do and why speeches, far from being an old-fashioned tool of political rhetoric, still matter in today's political arena.

What Speechwriters Do

In 1997 the White House held a party on the eve of President Bill Clinton's State of the Union address. President Clinton supposedly introduced one of his speechwriters to guests by saying, "This is the guy who types up my speeches."

No matter how brilliant a writer a principal is—and President Clinton is, by all accounts, known to be an exceptional writer—there are few speechwriters who fall under the category of overpaid stenographer.

The ideal speechwriter is a thought partner to a principal. She brings smart ideas to the table, makes everyday prose sing or soar, and advises on effective delivery techniques.

While the kinds of partnership between speechwriter and principal can differ vastly, the speechwriting process typically follows some version of the following:

- A principal agrees to speak at an event.
- The speechwriter or other staff members gather details about the event, including but not limited to the agenda and purpose of the event, the size and composition of the audience, the length of speech requested, any plans for press, and a list of other speakers.
- Based on this information, the speechwriter may work with staff or the principal to develop an outline for the speech.
- The speechwriter researches and drafts remarks.
- The speechwriter manages the review process, gathering edits from advisers, staff, and the principal and incorporating them into a final version formatted for delivery.

This process, and the overall role of a speechwriter, will depend on the size and sophistication of the team around a principal. Some writers work for a single principal and may have a large team to support their efforts. For example, White House speechwriters can rely on others to compile logistics, research background information, determine talking points and provide strategic guidance, and fact-check and approve language. Other speechwriters might work for a firm or freelance; they may draft a speech and send it off without ever knowing if edits are made or if remarks are even delivered.

Outside of speechwriting or public affairs firms, however, it is common for speechwriters to run the review process, sending a speech to staff, advisers, and the principal. This part of the job can be the biggest headache. People will almost always have conflicting views on remarks, and a good speechwriter will find some of these views lacking. As the keeper of the draft, the speechwriter may be empowered to make her own decisions about edits to accept or ignore, while always keeping in mind that the speech ultimately belongs to the principal. The ideas may come from others, but ultimately ownership lies with the principal.

Principals define this process as well. Some will want to be a part of every draft, defining and shaping ideas and drafting and editing language as a speech develops. Others will simply want to review a final text and make small changes.

In other words, speechwriters have varying degrees of control over final drafts, and this control depends on the nature of the relationship and the trust that exists in the partnership between writer and principal. The closer a speechwriter is to her principal, the more power she has in her pen and the greater her ethical responsibilities are likely to be.

Why Speeches Matter

In the age of digital political communication, it is tempting to view speeches as old-fashioned, even irrelevant political rhetoric. Technology offers many ways to navigate around media gatekeepers and instead take an argument straight to a target audience through websites, videos, emails, and online ads.

Thankfully for aspiring speechwriters, this reality has not threatened the power of speeches, for a simple reason: political leaders, elected officials, and influencers are still asked to speak in public. Political conventions, ceremonial events, dinners and rallies, prayer breakfasts, congressional hearings, business forums, and even Boy Scout meetings all provide a platform that political figures want and need to pursue their goals, and there is nothing like the political theater of a speech. A stage and a targeted, live audience are all a messenger needs to set moods, change minds, and shape beliefs.

Think of the speech President George W. Bush gave just three days after the 9/11 attacks in 2001.[2] He stood on top of a burned-out fire truck, surrounded by first responders, and spoke for just two minutes through a bullhorn: "I want you all to know that America today, America today is on bended knee, in prayer for the people whose lives were lost here, for the workers who work here, for the families who mourn. The nation stands with the good people of New York City and New Jersey and Connecticut as we mourn the loss of thousands of our citizens."

A rescue worker then shouted: "I can't hear you."

President Bush replied: "I can hear you! I can hear you! The rest of the world hears you! And the people who knocked these buildings down will hear all of us soon!"

In the words of the Canadian philosopher Marshall McLuhan, the message in President Bush's speech is in the medium. He spoke at what was essentially an active crime scene that did not lend itself to fancy rhetoric. His presence, his words, and that bullhorn conveyed solidarity and strength, resilience and resolve.

President Barack Obama made many similarly iconic speeches, such as when he sang "Amazing Grace" during his eulogy for the victims of the 2015 mass shooting at the Emanuel African Methodist Episcopal Church:[3] "If we can find that grace, anything is possible. If we can tap that grace, everything can change. Amazing grace. Amazing grace. Amazing grace, how sweet the sound, that saved a wretch like me; I once was lost, but now I'm found; was blind but now I see."

This is a speech that must be watched to achieve its full effect. At one of the most poignant moments, President Obama repeats "amazing grace," pausing to gain control over his emotions. Each time, the audience verbally responds to him. After another long pause, he begins to sing the old hymn. The audience claps and cheers. People rise to their feet and join him in song. The church band kicks in to accompany everyone. The vulnerability of the president is met by joy and encouragement; when the song ends, the president's tone shifts from vulnerable to resolved, and he calls out the names of each victim: "Clementa Pinckney found that grace. Cynthia Hurd found that grace. Susie Jackson found that grace. Ethel Lance found that grace. DePayne Middleton-Doctor found that grace. Tywanza Sanders found that grace. Daniel L Simmons, Sr. found that grace. Sharonda Coleman-Singleton found that grace. Myra Thompson found that grace."

Much of the power of this speech is in the delivery, in the way the president moves through the text, his decision to sing the hymn, and the audience's response to those choices. But he almost certainly talked with his speechwriting team about whether or not he should sing the hymn—news reports hint as much[4]—and how he could structure the speech to build a powerful moment regardless of whether the lyrics were sung or spoken.

Basic Ethics in Political Speechwriting

President Bush's 9/11 speech and President Obama's eulogy for the victims of the Emanuel shooting show what speeches are capable of when done at the highest level: they can convey and sway emotion in a way that comforts and unites a nation. But the vast majority of political speeches do not have that kind of high purpose.

Aristotle defined rhetoric as "the art of discovering all the available means of persuasion in a given situation." That leaves quite a bit of ethical wiggle room to explore within political speech, a space that is defined and shaped by political culture. To begin to explore that space, I first review some basic ethical guidelines.

The very existence of ghostwriters came about through changes in politics and policy making, which are now at a level of sophistication that requires staff and advisers. Principals rely on others to help them understand the details of congressional appropriations, the national health insurance industry, the legal statutes around tribal sovereignty, or the customs and culture of a foreign nation. Writing speeches is no different. It can be difficult and time-consuming, and therefore it can be outsourced.

This is true outside of politics as well. Business leaders and even celebrities use ghostwriters as well. But political speechwriting has its own set of ethical rules, building on some general ethical standards of writing and adopting others based on the unique rules of political rhetoric.

The culture of politics is a wide road with even wider shoulders. There are practices that may technically stay in the confines of the guardrails but are clearly off the road. An ethical speechwriter keeps all four wheels on the road at all times.

The first and most basic rule is simple: do not plagiarize. Do not copy sentences or paragraphs from a source and use it in a speech without credit. Plagiarizing, intentional or not, has derailed presidential campaigns and ruined writing careers. When researching, outlining, and drafting a speech, a speechwriter should be careful to distinguish between what is original writing and what she has pulled from outside sources.

The political twist on this rule is found in the more murky definitions of plagiarism, specifically borrowing ideas from others without giving credit. The political process requires many voices—advocates, experts, pundits, and politicians—who help to shape a narrative and build momentum. Building on others' ideas and rhetoric is message dissemination; it can be essential to pass a new law, defeat a ballot initiative, or elect someone to public office. So in politics, it is acceptable to borrow or expand on others' ideas without bothering to give them credit.

Obviously this would not be acceptable in academic or journalistic writing. But an honest look at political rhetoric will acknowledge that cribbing ideas or short turns of phrase is common practice and part of the political marketplace of ideas.

The political rhetoric used to argue for a single-payer health-care option versus a public option offers a strong example here. Senator Bernie Sanders is known for advocating Medicare for All, which is a cleverly framed single-payer plan. But that language was first used decades ago by a Republican senator who wanted to expand Medicare to cover everyone in the United States.[5]

In the 2020 presidential campaign, Mayor Pete Buttigieg billed his public option plan as "Medicare for All Who Want It," a concept that he borrowed from Senator Sanders's plan as well as a bill introduced by Senator Brian Schatz,[6] which as early as 2017 was characterized as "Medicaid for All Who Want It."[7]

Both Senator Sanders and Mayor Buttigieg have promoted these plans in their 2020 stump speeches and do not acknowledge that the language they use is far from their own original phrasing. But because the repetition of these two frames is required to build support for the ideas, their ownership of this language is deemed acceptable.

The key to this rule is to know that the line is clear and bright. Building on another political slogan, turn of phrase, or policy idea is fine; copying entire sections of a speech or publication is not.[8]

Responsibility to Your Audience

The most noble responsibility a speechwriter has is to her audience. It is also the one she is most likely to fail to uphold.

American political discourse is in a difficult state, full of euphemisms, base or toxic language, blatant pandering, and bald lies. This is not new; George Orwell's *Politics and the English Language* (1946) is proof that politics has long been distorted by destructive or deceptive language. But there is a national sense that we're searching for the bottom. According to the Pew Research Center, overwhelming majorities of Americans agree that our political debate has "become more negative . . . less fact-based . . . and less focused on issues" over the past few years.[9]

Americans don't want political discourse that sounds like a barroom brawl. Together, speechwriters and principals owe it to their audiences to search for the ceiling, not the floor, of political discourse. Political speeches should educate people about their rights and responsibilities as citizens. They should translate policy ideas into accessible, inclusive language. They should inspire and unite. Here we are failing, with high stakes in the balance.

The language scholar Victor Klemperer wrote about one of the most extreme examples of what happens when political rhetoric fails its ethical responsibilities to an audience in *The Language of the Third Reich*:

> But a speech was not only more important than it had been previously, it was also, of necessity, different in nature. In addressing itself to everyone rather than just select representatives of the people it had to make itself comprehensible to everyone and thus become more populist. Populist [*volkstumlich*] means more concrete: the more emotional a speech is, the less it addresses itself to the intellect, the more populist it will be. And it will cross the boundary separating populism from demagogy and mass seduction as soon as it moves from ceasing to challenge the intellect to deliberately shutting it off and stupefying it.[10]

Speechwriters should use the tools of rhetoric and persuasion with integrity. Everything from the facts used to support a thesis to the ways in which the speech puts an audience in a certain frame of mind should be considered through an ethical lens. There are three areas in which speechwriters should be particularly thoughtful about what they owe to their audiences: depicting or describing characters, ascribing motivation, and using good sources.

Any good story has a hero and a villain, but to what end? Speeches that use the frame of us versus them, of good guys versus bad guys, should be careful not to punch down. An extreme example of this is President Donald Trump, who often uses dehumanizing language to depict perceived bogeyman or political enemies. Here are remarks he made in 2018 on refugees:[11]

> At this very moment, large, well-organized caravans of migrants are marching towards our southern border. Some people call it an "invasion." It's like an invasion. They have violently overrun the Mexican border. You saw that two days ago. These are tough people, in many cases. A lot of young men, strong men. And a lot of men that maybe we don't want in our country. But again, we'll find that out through the legal process.

Speeches can make an intelligent argument against taking in refugees without demonizing them, without painting a false picture of who they are (many refugees today are women and children) or how they act (almost all refugees peacefully request asylum). It is unethical to craft a story that seeks to inspire fear and animosity toward people who are often helpless and out of options.

Here is a less extreme and more common example of unethical storytelling: the blaming of bureaucrats in Washington. Federal employees carry out orders from one of two bosses, the White House or Congress. They are critical to good governance, which requires high-performing employees to deliver mail, monitor the quality of our air and water, maintain our national parks, and make sure veterans have access to services. Many of them are veterans themselves, a group usually considered sacred in rhetoric from almost any political figure. Yet federal workers are an easy bogeyman for dysfunction, slow-moving processes, or unpopular policies.

Representative Paul Mitchell (R-MI) gave a floor speech on charter schools in January 2019 that offers a more nuanced example of this:

> I'm not here advocating a federal policy for school choice. Rather I'm advocating we make those options available through sharing information, highlighting models and encouraging states and communities to make sure they're meeting the needs of young people across America. Because as Congressman Biggs notes, the future of America is those young people. Parents, not Washington bureaucrats, I suggest no bureaucrats in states, know what's best for their children.[12]

Here "bureaucrats" is actually a euphemism for Rep. Mitchell's own party; Republican-appointed officials led the Trump administration's policies on charter schools and were also required to implement any and all laws passed by Congress. Mitchell's speech tries to pass the buck and create a false villain to blame for policies he doesn't like.

Mitchell's remarks also step up to the line of assigning motivation to his villain. He suggests, implicitly, that bureaucrats think they know better than parents what children need. This is another ethical challenge that speechwriters should navigate carefully. Speeches can encourage their audiences to question a character's judgment, but they should not question motive.

I once wrote a speech about a popular Democratic villain, Betsy DeVos, who happened to have a long track record of donating to Republican senators who were voting on her nomination to serve as US secretary of education. I included this fact in my speech and posed the question of how they could vote against her, unqualified and unpopular as she was, when she had already secured their loyalty through campaign contributions. During review, the principal took out a pen, circled the paragraph I've described, and wrote: *No. Never.* He was not comfortable—and I shouldn't have been, either—with saying so plainly that senators supported her because she essentially paid them to do so.

Finally, speechwriters owe it to their audiences to use sources that present a fact or reality with honesty and clarity. This is especially important because speeches don't always include citations, which usually make it into a speech only if they create an effect of credibility. For example, a Republican who can use a statistic from the Center for American Progress is essentially saying that even the other side agrees on the evidence of a problem. Or she may cite a report from the US Bureau of Labor Statistics, which is a trusted, reputable source for data.

If a source is not supporting an argument, speechwriters will likely leave it out to avoid clunking up a line. A good rule of thumb on ethical sourcing is that if a writer would be embarrassed to include the source—for example, noting that a figure is from Wikipedia or a crackpot on YouTube who would hurt credibility and persuasion—then another source should be found or the evidence should be left on the cutting-room floor.

Responsibility to Your Principal

The relationship between a speechwriter and principal at its best is a thought partnership; a speechwriter takes the stories, experiences, priorities, and ideas of a principal and arranges them into effective, compelling speeches that appeal to audiences and achieve a speaker's goals. Excellent speeches reflect the principal's voice and values, establishing her as a trustworthy, leading voice.

Some of the ethical responsibilities a speechwriter has to her audience also apply to her principal: craft a speech with integrity, ethical framing and storytelling, and strong sources. There should not be any mistakes—a bad source, a misleading statistic, an unverified story, or an uncited paragraph lifted from another writer—that could hurt a principal's credibility (and her press clips!).

Other ethical responsibilities are less obvious. Sometimes a principal will be open about having a speechwriter; others may be embarrassed or uninterested in promoting their staff's work; some people want absolute discretion and may even ask a speechwriter to sign a nondisclosure agreement. At each of these levels, the principal should be the one in the partnership to define if and how a speechwriter advertises her work. This can be beneficial for the writer as well, who may feel less burdened to reflect a principal's views in other settings, like social media.

Ultimately speechwriters should be thoughtful about what they share about a principal, especially if they have the kind of access that makes for a good thought partnership. Discretion is key.

A final responsibility to principals is to remember who owns the speech. (Hint: it's not the speechwriter.) A writer may feel strongly about the best way to structure an argument, frame a story, or grab an audience's attention and make the case for crafting language in a certain way, but the principal always has the final say.

Responsibility to Yourself

A speechwriter was once asked by his principal's chief of staff to draft a nice note of congratulations to a hugely controversial national security figure, who had just won an award. The speechwriter replied: "I don't write letters to war criminals. Get someone else to do it."

Politics offers many opportunities to "sell out." People may work for causes they don't believe in or promote a policy they wouldn't want for their own family or community. These decisions are personal, and speechwriters also make them. Having a set of principles and rules based on one's own moral feelings allows speechwriters to know when to say, "Not this one."

Speechwriters who work in the federal government have additional ethical obligations. The US government is clear that employees have a responsibility to both the government "and its citizens to place loyalty to the Constitution, laws and ethical principles above private gain. To ensure that every citizen can have complete confidence in the integrity of the Federal Government, each employee shall respect and adhere to principles of ethical conduct."[13]

Speechwriters in government or other traditional institutions of power should also be aware of the dynamics of power and political communication. The media look to people in power to explain events that have happened— and speeches are often the best tool for leaders to reach people. A speechwriter has an obligation to meet her own ethical standards and drive an honest speech process to account for actual events, not, as Noam Chomsky put it, to "disguise reality in the service of external power."[14]

Final Thoughts

At all levels—from a local mayor's office to the White House—speechwriters help their principals meet their immediate goals. They can change perspectives, frame reality, and set the public's mood. They can have a hand in history. But they also come up against the pressures that come in any political communication job: to take the easiest route, to win at any cost, to not worry about whatever damage is being done to public discourse and democratic institutions. In these moments, speechwriters should return to their ethical responsibilities, to the obligations they have to their audience, their principal, themselves, and even their country. These duties should be their guide.

Notes

1 There are circumstances in which a ghostwriter will receive credit, such as when she has negotiated to be credited for a book she helped write or when her principal is regaling an audience with an embarrassing story about the speechwriter.
2 George W. Bush, "Bullhorn Address to Ground Zero Rescue Workers" (delivered in New York City, September 14, 2001), American Rhetoric, https://american rhetoric.com/speeches/gwbush911groundzerobullhorn.htm.
3 "Transcript: Obama Delivers Eulogy for Charleston Pastor, the Rev. Clementa Pinckney," *Washington Post*, June 26, 2015, https://www.washingtonpost.com/news/post-nation/wp/2015/06/26/transcript-obama-delivers-eulogy-for-charleston-pastor-the-rev-clementa-pinckney/.
4 Andrew Buncombe, "Remembering Obama's 2015 Speech at the Charleston Shooting Service, Where He Sang 'Amazing Grace,'" *Independent*, January 16, 2017, https://www.independent.co.uk/news/world/americas/barack-obama-charleston-church-shooting-speech-in-full-victoms-funeral-2015-amazing-grace-dylann-a7529641.html.
5 Abigail Abrams, "The Surprising Origins of Medicare for All," *Time*, May 2019.
6 Full disclosure: I worked for Senator Schatz when he introduced this bill, also known as the State Public Option Act.
7 Eric Levitz, "Democrats' New Health-Care Plan: Medicaid for All (Who Want It)," *New York*, August 2017.
8 See Melania Trump's remarks at the 2016 Republican National Convention for a clear example of plagiarism and political speech. https://www.newsweek.com/melania-trump-michelle-obama-plagarism-compare-speeches-full-text-481779.
9 Bruce Drake and Jocelyn Kiley, "Americans Say the Nation's Political Debate Has Grown More Toxic and 'Heated' Rhetoric Could Lead to Violence," Fact Tank, July 2019, https://www.pewresearch.org/fact-tank/2019/07/18/ameri

cans-say-the-nations-political-debate-has-grown-more-toxic-and-heated-rhetoric
-could-lead-to-violence/.

[10] Victor Klemperer, *The Language of the Third Reich: LTI Lingua Tertii Imperii; a Philologist's Notebook* (London: Bloomsbury Academic, 2013).

[11] "Remarks by President Trump on the Illegal Immigration Crisis and Border Security," November 1, 2018, https://www.whitehouse.gov/briefings-statements/remarks-president-trump-illegal-immigration-crisis-border-security/.

[12] "User Clip: Rep. Paul Mitchell on School Choice," January 17, 2019, CSPAN, https://www.c-span.org/video/?c4826305/user-clip-rep-paul-mitchell-school-choice.

[13] US Office of Government Ethics, "Standards of Ethical Conduct for Employees of the Executive Branch," n.d., accessed October 2019, https://www.oge.gov/web/oge.nsf/0/076ABBBFC3B026A785257F14006929A2/$FILE/SOC%20as%20of%2081%20FR%2081641%20FINAL.pdf.

[14] Mitsou Ronat and Noam Chomsky, *Language and Responsibility: Based on Conversations with Mitsou Ronat* (New York: Pantheon Books, 1977), 5.

15

Identity Crisis
The Blurred Lines for Consumers and Producers of Digital Content

Cheryl Contee and Rosalyn Lemieux

Yesterday and Today

Today's rapid-fire, digitized world has created new frontiers for pushing the boundaries of ethics in political communication. Yet humans have explored the nuances of ethical political discourse since ancient times. The philosopher Socrates was tried in Athens around 399 BCE for moral corruption and impiety in part because he had politically supported a prior set of authoritarian rulers. A democratic Athenian jury of his peers found that Socrates's speech was harmful to society, and he was condemned to commit suicide by drinking hemlock.

We may lament the scourge of confusing fake news and outright lies in contemporary discourse, but America has faced similar issues before during the period of "yellow journalism" beginning in the 1890s. The term described communication practices of competitive New York City–based newspapers, which included frightening or misleading headlines in large print, cherry-picked to alarm readers, inflammatory images (drawings, pictures, cartoons), staged photos, populist sentiments, and heavy use of faked interviews and pseudoscience from "experts." Sound familiar?

William Randolph Hearst and Joseph Pulitzer, two influential New York City–based publishers, were fighting for sales. They pushed aside responsible journalism and used their papers and reporters to disseminate biased and/or inaccurate stories to drive public opinion toward desired opinions. Many historians believe that yellow journalism contributed to America's entry into the Spanish-American War and to the assassination of President William McKinley in 1901. At one point Hearst—who supported US intervention in Cuba against the Spanish, who at that time ruled the island and were facing an uprising—reportedly told one of his illustrators sent to cover the revolution, "You furnish the pictures. I'll furnish the war" (PBS n.d.).

Public opinion, clarifying court cases, and changing mores in the newspaper industry eventually led to a higher ethical standard more in keeping with the special protections for the press as enshrined in the US Constitution. The Federal Communications Commission (FCC) introduced the Fairness Doctrine in 1949. The Fairness Doctrine required that all holders of broadcast licenses "should include discussions of matters of public importance in their broadcasts, and that they should do so in a fair manner" (Matthews 2011). In 1987 the FCC revoked the Fairness Doctrine, which has led to significant changes in opportunities for communicators along the political spectrum in public platforms both old and new.

Today we again face a loosening of ethics in American political discourse. President Donald Trump has credibly been accused by fact-checkers of telling more than twelve thousand lies during his administration. Online ads that distort the truth abound, which is an issue when Pew Internet's research has found that two-thirds of Americans get their news first from Facebook, the most popular social network in the world. News coverage on TV and via websites is too often slanted toward one worldview or another, the motive being profit, propaganda, or both.

What is new in our contemporary world is that the line between producer and consumer has become blurred. When an Instagram influencer can become a political pundit, how does that change the game? Should it be possible to make a lot of money spreading fake news that influences public opinion on Twitter and Facebook? How do ethics come into play when those consuming political content are also the people commenting on, sharing, and creating content in response? What responsibilities do political communicators have in a new era in which artificial intelligence makes it possible to micro-target individuals at scale with messages precisely tailored to trigger a specific emotional response?

In the following sections we dig deeper.

The Self as Lens: Identity and Intent

As someone who seeks to enter the world of political communication, you must look to the self. You probably have already engaged in political discourse in some form, mostly likely on the internet. You may have liked a certain story or shared, retweeted, or commented. Perhaps you've created your own YouTube video in which you express your political opinions in response to events or other commentary.

Today anyone with a smartphone has at her fingertips everything she needs to practice polished political punditry if she chooses. Yet ultimately, others may judge political communication from the standpoints of identity and intent.

First let's tackle identity. There are many ways in which we define who we are and our authority to express a cogent opinion on a given matter. For example, perhaps it is part of your job to express an opinion. In this case, your identity as an elected representative or as a credentialed, employed journalist is key. Or perhaps you are a CEO or employee or client/customer of a company in the news. Or an event has happened in your region that you have experienced with your neighbors. Finally, you may belong to a group for whom an issue has special relevance and impact, such as an ethnic group, a disability, an age cohort, a specific gender, or marital status.

America was once limited in terms of the voices whose identities were legitimized to speak as authorities on political topics. Historically, upper-class white males were the ones who both decided which events, stories, or policies were most important and which people were allowed to speak in public about them.

Today there is more diversity than ever on our airwaves, in print, and online, and because of the proliferation of channels and platforms, little stands in the way of anyone reaching thousands or millions with political commentary, regardless of one's identity. Yet we can begin to create a formal definition of the political communicator as someone who is

a. inside *government,*
b. acting as a *consultant* to political actors and policy makers,
c. serving as *campaign staff* for an issue or a candidate,
d. creating content as *media professional* or as an *influencer,*
e. serving as an *activist,* or
f. an *everyday person* who expresses an opinion.

While there are many identities from which you might communicate on political matters, you must also consider the identities of the different audience segments your communications may reach. How do the digital identities of others impact you as a professional?

As previously mentioned, the reality is that everyone right now can be a political communicator, whether you are an influencer or a random person who engages in online dialogue. The impact you can have and the level of seriousness with which you should approach your engagement might be much higher if you are an elected official, campaign staff member, or media professional.

If you are a political professional who does not adhere to basic values such as truthfulness and balance, there can be consequences. Lies can create confusion among citizens about the facts surrounding an event or trend, leading to poor policy making or failure to create policies. Unprofessional political dialogue can incite others to violence or encourage harassment of those with differing desires or opinions. Finally, it's possible to nurture mistrust in the system and decrease civic engagement, which should be the opposite of the goal of any ethical political communication strategy.

It is now often the case that a person can migrate from being an influencer, commenting or engaging in activism, to become a political pro on the inside of the action. Are the ethics different on either side? The authors of this chapter argue that there is from our own experiences. Cheryl Contee was one of the cofounders of Jack and Jill Politics, a politics and pop culture blog targeted at African Americans (and those who love them). Cheryl's influence in the world of politics grew as a result of the blog's cultural impact on US and international political discourse, and ultimately she became an independent consultant with her own practice, focused on digital organizing and outreach for causes and campaigns.

Similarly, as an early "digital grassroots campaigner" in the late 1990s, Roz Lemieux saw the power of digital tools to meaningfully engage supporters at scale—first at the Feminist Majority and then at MoveOn.org. Later she helped train hundreds of other progressive campaigners through the New Organizing Institute's "boot camps" and connect thousands through Rootscamp, all with the intention of lifting up the voices of progressives, online and off.

But when an email from your organization or candidate can drive thousands to act—say, reciting your script at a town hall or texting your (targeted) friends—is A/B testing ethical? Is using the subject that gets the most clicks because it is the most inflammatory ethical? Everyone thinks they are working for the good guys and gals. The level of responsibility increases once you are speaking on behalf of or under the auspices of an organization, a candidate, a media outlet, or the government because your greater authority and the impact you can have on many more people.

That doesn't mean that if you represent another form of identity, such as an aggrieved minority group, that you are off the ethical hook! In fact, it can ultimately weaken your objectives if you are found to be communicating using distorted, inaccurate, or blatantly false motives or information. Yet we argue from personal experience that the stakes become even higher when you represent or advise large organizations or those that reach large numbers of people. It's important to push hard against the framework you were handed and ensure that you understand the arguments of those who oppose your position.

This brings us to intent. What impact do you intend to have, and how does that intersect with your identity? Before you engage in political communication, especially if you are operating in a professional context, consider what your goal may be. Think about applying critical thinking and breaking out of your echo chamber to hear multiple perspectives and facts, which can then strengthen your argument. Reflect on the checks and balances you are using to ensure you have the full picture instead of being led along by others' opinions.

Is your intention to inspire people, including policy makers? Is it to inform, enlighten, and entertain? Or is it to obfuscate, confuse, and discourage? Have you deeply interrogated the potential ramifications of your political speech? Beyond your intent (which you may believe is pure), what are the worst-case scenarios that could happen?

Naturally there is a difference between an opinion and a news report. However, both need to be based in a full set of facts. You can advocate a position or narrate an event with neutrality, but it is unethical to twist the truth to suit your argument or account. Most people don't think they are twisting the facts, but the onus is ultimately on you. If your career is as a professional communicator, it is incumbent upon you to see the other point of view and investigate your facts. Pull your intent apart and then build your argument based on as complete an understanding of the issue at hand as possible. The pace of campaigns today may appear to make this more challenging, yet a quick search engine ping or Wikipedia jog can be quite illuminating!

Substance as Lens: The Ethics of Content

Despite being grounded in a strong sense of individual ethics, the pace and pressure of the campaign world can easily cloud day-to-day decisions about *content*. This section addresses three distinct types of political communications that we argue are by nature unethical: deliberate deception, incitement to violence against individuals or groups, and suppression of civic engagement.

A commonly agreed upon definition of a lie is that it is "a statement made by one who does not believe it with the intention that someone else shall be led to believe it" (Isenberg 1973, 248).

Let's assume for a moment that you will never choose to publish what you yourself consider a blatant lie, for example, "I know A is true, yet I'm going to say A is false." (If you are willing to do that, a chapter on communication ethics is unlikely to sway you.) In politics, the "gray area" appears when short-term stakes feel high. If your candidate or cause loses, it can feel like the window of opportunity to advance "the good" (as you define it) will close. Communications cadence is frequently crisis driven, whether the crises are real or manufactured. And too frequently, you will be fighting *deliberate* disinformation campaigns—not only by explicit political opponents, but also by shadow political groups (Bansal et al. 2019), foreign operatives (Romm and Stanley-Becker 2019), and even bots posing as real humans (Howard 2018).

In such circumstances, even political communicators who would consider an outright lie unethical can be tempted to deceive through framing, tone, omission, or implication. On day 100 of a campaign, running up against a fund-raising deadline, writing tomorrow's appeal at 3:00 a.m., and fueled by nothing but caffeine and passion, "morally right" and "clickable" can start to look like the same thing. In a world where you may only have a sound bite or meme to catch a potential supporter's attention, what else can you do?

In short, we can look to the ethical frameworks established to provide such guidance—both in history and other fields that face a similar dilemma. While there are many examples of lies that might have a neutral or even beneficial impact when considered individually, Bok (1978) argues for the "Principle of Veracity"—that is, a strong moral presumption against lying, inclusive of a requirement to tell the *whole* truth, based on the social cost of living in a world without trust. Without the ability to presume widespread truth telling, we would not be able to trust our education or what we read in books. In principle, we would have to find out everything firsthand, which is of course impossibly limiting. The very foundation of our society, *particularly* a democracy, in which we've entrusted each other with critical governance decisions, is made possible by pervasive trust.

Interestingly, Bok's "Principle of Veracity" is foundational in health-care ethics. The classic health-care example is "informed consent"—that is, the principle that patients have the right to all the (sometimes grim) information about their own circumstances. There are only very slim exceptions in which a provider may withhold information in the best interest of the patient, where it could be outweighed by the "do no harm" principle, for example, in pediatrics or where suicide is a risk. In other words, if there isn't an immediate mortal threat to the adult patient, the provider is ethically required to provide *all* the information to the patient about her or his condition, *even if* the provider believes that obfuscation would benefit the patient. Why? The impact of such choices on the profession—destroying the foundation of patient-provider trust on which the health-care industry is built—is considered so threatening that this principle is enshrined in both medical education and practitioner culture.

In some ways that threat has been realized. Mistrust in doctors has been shown to correlate with unhealthy behaviors in patients and failure to consistently take medication or get vaccinated, as well as to hamper medical innovation (The Advisory Board 2018). Trust in doctors has plummeted by 75 percent since 1966 (Blendon, Benson, and Hero 2014). The consequences of *this* trust deficit, combined with a mistrust of government, can be catastrophic, as we have seen recently with the reemergence of vaccine-preventable diseases like measles. Measles once "ranked high among the leading killer of children worldwide, when it caused an estimated 2.6 million deaths annually" (Hotez 2019), was nearly defeated, and is now on the rise again as a result of the "medical freedom" movement, fueled in part by mistrust of government, for example, claims of a "vast conspiracy" by the US Centers for Disease Control (DeNoon n.d.).

In politics, where the paths to being a "practitioner" are more varied—and the line between layperson and professional is less well-defined—we have failed to implement even such basic guardrails around truth telling. And it shows. The Pew Research Center conducted a survey in December 2016 in which 64 percent of Americans reported feeling "a great deal of confusion" about basic facts in the news. And in 2019 Pew found that 64 percent said they find it hard to tell what's true when elected officials speak (Rainie, Keeter, and Perrin 2019) (see figure 15.1).

Hannah Arendt, a German American philosopher and influential political theorist, presents a more nuanced view of the vulnerability of political communications to deception in a 1971 essay titled "Lying in Politics," written shortly after the release of the Pentagon Papers:

A characteristic of human action is that it always begins something new. [. . .] Such change would be impossible if we could not mentally remove ourselves from where we physically are located and imagine that things might as well be different from what they actually are. In other words, the deliberate denial of factual truth—the ability to lie—and the capacity to change facts—the ability to act—are interconnected; they owe their existence to the same source: imagination. (Arendt 1971)

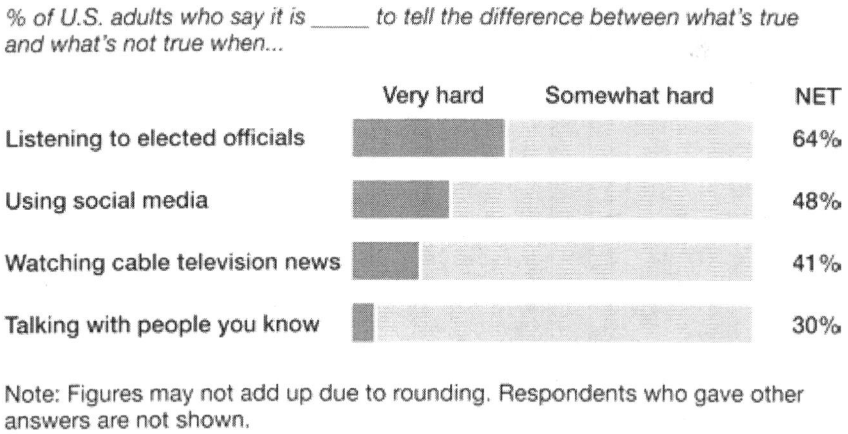

% of U.S. adults who say it is _____ to tell the difference between what's true and what's not true when...

	Very hard	Somewhat hard	NET
Listening to elected officials			64%
Using social media			48%
Watching cable television news			41%
Talking with people you know			30%

Note: Figures may not add up due to rounding. Respondents who gave other answers are not shown.

Figure 15.1.   Nearly two-thirds of adults find it hard to tell what's true when elected officials speak.

The nature of politics is that we are *inventing* society together. Papova (2016) quotes Hannah Arendt, noting that this requires a "relative freedom from things as they are." "Hence, when we talk about lying . . . let us remember that the lie did not creep into politics by some accident of human sinfulness. Moral outrage, for this reason alone, is not likely to make it disappear."

Furthermore, all deception is not strictly lying. Arendt warns of "public-relations managers in government who learned their trade from the inventiveness of Madison Avenue" (Arendt 1971). One could argue that this "trade," aka marketing, has become the standard practice of political communication fifty years later. No modern communication practice would be complete without A/B tested copy, visually captivating imagery, an advertising budget, and an influencer strategy.

Arendt asserts that the use of public relations tools, while effective in driving consumers' purchase choices, are limited in their ability to drive consumers to "buy" opinions and political views. Fifty years on, evidence seems to point in a different direction. In a 2014 study published in the *Proceedings of the National Academy of Sciences of the United States of America*, researchers from Cornell University and the University of California revealed that Facebook users experienced "emotional contagion" based on the content of their feeds. According to the abstract:

> We show, via a massive (N = 689,003) experiment on Facebook, that emotional states can be transferred to others via emotional contagion, leading people to experience the same emotions *without their awareness*. We provide experimental evidence that emotional contagion occurs without direct interaction between people (exposure to a friend expressing an emotion is sufficient), and in the complete absence of nonverbal cues. (Kramer, Guillory, and Hancock 2014; emphasis added)

Public outrage centered around the fact that nearly 700,000 Facebook users had been included in a psychological experiment without their consent. But perhaps more concerningly, the study proved what many had feared: *that we humans are disturbingly easy to manipulate.*

While the research was published in 2014, the experiment itself had been conducted in 2012. That same year, Facebook filed a patent on "determining user personality characteristics from social networking system communications." The patent suggests that "stored personality characteristics may be used as targeting criteria for advertisers . . . to increase the likelihood that the user . . . positively interacts with a selected advertisement" (Nowak and Eckles 2017).

In March 2018 a second Facebook scandal emerged: a British firm called Cambridge Analytica had harvested data from between thirty and eighty-seven million user profiles and used that information for voter persuasion. Again the controversy centered around the data breach: How could Facebook let such a massive amount of user data get into the hands of a commercial entity without user consent? But the data that trained the Cambridge Analytica model how to persuade voters were obtained *with* user consent, from approximately thirty-two thousand US voters who were paid $2–$5 to take online personality tests. "The personality surveys use [those] 120 questions to profile people along five discrete axes—the 'five factors' model, popularly called the 'Ocean' model after one common breakdown of the factors: openness to experience, conscientiousness, extraversion, agreeableness and neuroticism" (Hern 2018).

The combination of these personality tests, extensive data from the profiles of Facebook users who had accepted payments for taking the personality tests *and* all of their Facebook friends (the breach), other available data on individuals such as their voting records, and machine learning to analyze these patterns at scale enabled Cambridge Analytica to develop a sophisticated, 253-point psychometric model. That model enabled the development of highly personalized advertisements that were designed to trigger specific emotional responses in their viewers. Former employee and whistleblower Christopher Wylie described the "actual issues" as "plain white toast" and the data as a tool to add the right flavor to appeal to each individual. The model was used by Republican Ted Cruz in his 2016 presidential campaign (Davies 2015).

The Trump campaign also utilized Cambridge Analytica in 2016 (Lapowsky 2016a). While it is unclear if the campaign benefited from the same modeling service, the firm did conduct hundreds of thousands of voter surveys to identify geographic clusters of persuadable voters. At the same time, the Republican National Committee (RNC) collaborated with Trump's digital team to maximize social media engagement through targeting. On the day of the third presidential debate, the RNC released *175,000 variations of the same Facebook ad*, which its director of advertising Gary Coby called "A/B testing on steroids" (Lapowsky 2016b).

While Cambridge Analytica has received much of the attention because the scandal surrounding its acquisition of Facebook data landed Mark Zuckerberg in front of the US Congress, the psychographic-targeting tactics are not uncommon at all. Neither are these techniques confined to Republican campaigns. Barack Obama's 2012 presidential campaign is widely credited with introducing "big data" (DataFloq 2013) as a tool, using similar opt-in techniques on Facebook to "suck out the whole social graph" and leverage that for targeted political messaging (Davidsen 2018a). The idea was twofold: that young voters were unreachable via traditional methods, given that more than half did not have listed phone numbers, and that even if they did, they did not trust information coming directly from campaigns. They trusted information coming from friends. "More than 600,000 supporters followed through [on the ask to share targeted content] with more than 5 million contacts, asking their friends to register to vote, give money, vote or look at a video designed to change their mind[s]" (Scherer 2012).

These examples are striking because they reveal both that it is possible to manipulate (or "persuade") *political* opinions using modern marketing techniques and that political campaigns are doing this at scale, frequently leveraging data obtained without user consent. So where should political communicators draw ethical lines? We could start by breaking down "what happened" in these high-profile cases into three buckets:

1. The info you have: collection of personal data at scale
2. How you use it to target: psychographic profiling for targeting
3. What you are saying: A/B testing and the content of the messages themselves

Regarding bucket 1, there have been sweeping policy changes since 2016, with the European Union (EUGDPR n.d.), Maine (Musil 2019), and California (State of California, Department of Justice n.d.) leading the way on consumer data and privacy protection. Paradoxically, consumers *say* they are concerned about privacy risks but consistently embrace data sharing in exchange for convenience or free services (Symantec 2019). Between new government regulations and shifts in corporate policy at major social networks, it is today largely impossible to do the kind of "social graph" data mining that caused such concern in the Cambridge Analytica case. Consumers still can be induced to give up their own personal data, but they are largely prevented from giving up their friends' data. Younger generations exhibit a stronger awareness of personal data and are more willing to take action to manage it on social media accounts (Help Net Security 2019), so this feels like a problem en route to being solved, at least through the lens of "ethical political communications" (less so of cybersecurity).

Regarding number 2, the ship has sailed in the other direction. Psychographic data are part and parcel of "modern marketing" practice, embraced by mainstream companies like Hubspot (Meredith n.d.), with dozens of vendors offering profiling services. Targeting individuals with personalized messaging about everything from diapers (Hill 2012) to Porsches (CB Insights 2018) to planned giving (McCarville 2018) has been commonplace for the better part of a decade and doesn't seem to be going away. If marketers can use these methods to target commercial ads, it can be reasonably expected campaigns will do the same. In fact, campaigns have been adapting those "modern marketing" techniques to the political space in recent years by creatively blending marketing and data, for example, tying browser-based cookie tracking to voting history available via the public voter file (DSPolitical n.d.). While this type of targeting was once in an ethical gray area, trends indicate the public is increasingly aware that they are trading data privacy for convenience, free services, and targeted communications (65% of Consumers Question How Brands Are Using Their Data 2019)—and they continue to opt in.

If we concede that targeting based on personal data, freely available or given, is ethical—and mining second-degree or social graph data is not— then what remains is the message itself. If a campaign can cook up 175,000 variations of Christopher Wylie's "plain white toast" to ensure it is delivered in the most palatable possible form for a particular individual, can all those variations accurately represent a true statement, let alone the authentic voice of a candidate? It depends.

Looking a little closer at the 2012 and 2016 presidential cycle examples previously cited, the implications of large-scale targeted messaging on social media appear to be quite different depending on the content being delivered. According to a former campaign staffer, who provided the image shown in figure 15.2 (Davidsen 2018b), the Obama campaign used social

OBAMA BIDEN

Harper --

North Carolina's got a big day today, and you can help.

Folks in our state start voting today, and it's a unique opportunity for us all to make a difference for President Obama and other Democrats, right out of the gate.

Here's where you come in: We're getting the word out about the start of early voting, and your connections with voters in this battleground state can get more people to the polls.

Reach out to the folks you know in North Carolina using Facebook **and let them know they can vote, RIGHT NOW.**

Jon Ruth

With just a few clicks your friends can find their nearest polling location, and your message could be what gets them out to cast a decisive vote in our critical battleground state.

In 2008, over 60 percent of the votes in North Carolina were cast before Election Day. President Obama narrowly won the state by only 14,000 votes out of 4.3 million cast -- which means critical early votes likely made the difference.

We need to make this year even bigger if we're going to win North Carolina again, and that starts with you.

So reach out to Jon right now:

Figure 15.2.   Targeted email.

data to target shareable messaging to supporters with friends in key states, for example, to drive early voting.

Where the targeting becomes truly concerning is when authentic content—what the campaign or candidate truly represents—becomes nothing more than a bland vehicle on which to deliver inflammatory or triggering words dropped in "Mad-Libs style" to elicit the predicted response. "Unfortunately, what [Cambridge Analytica] found was that the most effective personality messaging is based on fear," according to Brittany Kaiser, another former employee (Kates 2019).

Wiley cites the example of immigration, where images of walls were effective with "Conscientious" profiled conservative voters. "If you show that image, some people wouldn't get that that's about immigration, and others immediately would get that." Dog-whistle content like this—designed to appeal to a specific group of people while sounding innocuous to the general population—is increasingly being used to keep fringe groups engaged (Scott 2018). Micro-targeting is an ideal vehicle to deliver such content, and social networks are an ideal environment to drive message saturation among a fringe target population. The ethical lines are clear here. Dog-whistle politics is inherently dishonest, given that it is designed to obscure the true message from a general population. Worse, these messages are also very often subtle incitement to violence against individuals and groups, or at least can be interpreted as such by those predisposed to violence (Lind 2018).

Another GOP ad attacked same-sex marriage to boost right-wing turnout. "It's funny," Wiley said, "because this is so offensive and implicitly homophobic, but it's a team of gays that created it" (Hern 2018). Though not new, the use of external consultants and third parties disconnected from the purpose of the campaign creates additional space for unethical communications practice to arise. When working or volunteering with a campaign *because* your personal values align with its mission, it is a comparatively easy decision to quit or refuse to comply if that campaign makes requests that don't align with the values that drew you there in the first place. If you are an outside consultant, it can be too easy to distance yourself from unethical content on the basis of it being "work for hire."

In *Elle*'s profile of Brittany Kaiser, she describes the dissonance between her personal politics—having volunteered for Howard Dean in 2004, interned for Barack Obama in 2008, and voted for Bernie Sanders in the 2016 primary—and her work for Leave.EU and the Trump campaign, among others, as a form of professionalism: "Just because I wouldn't vote for them doesn't mean I shouldn't tell them how to use these tools," Kaiser says, explaining her way of thinking at the time. "A lot of people are uncomfortable with that. I'm not" (Chon 2019).

When pressed by David Carroll[1] in *The Great Hack* to explain her apparent flip of allegiance, Kaiser recalls the financial straits her family faced after her father lost his job after the 2008 financial crisis and how her family lost their home. Alexander Nix, then future CEO of Cambridge Analytica, seemed to value her experience—elevating her career to a new level and providing much-needed income—in a way that Democrats and the Obama campaign had not (Chon 2019).

If the passion-fueled adrenaline rush of a campaign poses a risk of blurred lines, so do the ego boost and hefty paycheck that successful strategists can attract as consultants once the campaign is over. Kaiser's willingness to overlook the content of her clients' campaigns under the guise of "professionalism" in order to advance her career recalls Hannah Arendt's *Eichmann in Jerusalem*. Adolf Eichmann, a high-ranking Nazi officer charged with facilitating and managing the logistics involved in the mass deportation of Jews to ghettos and extermination camps during World War II, is described by Arendt as displaying no guilt for his actions during the trial that ultimately led to his death by hanging, *claiming he bore no responsibility because he was simply doing his job* (Arendt 1963).

Even under totalitarianism, Arendt insists, moral choice remains—and she recommends as "required reading in political science for all students" the story of Denmark under Nazi occupation.

While not comparable to the Nazi terror of World War II, the manic pace of communication in a world of 24/7 news coverage, social media, and always-on devices can make it hard for anyone (Vincent 2016) to think clearly. As a political communications professional tasked with winning hearts and minds in the midst of that melee, you may find the ethical practices that seem obvious in a classroom setting feel fuzzier "in the field." Whether you are intoxicated by the rush of a campaign or the swelling pride that your first big client or high-paying job brings, remember that history will not judge kindly ethical compromises made to gain a quick win—for a campaign or for your career.

As a starting point, get in the habit of asking yourself: Is this communication *deceptive* in framing, tone, omission, or implication? Could it be construed to *incite violence* against individuals or groups, for example, based on triggering language? Does it *discourage* any segment of the electorate from voting or other civic engagement? Perhaps more important, before you join *any* campaign, invest in learning how to ground yourself,[2] check your own moral compass, and practice saying "no" to the opportunities that point you in the wrong direction.

Conclusion

Political communication has been a laboratory for exploring the application of ethical theory in practice since ancient times. Innovations in how people promote their preferred spokespeople, ideologies, and policies through new platforms are creating new opportunities to experiment with old concepts.

As of this writing, the founder of Facebook, Mark Zuckerberg, has informed the public that a platform that two-thirds of Americans use to receive news (Shearer and Matsa 2018) will not limit or police facts in the political advertisements reaching the eyeballs of millions, if not billions, of people. He stated on October 17, 2019, in a speech at Georgetown University to students just like you:

> "I believe that when it's not absolutely clear what to do, we should err on the side of greater expression. . . . There are many more ads about issues than there are ads about elections. Do we ban ads about healthcare, immigration or women's empowerment?" he said. "If you're not going to ban those, does it really make sense to give everyone else a voice in political debates except for the candidates themselves?" (Rodriguez 2019)

Zuckerberg also says the company has considered banning all political ads. Another emerging network among young people worldwide, TikTok, already bans political advertising, in part due to pressure around both pro-Chinese government and pro-LGBTQ+ messages. Blake Chandlee, TikTok vice president of global business solutions and a former Facebook executive, says, "We will not allow paid ads that promote or oppose a candidate, current leader, political party or group or issue at the federal, state or local level—including election-related ads, advocacy ads or issue ads" (Perez 2019).

TikTok says that banning political ads will protect the culture of the platform as an arena of positive creative self-expression, yet the company may also think that this policy will inoculate it as a target of governmental regulation and outright bans in nations that feel threatened by political discourse on the platform, which has happened to popular platforms such as Facebook and Twitter in authoritarian countries like Egypt, Turkey, China, and Iran.

Which company has the most ethical strategy for its business or for society, Facebook or TikTok? How will candidates, journalists, academics, and governments respond? We don't yet know, and you are one of the people who will help determine the outcome. Whether you become a government official, a Facebook or TikTok employee in the policy or news department, a journalist, an editor, an online influencer, or a staff member for a candidate for public office, your daily decisions will contribute to the future of ethics in political communication. Your actions will have a ripple effect on the rest of society, its history, and its laws beyond even your good intentions. How will your personal beliefs and experiences, along with the wisdom of the ages, align with how you practice the art of political communication? And how will you adjust to unforeseen consequences of your actions and speech in the political arena?

In an uncertain time whose history is still being written, in part by you, we might turn to Simone de Beauvoir, who wrote extensively on the ethics of ambiguity:

> Regardless of the staggering dimensions of the world about us, the density of our ignorance, the risks of catastrophes to come, and our individual weakness within the immense collectivity, the fact remains that we are absolutely free today if we choose to will our existence in its finiteness, a finiteness which is open on the infinite. And in fact, any man who has known real loves, real revolts, real desires, and real will knows quite well that he has no need of any outside guarantee to be sure of his goals; their certitude comes from his own drive. (Beauvoir 1948, 159)

Notes

1   A Parsons School of Design professor who sued Cambridge Analytica to get his data back.
2   There are many viable approaches here, for example, establishing a practice of mindfulness meditation.

References

The Advisory Board. 2018. "Trust in Doctors Has Plummeted by 75%: What Can Be Done?" February 16. Accessed October 28, 2019. https://www.advisory.com/daily-briefing/2018/02/16/trusting-medical-professionals.

Arendt, Hannah. 1963. "Eichmann in Jerusalem—I." *New Yorker,* February 16. Accessed October 30, 2019. https://www.newyorker.com/magazine/1963/02/16/eichmann-in-jerusalem-i.

———. 1971. "Lying in Politcs: Reflections on the Pentagon Papers." *New York Review of Books,* November 18. Accessed October 28, 2019. https://www.nybooks.com/articles/1971/11/18/lying-in-politics-reflections-on-the-pentagon-pape/.

Bansal, Samarth, Gopal Sathe, Rachna Khaira, and Aman Sethi. 2019. "How Modi, Shah Turned a Women's NGO into a Secret Election Propaganda Machine." *HuffPost,* May 4. Accessed October 28, 2019. https://www.huffingtonpost.in/entry/how-modi-shah-turned-a-women-s-rights-ngo-into-a-secret-election-propaganda-machine_in_5ca5962ce4b05acba4dc1819.

Beauvoir, Simone de. 1948. *The Ethics of Ambiguity.* Translated by Bernard Frechtman. New York: Citadel Press.

Blendon, Robert J., John M. Benson, and Joachim O. Hero. 2014. "Public Trust in Physicians—U.S. Medicine in International Perspective." *New England Journal of Medicine* 371: 1570–1572. Accessed October 28, 2019. https://www.nejm.org/doi/full/10.1056/NEJMp1407373#t=article.

Bok, Sissela. 1978. *Lying: Moral Choice in Public and Private Life.* New York: Pantheon Books.

CB Insights. 2018. "What Is Psychographics? Understanding The 'Dark Arts' of Marketing That Brought Down Cambridge Analytica." *Research Briefs,* June 7. Accessed October 28, 2019. https://www.cbinsights.com/research/what-is-psy chographics/.

Chon, Gina. 2019. "Breakingviews—Review: Blaming Big Data Is Political Diversion." *Reuters,* July 7. https://www.reuters.com/article/us-usa-technology-break ingviews/breakingviews-review-blaming-big-data-is-political-diversion-id USKCN1UE1NL (accessed October 28, 2019).

DataFloq. 2013. "Obama Changed the Political Campaign with Big Data." January 24. Accessed October 28, 2019. https://datafloq.com/read/big-data-obama -campaign/516.

Davidsen, Carol. 2018a. "An example of how we used that data to append to our email lists." Twitter, March 18, 2018, 7:53 p.m. https://twitter.com/cld276/ status/975565844632821760.

———. 2018b. "Facebook was surprised we were able to suck out the whole social graph. . . ." March 18, 2018, 11:02 p.m. https://twitter.com/cld276/sta tus/975568130117459975.

Davies, Harry. 2015. "Ted Cruz Using Firm That Harvested Data on Millions of Unwitting Facebook Users." *Guardian,* December 11. Accessed October 28, 2019. https://www.theguardian.com/us-news/2015/dec/11/senator-ted-cruz -president-campaign-facebook-user-data.

DeNoon, Daniel J. n.d. "Did CDC Conspire to Hide Vaccine Risk?" WebMD. Accessed October 28, 2019. https://www.webmd.com/children/vaccines/ news/20110227/did-cdc-conspire-to-hide-vaccine-risk#1.

DSPolitical. n.d. "About Us." Accessed October 28, 2019. https://www.dspolitical .com/about-us/.

EUGDPR. n.d. Accessed October 28, 2019. https://eugdpr.org/.

Help Net Security. 2019. "Consumers Concerned about Privacy but Willing to Take Risks for Convenience." April 3. Accessed October 28, 2019. https://www .helpnetsecurity.com/2019/04/03/consumers-concerned-about-privacy/.

Hern, Alex. 2018. "Cambridge Analytica: How Did It Turn Clicks into Votes?" *Guardian,* May 6. Accessed October 28, 2019. https://www.theguardian.com/ news/2018/may/06/cambridge-analytica-how-turn-clicks-into-votes-christo pher-wylie.

Hill, Kashmir. 2012. "How Target Figured Out a Teen Girl Was Pregnant Before Her Father Did." *Forbes,* February 16. Accessed October 28, 2019. https:// www.forbes.com/sites/kashmirhill/2012/02/16/how-target-figured-out-a -teen-girl-was-pregnant-before-her-father-did/#c4494a866686.

Hotez, Peter. 2019. "America and Europe's New Normal: The Return of Vaccine-Preventable Diseases." *Pediatric Research* 95: 912–914. Accessed October 28, 2019. https://www.nature.com/articles/s41390-019-0354-3.

Howard, Philip N. 2018. "How Political Campaigns Weaponize Social Media Bots." *IEEE Spectrum,* October 18. Accessed October 28, 2019. https://spectrum.ieee .org/computing/software/how-political-campaigns-weaponize-social-media-bots.

Isenberg, Arnold. 1973. "Deontology and the Ethics of Lying." In *Aesthetics and Theory of Criticism: Selected Essays of Arnold Isenberg,* by Arnold Isenberg, 245–264. Chicago: University of Chicago Press.

Kates, Graham. 2019. "'The Law Doesn't Protect You' or Your Financial Secrets, Says Cambridge Analytica Whistleblower." *CBS News*, October 23. Accessed October 28, 2019. https://www.cbsnews.com/news/the-law-doesnt-protect -your-most-private-financial-secrets-says-cambridge-analytica-whistleblower/.

Kramer, Adam D. I., Jamie E. Guillory, and Jeffrey T. Hancock. 2014. "Experimental Evidence of Massive-Scale Emotional Contagion through Social Networks." *Proceedings of the National Academy of Sciences*. 111, no. 24: 8788–8790. Accessed October 28, 2019. https://www.pnas.org/content/111/24/8788.full.

Lapowsky, Issie. 2016a. "A Lot of People Are Saying Trump's New Data Team Is Shady." *Wired*, August 15. Accessed October 28, 2019. https://www.wired .com/2016/08/trump-cambridge-analytica/.

———. 2016b. "Here's How Facebook Actually Won Trump the Presidency." *Wired*, November 15. Accessed October 28, 2019. https://www.wired.com/2016/11/ facebook-won-trump-election-not-just-fake-news/.

Lind, Dara. 2018. "The Conspiracy Theory That Led to the Pittsburgh Synagogue Shooting, Explained." Vox, October 29. Accessed October 28, 2019. https:// www.vox.com/2018/10/29/18037580/pittsburgh-shooter-anti-semitism-rac ist-jewish-caravan.

Matthews, Dylan. 2011. "Everything You Need to Know about the Fairnesss Doctrine in One Post." *Washington Post*, August 23. Accessed October 28, 2019. https://www.washingtonpost.com/blogs/ezra-klein/post/everything-you -need-to-know-about-the-fairness-doctrine-in-one-post/2011/08/23/gIQAN 8CXZJ_blog.html.

McCarville, Jill. 2018. "Wealth Data: 5 Ways to Learn More About Your Prospect's Capacity to Give." The Giving Institute, December 12. Accessed October 28, 2019. https://www.givinginstitute.org/news/431160/Wealth-Data-5-Ways-to -Learn-More-About-Your-Prospects-Capacity-to-Give.htm.

Meredith, Alisa. n.d. "How to Use Psychographics in Your Marketing: A Beginner's Guide." Hubspot. Accessed October 28, 2019. https://blog.hubspot.com/ insiders/marketing-psychographics.

Musil, Steven. 2019. "Maine Governor Signs Strict Internet Privacy Protection Bill." Cnet, June 6. Accessed October 28, 2019. https://www.cnet.com/news/ maine-governor-signs-internet-privacy-protection-bill/.

Nowak, Michael, and Dean Eckles. 2017. Determining user personality characteristics from social networking system communications and characteristics. US Patent 9740752 B2, filed June 3, 2016, and issued August 22, 2017.

Papova, Maria. 2016. "Lying in Politics: Hannah Arendt on Deception, Self-Deception, and the Psychology of Defactualization." Brain Pickings, June 15. accessed October 30, 2019. https://www.brainpickings.org/2016/06/15/lying-in-poli tics-hannah-arendt/.

PBS. n.d. "Yellow Journalism." n.d. Accessed October 28, 2019. https://www.pbs .org/crucible/bio_hearst.html.

Perez, Sarah. 2019. "TikTok Explains Its Ban on Politcal Advertising." TechCrunch, October 3. Accessed October 28, 2019. https://techcrunch.com/2019/10/03/ tiktok-explains-its-ban-on-political-advertising/.

Rainie, Lee, Scott Keeter, and Andrew Perrin. 2019. Pew Research Center, July 22. Accessed October 28, 2019. https://www.people-press.org/2019/07/22/trust-and-distrust-in-america/.

Rodriguez, Salvador. 2019. "Mark Zuckerberg: I Thought about Banning Political Ads from Facebook, but Decided Not To." CNBC, October 17. Accessed October 28, 2019. https://www.cnbc.com/2019/10/17/mark-zuckerberg-says-he-wont-ban-political-ads-on-facebook.html.

Romm, Tony, and Isaac Stanley-Becker. 2019. "Facebook Fine-tunes Disinformation Defenses but Leaves Controversial Political Ad Rules Intact." *Washington Post*, October 21. Accessed October 28, 2019. https://www.washingtonpost.com/technology/2019/10/21/facebook-fine-tunes-disinformation-defenses-but-leaves-controversial-political-ad-rules-intact/.

Scherer, Michael. 2012. "Friended: How the Obama Campaign Connected with Young Voters." *Time*, November 20. Accessed October 28, 2019. http://swampland.time.com/2012/11/20/friended-how-the-obama-campaign-connected-with-young-voters/.

Scott, Eugene. 2018. "2018: The Year of Dog Whistle Politics." *Washington Post*, November 14. Accessed October 28, 2019. https://www.washingtonpost.com/politics/2018/11/14/year-dog-whistle-politics/.

Shearer, Elisa, and Eva Katerina Matsa. 2018. "News Use Across Social Media Platforms 2018." Pew Research Center, September 10. Accessed October 28, 2019. https://www.journalism.org/2018/09/10/news-use-across-social-media-platforms-2018/.

"65% of Consumers Question How Brands Are Using Their Data." 2019. *Security Magazine*, July 18. Accessed October 28, 2019. https://www.securitymagazine.com/articles/90561-of-consumers-question-how-brands-are-using-their-data.

State of California, Department of Justice. n.d. California Consumer Privacy Act. Accessed October 28, 2019. https://oag.ca.gov/privacy/ccpa.

Symantec. 2019. "Control Versus Convenience: Consumers Weigh in on Their Own Privacy in New Norton LifeLock Report." March 27. Accessed October 28, 2019. https://investor.symantec.com/About/Investors/press-releases/press-release-details/2019/Control-Versus-Convenience-Consumers-Weigh-in-on-Their-Own-Privacy-in-New-Norton-LifeLock-Report/default.aspx.

Vincent, James. 2016. "Twitter Taught Microsoft's AI Chatbot to Be a Racist Asshole in Less Than a Day." The Verge, March 24. Accessed October 28, 2019. https://www.theverge.com/2016/3/24/11297050/tay-microsoft-chatbot-racist.

16

The Ethics of Lobbying

Matthew L. Johnson and Israel S. Klein

Background

In the 2005 film *Thank You for Smoking*, tobacco lobbyist Nick Naylor, played by Aaron Eckhart, testifies before a congressional hearing in opposition to adding warning labels to cigarette packages. He spars with the senators, telling them that smoking can offset Parkinson's disease, that the real number one killer of Americans is cholesterol, and that if cigarettes should have a warning label on them, so should Vermont's cheddar cheese.

Legendary film critic Roger Ebert wrote of the film, "The target of the movie is not so much tobacco as lobbying in general, which along with advertising and spin-control makes a great many evils palatable to the population."[1]

Movies like *Thank You for Smoking* and TV shows like *House of Cards* portray lobbying, and politics generally, in a negative light. The truth is that Hollywood and the media give a distorted view of the reality of lobbying. Although there are undoubtedly some lobbyists (like those discussed here) who give the profession a bad name, they are the minority.

In 2006 lobbyist Jack Abramoff pled guilty to conspiracy, fraud, and tax evasion for offering gifts to government officials, funneling donations to lawmakers, and conspiring with former congressional staff members to engage in lobbying prior to the expiration of their one-year lobbying ban.[2] In 2011 Paul Magliocchetti was sentenced to twenty-seven months in prison for contributing hundreds of thousands of dollars in illegal donations through third parties in an effort to increase his lobbying firm's prestige and curry influence.[3] More recently, in 2019 Paul Manafort was sent to jail for failing to register as a foreign agent or lobbyist on behalf of the Ukrainian government.[4] Like a baseball umpire who makes a bad call, the public only knows a lobbyist's name when that person messes up. One result is that the public has a negative view of the profession.

Public Opinion of Lobbyists

Public opinion of lobbying has deteriorated over recent decades. The earliest recorded public opinion poll about lobbying was taken by Gallup in 1949. The poll asked, "Will you tell me what a lobbyist in Washington is?" Fifty-five percent of respondents provided generally correct answers identifying the role/function of a lobbyist.[5] Only 2 percent of respondents described a lobbyist as someone who seeks favors or special privileges from Congress or used derogatory language to describe lobbyists. Years later, in 1990 a *USA Today* poll asked how much of a threat lobbying in politics posed to American democracy. While 29 percent said that lobbying is no threat at all to democracy, 43 percent said it was a somewhat serious threat, and 21 percent said it was a very serious threat.[6]

More recent polling puts lobbying in an even more negative light. A 2011 Gallup poll found that 71 percent of Americans think lobbyists have too much power and influence in society.[7] A 2017 poll found that only 8 percent of Americans believe lobbyists have very high or high standards for honest and ethical behavior. That number was actually an all-time high mark. The rest of the 2017 Gallup data, shown in figure 16.1, show lobbyists performing poorly compared to other professions.[8]

It's worth noting that most Americans have never met a lobbyist. However, the profession's reputation is so poor that it still consistently ranks as the least trusted in America. In modern times, members of Congress also consistently rank poorly in public opinion polls. While most people consider their own member of Congress to be trustworthy, they think of other members of Congress and Congress in general poorly. What in the past was hardly talked about outside of Washington has become a highly salient issue nationwide. In fact, a 2018 Pew Research poll found that 47 percent of Americans think that reducing the influence of lobbyists and

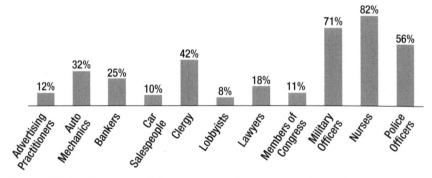

Figure 16.1.   Percent of Americans who view each profession as having very high/high honesty and ethical standards.

special interest groups in Washington should be a top priority for Congress and President Donald Trump.[9]

This change in public opinion about lobbying is mirrored in statements by public officials. Then-senator John F. Kennedy said in 1956: "Lobbyists are in many cases expert technicians and capable of explaining complex and difficult subjects in a clear, understandable fashion. They engage in personal discussions with Members of Congress in which they can explain in detail the reasons for positions they advocate. . . . [They] serve a very useful purpose and have assumed an important role in the legislative process."[10]

Today, a majority of 2020 Democratic presidential candidates won't take political contributions from registered federal lobbyists, and the latter have become a bipartisan punching bag. Senator Bernie Sanders, in his 2016 campaign, said, "A handful of super-wealthy campaign contributors have enormous influence over the political process, while their lobbyists determine much of what goes on in Congress."[11] Rhetoric like this is becoming commonplace, but it is also grossly oversimplified. Nick Allard, a lobbyist and the former dean of Brooklyn Law School, wrote in 2014: "Lobby bashing is almost irresistible in the present climate—like scratching a rash. While it may feel good at the time, it actually makes things worse. It breeds distrust of Government at a time when building trust is needed."[12]

In the authors' experience, the vast majority of lobbyists behave ethically. Nevertheless, scandals and the steady stream of former lawmakers and staff becoming lobbyists fuel the negative impression of the industry. An article in the *Atlantic* stated in May 2018: "Of the nearly four dozen lawmakers who left office after the 2016 election, one-fourth stayed in Washington, and one in six became lobbyists. . . . The numbers were even higher for those who departed after the 2014 midterms."[13] The media's focus on lobbying by large corporations does not help the public perception of the profession, either. But the fact is that all different types of organizations have lobbyists who advocate for their policy preferences. Hundreds of groups, like the World Wildlife Fund, American Heart Association, and Catholic Charities of America, spend millions of dollars on lobbying each year. Typically, there are lobbyists on every side of a given issue. No one interest has a monopoly on lobbying or advocacy. This chapter provides an overview of the lobbying profession and examines ethical issues in the field of lobbying.

What Is Lobbying?

Lobbying is an attempt to influence government action through communication. Nick Allard notes: "The most basic function of the lobbyist is to educate by providing information."[14] The practice of lobbying is older than America itself. Jacob Straus of the Congressional Research Service wrote in

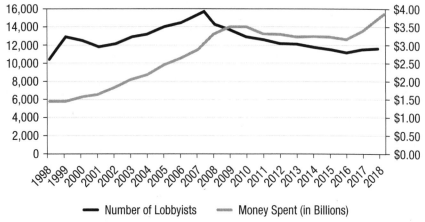

— Number of Lobbyists ▬▬ Money Spent (in Billions)

Figure 16.2. Registered lobbyists and spending per year.

2015: "The right of citizens to petition government has long been considered a protected and fundamental aspect of the citizen-government dynamic. The right to petition government was so deeply rooted in American life, that while it was not explicitly addressed in the Constitution, it was immediately included in the Bill of Rights"[15] in the First Amendment.

Lobbying spending, defined as expenditures spent on lobbying services by a registered client, has increased nationally. This does not include campaign contributions, discussed later in this chapter. While the number of federal lobbyists has decreased since its peak in 2007, lobbying expenditures are approaching an all-time high. Figure 16.2 illustrates the trend using data from the Center for Responsive Politics.

How much a company or industry decides to spend on lobbying per year typically depends on the size of that industry/company/organization and if there are any controversies or major pieces of legislation about its area of concern being considered by Congress. For some general perspective, table 16.1 shows the cumulative top five lobbying spenders for companies and industries since 1998, according to the Center for Responsive Politics.

Table 16.1. Top Lobbying Spenders

Top Lobbying Industries Since 1998	Top Lobbying Groups Since 1998
Pharmaceuticals/health products	US Chamber of Commerce
Insurance	National Association of Realtors
Electric utilities	American Medical Association
Electronic manufacturers/equipment	American Hospital Association
Business associations	PhRMA

These data reveal a few things. First, the top two industries in terms of lobbying and three of the top five associations are related to health care. Health care is a constant topic of conversation on Capitol Hill. According to a November 2018 Gallup poll, health care is the most important issue to voters.[16] According to the Centers for Medicare and Medicaid Services, health-care spending was almost 18 percent of GDP in 2017 and is projected to be 19.5 percent of GDP in 2027.[17] The other trend to note is that these companies or associations all represent various business interests. Since 2013, all but one of the top five yearly lobbying spenders has been a public corporation or business association. According to preeminent lobbying scholar Lee Drutman in 2015, "For every dollar spent on lobbying by labor unions and public-interest groups together, large corporations and their association now spend $34. Of the 100 organizations that spend the most on lobbying, 95 consistently represent business."[18] While these numbers may have changed slightly since that statement was made, it's clear that lobbying is seen as an important business expenditure for corporations. Therefore, it is no surprise that the US Chamber of Commerce has been by far the single largest lobbying spender in Washington over the past two decades. The group, which represents business interests broadly, has spent $1.5 billion in lobbying since 1998. The next closest entity is the National Association of Realtors, which spent $568 million.[19] To provide some context, labor unions as a whole have spent $839 million on lobbying in the same time period,[20] split among nearly one hundred public sector, transportation, industrial, and building trades, and miscellaneous unions. Whether it be through a corporate office in DC or through a hired lobbyist, major businesses are generally well-represented in Washington. Three case studies illustrate how companies lobby when their industry is under increased scrutiny by lawmakers.

Case Studies

In 2012, President Barack Obama signed the bipartisan Jumpstart Our Business Startups Act, aka the JOBS Act. This legislation made it easier for emerging businesses to raise capital (especially through means like crowdfunding), loosened SEC regulations on small businesses, and was intended to spur investment. The bill passed 73–26 in the Senate, with 27 Democrats joining all Republicans in voting for the bill.[21] In the House, the bill passed with a bipartisan 390–23 majority.[22] While the bill was somewhat controversial, its passing in such a bipartisan fashion can be attributed to a small but focused lobbying effort. According to the Lobbying Disclosure Act Database, 136 companies or associations mentioned the JOBS Act by bill number in their 2012 LDA reports.[23] These groups spent a combined $858 million lobbying on a variety of issues that year. Groups that mentioned the JOBS Act in their lobbying that year include names that would make sense for legislation involving investment and the technology industry: business associations, startups, banks, and finance groups. However, others who lobbied on this piece of legislation include the AFL-CIO, the Nuclear Energy Institute, General Motors, and the American Apparel & Footwear Association.

The next example is not as clear-cut in terms of winning and losing. Much of congressional attention in 2009 was centered on the Patient Protection and Affordable Care Act (aka Obamacare). The *New York Times* described the bill as "the most expansive social legislation enacted in decades."[24] Undoubtedly Obamacare had a massive impact on the healthcare system in the United States. Therefore, it should be no surprise that lobbyists from a variety of industries tried to influence and shape the legislation. An analysis by the Center for Public Integrity of Senate lobbying disclosure forms found "that more than 1,750 companies and organizations hired about 4,525 lobbyists—eight for each member of Congress—to influence health reform bills in 2009."[25] The analysis found that 207 hospitals, 105 insurance companies, 85 manufacturing companies, and 745 trade/advocacy organizations lobbied on the bill. Consumer advocates, unions, and patient groups also lobbied on the bill. According to Beth Leen, a Rutgers University professor who specializes in lobbying, a typical issue in Washington usually attracts fifteen interest groups.[26] Per the Center for Responsive Politics, the top industry by far in terms of lobbying that year was pharmaceuticals/health products.[27] That industry spent more than $271 million on lobbying. PhRMA, Pfizer, Blue Cross/Blue Shield, AARP, the American Medical Association, and the American Hospital Association made up six of the top ten lobbying spenders that year.[28]

Recently technology and social media companies have come under increased scrutiny on Capitol Hill. Silicon Valley giants like Facebook, Amazon, Apple, and Google have been the subject of hearings and investigations into issues ranging from data privacy to antitrust. Their lobbying spending has correspondingly increased. In 2012, for example, the four companies spent a combined $26.54 million on lobbying. In 2018 the four companies spent a combined $55.47 million.[29] As these companies grew and became increasingly central components of the US economy, so did their presence in Washington, DC. A June 2019 *New York Times* headline that declared "Tech Giants Amass a Lobbying Army for an Epic Washington Battle"[30] adequately describes the current situation. Tech companies have become sophisticated lobbying machines, with policy interests far more diverse than when they opened their first DC outposts. For example, in its 2019 second-quarter lobbying disclosure, Google revealed that it had lobbied on the following issues: advertising, copyright, consumer issues, education, foreign relations, health issues, homeland security, immigration, labor issues, science/technology, small business, telecommunications, trade, criminal justice, and taxation.[31]

Campaign Contributions

While this chapter is largely focused on lobbying, it is worth noting that there are other political activities that relate to lobbying. One is campaign contributions from individuals or political action committees (PACs). It is important to note that campaign contributions over $200 are required to be disclosed and are listed on the Federal Election Commission website. In addition, lobbyists are required to disclose campaign contributions semiannually. The Hollywood depiction of lobbyists and campaign contributions usually portrays a corrupt system that involves a quid pro quo relationship. However, as Nick Allard writes, "The simple truth is that our government cannot be bought. If it were that easy—if all it took to prevail was to buy a few steaks, sponsor a golf trip, or make campaign contributions—then anyone could do it, and there would be no reason to hire a professional lobbyist."[32]

While the largest spenders in elections are partisan groups, labor, business, or industry-specific interest groups can spend independently in elections as well. This is largely done through PACs. In 2018, excluding explicitly partisan groups, the ten largest PAC sources for campaign contributions to Democratic candidates included the American Association for Justice (the leading lobby organization for plaintiffs' attorneys), the National Association of Realtors, and eight unions, the biggest donor being the International Brotherhood of Electrical Workers.[33] For Republicans, among the top ten PACs were the American Bankers Association, National Auto Dealers Association, AT&T, and the National Beer Wholesalers Association.[34] In 2018, of the twenty candidates who received the most personal donations from lobbyists, fourteen were Democrats.[35]

Types of Lobbyists

There are different types of lobbyists and lobbying firms. In general, lobbyists are divided into two distinct types: in-house lobbyists and external or contract lobbyists. In-house lobbyists are employed by businesses or organizations to lobby full-time on behalf of their employers or clients. An example of this is a Comcast employee who is a registered lobbyist and lobbies solely for Comcast. External lobbyists may work for a lobbying firm or work solo and lobby on behalf of their clients. An external lobbyist will usually have multiple clients for which they lobby. A lobbyist could specialize in a particular industry or have a broad base of clients. The authors built their firm to represent clients in a variety of industries. Lobbying clients can be businesses, nonprofits, trade associations, unions, state or local governments, individuals, or even foreign entities.

There are also many different types of lobbying firms. Lobbying firms can be single party (only employing Republicans or Democrats) or bipartisan, large or small, broad based or issue specific, or part of a law firm or larger public affairs firm or stand alone.

The Ethics of Lobbying

Lobbyists, like journalists, are not licensed. Both have a First Amendment right to their expression. Lobbyists do not take a bar exam as lawyers do and do not have any educational requirements. There are no ethics requirements or code of conduct other than the US criminal code. Plenty of moral gray areas exist in the field of lobbying, and lobbyists have to use their own judgment. The only affirmative legal requirement for lobbying in general is disclosure. This disclosure is mandated by the Lobbying Disclosure Act (LDA) and Foreign Agents Registration Act (FARA). Federally registered lobbyists disclose all of their lobbying clients and what they pay their firms quarterly. They also disclose their federal campaign contributions. Both of these disclosure documents can be found on public websites maintained by the US House of Representatives and Senate.

Laws Regulating Lobbying

Lobbying is governed and defined by the Lobbying Disclosure Act of 1995. A federal lobbying registration is required if "any individual (1) who is either employed or retained by a client for financial or other compensation (2) whose services include more than one lobbying contact; and (3) whose lobbying activities constitute 20 percent or more of his or her time in services for that client over any three-month period."[36] The act defines lobbying contact as "any oral, written, or electronic communication to a covered official that is made on behalf of a client," while lobbying activities include lobbying contacts and "preparation or planning activities, research, and other background work that is intended, at the time of its preparation, for use in contacts, and coordination with the lobbying activities of others."

This definition sometimes produces confusion, but essentially if an individual is paid, meets with government officials twice, and spends 20 percent of his or her time with a client lobbying, he or she must register as a lobbyist. Lobbying requirements vary greatly at the state level.[37]

The Foreign Agents Registration Act (FARA) of 1938 requires individuals who act on behalf of a "foreign principal" to register if they meet a wide variety of criteria. Foreign principal applies not only to foreign governments, but also to foreign political parties, foreign nationals, and certain foreign-based businesses.[38] Furthermore, acting on behalf of a foreign principal does not solely refer to lobbying, but also to advising, public relations work, or other nonlobbying types of consulting. Covington and Burling wrote in their 2019 FARA guide that "FARA is a complicated, arcane, and loosely worded statute. Whether registration is triggered is highly fact dependent, turning on whether agency exists, the nature of the activities conducted by the agent, and whether any of FARA's amorphous 'exemptions' apply."[39] Lobbyists who lobby on behalf of foreign entities that are not governments or political parties register under the aforementioned LDA regime, a key exemption to FARA. Therefore, there are only about 450 active FARA registrations (compared to about 18,000 LDA registrations), mostly for public relations work. Work on behalf of foreign governments or individuals can be lucrative but fleeting and resource intensive. However, there could be some situations in which lobbyists have to register under FARA.

A few other regulations exist for lobbyists. A recent one is the Justice Against Corruption on K Street Act (known as the JACK Act), passed in 2019 in response to Jack Abramoff's post-prison lobbying activity. This act requires registered lobbyists to disclose a lobbyist's convictions for federal or state criminal offenses such as bribery, extortion, embezzlement, and tax evasion.[40] Finally, the Honest Leadership and Open Government Act became law in 2007.[41] This act increased disclosure requirements, placed restrictions on gifts from lobbyists, and required mandatory disclosure of earmarks in expenditure bills. This act also increased the cooling-off period for former members of Congress and their staff.

This cooling-off period is also known as a "lobbying ban." The Senate Select Committee on Ethics summarizes: "Former Senators are banned for two years from contacting the Senate and House of Representatives. Former officers and 'senior staff' are banned for one year from contacting only the Senate. And all former Senate employees, even if not senior," cannot lobby their former office for one year.[42] The House Committee on Ethics specifies that for one year, former members "may not seek official action from any current Member, officer, or employee of either the Senate or the House," while former staffers cannot lobby their former offices for one year.[43] An executive order issued by President Trump shortly after taking office prohibits political appointees in his administration from lobbying their former agencies for five years after leaving the executive branch, lobbying the administration for the remainder of its term, lobbying that would require FARA registration in perpetuity, and engaging in any activity for two years related to their role in the administration.[44] An executive order issued on the first day of President Barack Obama's term prohibited political appointees from lobbying the administration for the remainder of its term and from lobbying for two years after leaving government.[45] It should be noted that there is no post-administration enforcement mechanism for an executive order.

Revolving Door

Lobbying bans are in place to address the "revolving door," which refers to former government officials becoming lobbyists and lobbyists becoming government officials and lobbying their former government offices or departments. According to a 2011 analysis from research at the London School of Economics, 41.6 percent of all registered lobbyists have prior government experience. Furthermore, the study found that 22.9 percent of lobbyists are former congressional staffers.[46] Another study looked at the employment of former members of Congress from 1976 to 2012. The study found that 27 percent of former House members and 31 percent of senators became registered lobbyists. The researchers found that party and committee leaders are more likely to become lobbyists.[47] A more recent analysis by the Center for Responsive Politics identified companies in the health, finance, and electronics industries as the most likely to hire lobbyists with prior government experience.[48] It should surprise no one that a large percentage of lobbyists have government experience, since a lobbyist's job is to help organizations navigate the federal government. On Capitol Hill and in an administration, time is a limited resource, and with so many complicated issues to tackle, it is impossible to be an expert on all of them as a member of Congress or staff member. A survey by the Policy Counsel found that more than two-thirds of congressional staffers say that lobbyists are "necessary to the process" and are viewed as "collaborators" or "educators."[49]

Clients

Returning to the introductory vignette about the fictional tobacco lobbyist in *Thank You for Smoking*, how does one decide what company or cause he or she will lobby on behalf of? Are there issues that a lobbyist may want to avoid? Are there other issues a lobbyist would work pro bono to further? Does a person who has chosen to be a lobbyist have any choice in who or what she or he represents? What are the consequences of declining to work on certain issues or for certain clients?

Many individuals at large lobbying, law, or public relations firms may not have the option to say "no" to working with a personally objectionable client if they want to keep their jobs. These firms may or may not give employees the opportunity to decline projects they find objectionable. However, some lobbyists may have bright lines that are respected by their employers. For example, some may not be interested in working on foreign government clients or tobacco or alcohol companies. Other lobbyists may not want to work on ideological issues such as the death penalty or abortion.

A business, foreign country, or ideological interest group is entitled to petition the federal government but is not entitled to employ a particular lobbyist. A lobbyist might not want to jeopardize his or her reputation or an existing client's interests with questionable new client engagements. Firms have different priorities and different values.

Another bright line a lobbyist could set is not to take on a client that disagrees with the position of a former boss. This dynamic is particularly present when a lobbyist is a former congressional staffer. However, not taking on a client that disagrees with a former boss may not be a tenable position. Often the reason a particular lobbyist is hired is because of his or her relationship with a former boss and expertise in a particular issue. In addition, as a congressional staffer you might not have agreed with everything the boss said, but there is an expectation for you to toe the company line while on staff. As a lobbyist, you are expected to bring your expertise to the table to help a client. The job may also require presenting a position on an issue to your former boss that may be in conflict with his or her previous positions.

While there are many companies and trade associations that seek out lobbying help, there are also scores of countries that, either through their embassies in Washington or their foreign ministries, seek to lobby the US federal government. This may be to bolster or guide their own diplomatic efforts and can be traditional "shoe-leather"[50] lobbying, public and media relations, or developing relationships with think tanks and other nongovernmental organizations. Disclosure of these engagements is governed by FARA, not just the LDA. Acting as an agent for a foreign government without registering, accepting funds, and still trying to influence policy makers inside and outside the federal government is *not* a gray area of the law.

Comparisons to Law

It is instructive to compare the ethical obligations of lobbyists and lawyers. While both represent clients and are related to law, the professions have several key distinctions. Lawyers must earn and maintain a professional license, which requires a law degree, passing the bar exam, and being licensed to practice in a particular jurisdiction. Lobbying requires no credential, license, or degree. According to the American Bar Association's most recent National Lawyer Population survey, about 56,000 lawyers are licensed to practice in DC, and there are 1.35 million lawyers in the United States.[51] Last year, there were 11,655 federal lobbyists.[52]

In the law there are bar associations and clearly defined ethics. These are either organized by jurisdiction or for various special interests. Membership in state bar associations can be mandatory or voluntary. In general, these act as professional associations that provide services like continuing education, setting ethical rules for practitioners, and enforcing the professional code of conduct. A bar association can suspend a lawyer's license for unethical behavior. There is no equivalent for lobbyists. Formerly, the Association of Government Relations Professionals published a code of ethics and provided continuing education certificates.[53] When this organization shut down in 2016, The National Institute for Lobbying and Ethics was formed as a successor to "serve the needs of advocacy professionals by offering a professional association and an avenue for continuing education."[54] While its efforts should be applauded, it is not functionally analogous to state bar associations or the American Bar Association.

Another difference between lawyers and lobbyists is that in law, there is a principle that anyone involved in a legal trial deserves a zealous advocate. As a lawyer, you are not necessarily defined by the clients you take. If you work at a large law firm, you could be assigned a client you don't like. And as a public defender, you are assigned a variety of clients whom you might not voluntarily take on. However, the ethical obligation of a lawyer is to represent the client as a zealous advocate. Importantly, the ABA Model Rules of Professional Conduct state: "A lawyer's representation of a client, including the representation by appointment, does not constitute an endorsement of the client's political, economic, social, or moral views or activities."[55]

As discussed previously, a lobbyist can choose the clients to represent. And these clients will reflect on a lobbyist's reputation. Representing someone on Capitol Hill, before a federal agency, or at the White House is very different from representing someone in a court of law. There are heightened reputational concerns for a lobbyist depending on the clients he or she takes on. Lobbyists also may take on clients that interest them personally. This can be done either pro bono or for a fee. Pro bono work is more common in the legal profession than in lobbying.

Finally, there is a distinction between how conflicts of interest are dealt with in law and with lobbyists. Rule 1.7 of The DC Rules of Professional Conduct clearly states: "A lawyer shall not advance two or more adverse positions in the same matter."[56] At some large lobbying firms, internal firewalls may exist that might result in two conflicting clients being represented. However, other firms operate with a default of asking for permission from legacy clients, not forgiveness. If a new potential client is tangentially related to an existing client, it is recommended to have an open and honest conversation with the existing client to make sure that client is comfortable with any arrangement you are proposing.

Why It Is in a Lobbyist's Best Interest to Be Ethical

Not only should a lobbyist be ethical for morality's sake, it is also best for business. Richard Branson once said, "All you have in business is your reputation—so it's very important that you keep your word."[57] To be a successful lobbyist, it is best practice to be trustworthy and honest. Julie Reynolds explained in *Washington Lawyer* in 2006, "In lobbying, credibility and reputation are the coin of the realm—a lobbyist cannot be effective if his contact believes him untrustworthy or unprepared. Missteps in integrity or information can be disastrous for a lobbyist's career."[58]

This is so because most lobbying, in the terms of game theory, is an iterated, or repeated, game. Mikhael Shor, an economics professor at the University of Connecticut, defines an iterated game as one "when players interact a similar stage game numerous times. . . . Unlike a game played once, a repeated game allows for a strategy to be contingent on past moves, thus allowing for reputation effects and retribution."[59] Practically, a Hill office or government agency will remember you from when you came in last time. They will remember what you said, if what you said turned out to be true, and if you shared information they gave you in confidence. This interaction also plays out with clients and potential clients. In repeated interactions, maintaining your reputation is paramount. If you destroy your credibility for a single win, you're likely not going to last a long time in this business.

Notes

Our first intern and current associate, Jeremy Marsh, along with our summer policy fellows, Rachael Packard, Caroline Rao, and Lily Martin, helped us to research and assemble the materials for this chapter. We are grateful for their hard work and Jeremy's help in keeping us on track.

1 Jason Reitman, dir., *Thank You for Smoking* (Beverly Hills, CA: Room 9 Entertainment, 2006), film.

2 Anne E. Kornblut, "G.O.P. Lobbyist Pleads Guilty in Deal With Prosecutors," *New York Times*, January 3, 2006, https://www.nytimes.com/2006/01/03/politics/gop-lobbyist-pleads-guilty-in-deal-with-prosecutors.html.

3 Department of Justice, "Lobbyist Sentenced to 27 Months in Prison for Role in Illegal Campaign Contribution Scheme," January 7, 2011, https://www.justice.gov/opa/pr/lobbyist-sentenced-27-months-prison-role-illegal-campaign-contribution-scheme.

4 Brian Bennett, "Paul Manafort's Sentence May Start Cleaning Up the Shady Lobbying He Pioneered," *Time*, March 13, 2019, https://time.com/5550831/paul-manafort-sentencing-lobbying/.

5 Gallup Organization, Gallup Poll, March 1949, https://ropercenter-cornell-edu.proxygw.wrlc.org/CFIDE/cf/action/ipoll/questionDetail.cfm?keyword=lobby%20or%20lobbying%20or%20lobbyist&keywordoptions=1&exclude=&excludeOptions=1&topic=Any&organization=Any&label=&fromdate=1/1/1935&to-Date=&stitle=&sponsor=&studydate=March%2019-24,%201949&sample=1500&qstn_list=&qstnid=8837&qa_list=&qstn_id4=8837&study_list=&lastSearchId=317679018585&archno=USAIPO1949-0439&keywordDisplay=.

6 Gordon Black/USA Today Poll, June 1990, https://ropercenter-cornell-edu.proxygw.wrlc.org/CFIDE/cf/action/ipoll/questionDetail.cfm?keyword=lobby%20or%20lobbying%20or%20lobbyist&keywordoptions=1&exclude=&excludeOptions=1&topic=Any&organization=Any&label=&fromdate=1/1/1935&

toDate=&stitle=&sponsor=USA%20Today&studydate=June%2025-26,%20
1990&sample=811&qstn_list=&qstnid=220563&qa_list=&qstn_id4=220563&
study_list=&lastSearchId=317679018585&archno=USUSATY1990-3213&key
wordDisplay=.

7 "Americans Decry Power of Lobbyists, Corporations, Banks, Feds" Gallup Organization, April 11, 2011, https://news.gallup.com/poll/147026/americans-de
cry-power-lobbyists-corporations-banks-feds.aspx.

8 Jeff Jones and Lydia Saad, "2017 Honesty and Ethics," Gallup Organization,
December 4–11, 2017, https://news.gallup.com/poll/224645/2017-honesty
-ethics.aspx.

9 "Economic Issues Decline Among Public's Policy Priorities," Pew Research Center, January 2018, https://www.people-press.org/wp-content/uploads/sites/4/
2018/01/1-25-18-Priorities-release1.pdf.

10 Senator John F. Kennedy, "To Keep the Lobbyist Within Bounds," https://
tinyurl.com/JFKLobbyQuote.

11 Senator Bernie Sanders, "Speech on Democratic Socialism" (Washington, DC,
November 19, 2015), Common Dreams, https://www.commondreams.org/
news/2015/11/19/sanders-delivers-speech-democratic-socialism.

12 Nick Allard, "The Seven Deadly Virtues of Lobbying," *Election Law Journal* 13,
no. 1 (2014): 210–219, https://brooklynworks.brooklaw.edu/cgi/viewcontent
.cgi?referer=https://www.google.com/&httpsredir=1&article=1532&context=
faculty.

13 Russell Berman, "An Exodus from Congress Tests the Lure of Lobbying," *Atlantic*, May 1, 2018, https://www.theatlantic.com/politics/archive/2018/05/lob
bying-the-job-of-choice-for-retired-members-of-congress/558851/.

14 Nick Allard, "Lobbying Is an Honorable Profession: The Right to Petition and
the Competition to be Right," *Stanford Law & Policy Review* 19 (2008): 23–68,
https://brooklynworks.brooklaw.edu/faculty/43/.

15 Jacob R. Straus, "The Lobbying Disclosure Act at 20: Analysis and Issues for Congress," Congressional Research Service, December 1, 2015, https://fas.org/sgp/
crs/misc/R44292.pdf.

16 Frank Newport, "Top Issues for Voters: Healthcare, Economy, Immigration," Gallup Organization, November 2, 2018, https://news.gallup.com/poll/244367/
top-issues-voters-healthcare-economy-immigration.aspx.

17 "NHE Fact Sheet," Centers for Medicare & Medicaid Services, April 26, 2019,
https://www.cms.gov/research-statistics-data-and-systems/statistics-trends-and
-reports/nationalhealthexpenddata/nhe-fact-sheet.html.

18 Lee Drutman, "How Corporate Lobbyists Conquered American Democracy,"
Atlantic, April 20, 2015, https://www.theatlantic.com/business/archive/2015/
04/how-corporate-lobbyists-conquered-american-democracy/390822/.

19 "Top Spenders," Center for Responsive Politics, September 19, 2019, https://
www.opensecrets.org/lobby/top.php?showYear=a&indexType=s.

20 "Labor: Lobbying, 2019," Center for Responsive Politics, https://www.open
secrets.org/industries/lobbying.php?cycle=2020&ind=P.

21 "Reopening American Capital Markets to Emerging Growth Companies Act of
2011: Roll Vote No. 55," March 22, 2012, https://www.senate.gov/legislative/

LIS/roll_call_lists/roll_call_vote_cfm.cfm?congress=112&session=2& vote=00055.

22 "Reopening American Capital Markets to Emerging Growth Companies Act of 2011: Roll Vote No. 110," March 8, 2012, http://clerk.house.gov/evs/2012/ roll110.xml.

23 "Query the Lobbying Disclosure Act Database," US Senate, https://soprweb .senate.gov/index.cfm?event=processSearchCriteria.

24 Sheryl Gay Stolberg and Robert Pear, "Obama Signs Health Care Overhaul Bill, with a Flourish," *New York Times*, March 23, 2010, https://www.nytimes .com/2010/03/24/health/policy/24health.html?_r=0.

25 Joe Eaton and M. B. Pell, "Lobbyists Swarm Capitol to Influence Health Reform," The Center for Public Integrity, February 24, 2010, https://publicintegrity.org/ health/lobbyists-swarm-capitol-to-influence-health-reform/.

26 Lewis Krauskopf, "Demands to Alter Obamacare Persist Even as Launch Nears," Reuters, August 23, 2013, https://www.reuters.com/article/us-usa-health care-lobbying/demands-to-alter-obamacare-persist-even-as-launch-nears-idUS BRE97M0UJ20130823.

27 "Top Industries, 2009," Center for Responsive Politics, https://www.opensecrets .org/lobby/top.php?showYear=2009&indexType=i.

28 "Top Spenders, 2009," Center for Responsive Politics, https://www.opensecrets .org/lobby/top.php?indexType=s&showYear=2009.

29 "Lobbying Database," Center for Responsive Politics, n.d., https://www.open secrets.org/lobby/.

30 Cecilia Kang and Kenneth P. Vogel, "Tech Giants Amass a Lobbying Army for an Epic Washington Battle," *New York Times*, June 5, 2019, https://www.nytimes .com/2019/06/05/us/politics/amazon-apple-facebook-google-lobbying.html.

31 "Lobbying Report," Clerk of the House of Representatives, Secretary of the Senate, July 22, 2019, https://soprweb.senate.gov/index.cfm?event=getFiling Details&filingID=65FBB30E-D962-4675-B879-4CE1E3329D85&filing TypeID=60.

32 Nick Allard, "Lobbying Is an Honorable Profession: The Right to Petition and the Competition to be Right," *Stanford Law & Policy Review* 19 (2008): 23–68, https://brooklynworks.brooklaw.edu/faculty/43/.

33 "Top 20 PAC Contributors to Democratic Candidates, 2017–2018," Center for Responsive Politics, https://www.opensecrets.org/pacs/toppacs.php ?Type=C&pac=A&cycle=2018&Pty=D.

34 "Top 20 PAC Contributors to Republican Candidates, 2017–2018," Center for Responsive Politics, https://www.opensecrets.org/pacs/toppacs.php ?Type=C&pac=A&cycle=2018&Pty=R.

35 "Lobbyists: Top Recipients," Center for Responsive Politics, https://www.open secrets.org/industries/recips.php?ind=K02&recipdetail=A&sortorder= U&mem=Y&cycle=2018.

36 "Lobbying Disclosure Act Guidance," Committee on Ethics, US House of Representatives, January 1, 2008, rev. January 31, 2017, https://lobbyingdisclosure .house.gov/amended_lda_guide.html.

37 "50 State Chart: Lobbyist Activity Report Requirements," National Conference of State Legislatures, May 15, 2018, http://www.ncsl.org/research/eth ics/50-state-chart-lobbyist-report-requirements.aspx.
38 "General FARA Frequently Asked Questions," US Department of Justice, https://www.justice.gov/nsd-fara/general-fara-frequently-asked-questions#3.
39 "The Foreign Agents Registration Act ("FARA"): A Guide for the Perplexed," Covington & Burling LLP, July 26, 2019, https://www.cov.com/-/media/files/ corporate/publications/2018/01/the_foreign_agents_registration_act_fara_a_ guide_for_the_perplexed.pdf.
40 Robert Kelner, Robert Lenhard, Zachary G. Parks, Derek Lawlor, and Brady Bender, "Congress Amends LDA Forms to Require Reporting of Lobbyist Convictions," Covington & Burling LLP, April 8, 2019, https://www.inside politicallaw.com/2019/04/08/congress-amends-lda-forms-to-require-reporting -of-lobbyist-convictions/.
41 Honest Leadership and Open Government Act of 2007, H.R. 2316, 110th Cong. (2007), https://www.congress.gov/bill/110th-congress/house-bill/2316.
42 "Guidance on the Post-Employment Contact Ban," Select Committee on Ethics, US Senate, May 24, 2012, https://www.ethics.senate.gov/public/index.cfm/ files/serve?File_id=bf9ea0f9-2593-4f49-83b3-f581f86b9098.
43 "Post-Employment Restrictions," Committee on Ethics, US House of Representatives, https://ethics.house.gov/outside-employment-income/post-employment -restrictions#emp_scope_restrictions.
44 "Ethics Commitments by Executive Branch Appointees," Exec. Order No. 13,770 (Jan. 28, 2017), https://www.whitehouse.gov/presidential-actions/executive-or der-ethics-commitments-executive-branch-appointees/.
45 "Ethics Commitments by Executive Branch Personnel," Exec. Order No. 13,490 (Jan. 21, 2009), https://obamawhitehouse.archives.gov/the-press-office/ethics -commitments-executive-branch-personnel.
46 Jordi Blanes i Vidal, Mirko Draca, and Christian Fons-Rosen, "Revolving Door Lobbyists," May 2011, http://personal.lse.ac.uk/blanesiv/revolving.pdf.
47 Lazarus, Jeffrey, and Amy Melissa McKay, and Lindsey C. Herbel, "Who Goes Through the 'Revolving Door'? Examining the Lobbying Activity of Former Congress Members and Staffers" (paper presented at American Political Science Association Annual Meeting2013), https://papers.ssrn.com/sol3/papers.cfm?ab stract_id=2300276.
48 "Top Industries," Center for Responsive Politics, n.d., https://www.opensecrets .org/revolving/top.php?display=I.
49 The Policy Council, "Changing of the Guard: 2007 State of the Industry for Lobbying and Advocacy," 2007.
50 Lobbying focused on one-on-one meetings with congressional staff and elected officials, which requires a lot of walking the halls and wearing out the leather on the soles of one's shoes.
51 "ABA National Lawyer Population Survey," American Bar Assocation, 2019, https://www.americanbar.org/content/dam/aba/administrative/market_ research/national-lawyer-population-by-state-2019.pdf.
52 "Lobbying Database."

53 "Code of Ethics," Association of Government Relations Professionals, n.d., http://grprofessionals.org/join-agrp/code-of-ethics.

54 "About Us," The National Institute for Lobbying & Ethics, n.d., https://lobby inginstitute.com/about-us/.

55 "Rule 1.2: Scope of Representation & Allocation of Authority Between Client & Lawyer," American Bar Assocation, n.d., https://www.americanbar.org/ groups/professional_responsibility/publications/model_rules_of_professional_ conduct/rule_1_2_scope_of_representation_allocation_of_authority_between_ client_lawyer/.

56 "Rules of Professional Conduct: Rule 1.7—Conflict of Interest: General Rule," The DC Bar, n.d., https://www.dcbar.org/bar-resources/legal-ethics/amended -rules/rule1-07.cfm.

57 "Richard Branson Quotes," BrainyQuote.com, 2019, https://www.brainyquote .com/quotes/richard_branson_770387.

58 Julie Reynolds, "Lawyer Lobbyists," The DC Bar, January 2006, https:// www.dcbar.org/bar-resources/publications/washington-lawyer/articles/janu ary-2006-lobbyists.cfm.

59 Mikhael Shor, "Iterated Game," in *Dictionary of Game Theory Terms*, n.d., http:// www.gametheory.net/dictionary/IteratedGame.html.

Index

About the Editor and Contributors

Editor

Peter Loge is an associate professor in the School of Media and Public Affairs at The George Washington University, the founding director of the Project on Ethics in Political Communication, a writer, and a strategic communication consultant. Loge has served in senior staff positions in the US House and Senate and in the Obama administration. His experience includes serving as a chief of staff in the House of Representatives during the Clinton impeachment proceedings. In early 2019 Loge launched the Project on Ethics in Political Communication to promote the study, teaching, and practice of ethics in political communication.

Contributors

Janet M. Atwill is a scholar of rhetoric in antiquity and a teacher of rhetoric and critical theory. She is the author of *Rhetoric Reclaimed: Aristotle and the Liberal Arts Tradition* (Cornell University Press), coeditor of *The Viability of the Rhetorical Tradition, Perspectives on Rhetorical Invention*, and coauthor of two textbooks on rhetoric and writing. She is presently completing *Rhetoric and the Display of Art*, which examines the role of material culture in the discourses of orators of the Roman Empire. Her publications include articles in *College English, Rhetoric Review, Pre/Text, Advances in the History of Rhetoric, Rhetorica*, and *PMLA*. Professor Atwill has been awarded fellowships by the Dumbarton Oaks-Harvard University Research Center in Byzantine Studies (Washington, DC), the National Endowment for the Humanities, and the Obermann Center for Advanced Studies and the Project on the Rhetoric of Inquiry at the University of Iowa. Her service to the profession includes being president of the American Society for the History of Rhetoric, chair of the executive committee of the MLA Division of History and Theory of Rhetoric and Composition, and a member of the board of directors of the Rhetoric Society of America. She has served on a number of editorial boards and is a referee for academic presses and journals.

Edward Brookover, Senior Partner at Avenue Strategies. Before joining Avenue Strategies, served as a senior adviser for President Donald Trump's campaign, managing the Trump delegate selection process. Earlier in the 2016 election cycle, Ed was the senior strategist, and later campaign manager, for the

"Dr. Ben Carson for President" campaign. Since 2001 Brookover has served as chair of political practice for the public affairs firm Greener and Hook, whose political clients included Governor Pat McCrory (R-NC), Speaker John Boehner (R-OH), and Congresswoman Michele Bachmann (R-MN). Prior to that Ed served as vice president of political affairs for Bonner & Associates. Brookover previously served as the national director of campaigns for all three Republican national committees and has served as a campaign adviser abroad. Brookover has been married to his wife, Barbara, for thirty-five years. They reside in Virginia. Ed is also the current president of the National Association of Republican Campaign Professionals.

Kenneth R. Chase is chair and associate professor of communication at Wheaton College (IL), where he teaches public speaking, rhetorical theory, and communication ethics. He has served as director of the Center for Applied Christian Ethics at Wheaton, president of the Religious Communication Association, and chair of the Communication Ethics Division of the National Communication Association. His essays on rhetorical theory and ethical rhetoric have appeared in various books and journals, including the *Quarterly Journal of Speech, Journal of Communication and Religion*, and *Bulletin for Biblical Research*. His forthcoming book, *Honoring Persuasion: Isocrates and the Ethics of Rhetoric*, argues for the contemporary value of Isocrates's political oratory.

Cheryl Contee is the award-winning CEO and cofounder of Do Big Things, a digital agency that creates new narrative and new tech for a new era focused on causes and campaigns. She is the author of the Amazon best seller *Mechanical Bull: How You Can Achieve Startup Success*. Cheryl was a cofounder of social marketing software Attentive.ly at Blackbaud, the first tech start-up with a black female founder onboard to be acquired by a NASDAQ-traded company. Her prior company, Fission, helped write the early source code for Crowdtangle, earning sweat equity in a successful social enterprise start-up acquired by Facebook in December 2016. Cheryl is proud to be a cofounder of the tech inclusion initiative #YesWeCode with Van Jones.

Alexander S. Duff, assistant professor of political science at the University of North Texas, writes widely on the history of political thought, and his publications on classical, modern, and contemporary political philosophy have appeared in both scholarly and popular publications. He has held fellowships from the Tocqueville Program for Inquiry into Religion and American Public Life at the University of Notre Dame and from the Program for the Study of the Western Heritage at Boston College, and he has taught at Skidmore College and College of the Holy Cross.

David A. Frank is a professor of rhetoric in the Robert D. Clark Honors College at the University of Oregon. The author and coauthor of six books and fifty journal articles, Professor Frank studies the use of rhetoric and argumentative reason in value conflicts. He writes and teaches courses on rhetorical history and theory, civil rights rhetoric, the Israeli-Palestinian relationship, and the prevention of genocide and mass atrocities. He has received research awards alone and in collaboration with colleagues from the Mellon Foundation, the Stanley Foundation, the National Endowment for the Humanities, the National Science Foundation, and the Korea Research Foundation. He and his colleague Robert Rowland were awarded the Kohrs-Campbell Prize in Rhetorical Criticism for their book *Shared Land/Conflicting Identity: Trajectories of Israeli and Palestinian Symbol Use*, and he was recognized with the "article of the year" award by the Communication and Religion Association. He served a five-year term as the academic dean of the Clark Honors College and has received six teaching awards during his career. Professor Frank is married to Marjorie Enseki, a retired kindergarten teacher. They have two sons, Michael (a student at Yale Law School) and Justin (a psychology major at the University of Oregon). Professor Frank has played racquetball for fifty years and can beat most players over the age of eighty.

Matthew L. Johnson is a principal and cofounder of the Klein/Johnson Group, where he creates comprehensive, winning strategies for a diverse set of clients on Capitol Hill and across Washington. For nearly a decade, Matt was a top policy aide and lawyer for Senator John Cornyn (R-TX) and the US Senate Committee on the Judiciary, where he was involved in the crafting of more than fifty bipartisan bills. Before founding the Klein/ Johnson Group, he worked as a senior principal at two of the leading public affairs firms in Washington. He is often quoted in national publications, among them the *Wall Street Journal*, the *Washington Post*, *USA Today*, and *Politico*. A native of Houston, Texas, Johnson is a graduate of the Medill School of Journalism at Northwestern University and The Law School at the University of Notre Dame.

Anson Kaye is a partner at GMMB, where he leads the firm's political team. In 2017, *Politico* named Anson to its "new guard power list," calling him a "go-to ad guru for top candidates." An award-winning media strategist, he has played a leading role in campaigns across the country, including helping to elect President Barack Obama. In 2018, Anson helped Democrats win races for governor, US Senate, US House of Representatives, and attorney general in states such as Wisconsin, Arizona, New Jersey, New York, Minnesota, and Maine, and he was a chief architect of some of the biggest campaign upsets in the country. Ads Anson has written, directed, and produced have been called "masterful," "powerful," "brilliant," and "the most memorable in years." His work extends outside the political realm as well; he has provided strategic counsel to national and multinational nonprofit and Fortune 500 clients such as the American Lung Association, Cisco Systems, and MGM Resorts International. Prior to joining GMMB, Anson served as a chief of staff on Capitol Hill and as communications director and senior policy adviser to the governor of Wisconsin, and he worked on campaigns across the country in roles including campaign manager, comms director, and field director.

Israel S. "Izzy" Klein is a principal and cofounder of the Klein/Johnson Group, where he represents over a dozen organizations in front of Congress and the administration. He held senior communications, policy, and political positions with Senators Chuck Schumer (D-NY) and Ed Markey (D-MA) for a dozen years. For the last decade, Klein has worked as a senior principal at a large public affairs firm and a managing partner at a boutique lobbying firm. Klein is a founding board member of the Jewish Democratic Council of America and the Government Affairs Industry Network. He is quoted extensively by leading news organizations, writes op-eds, and serves on kitchen cabinets or finance committees for various members of the House and Senate. A native of West Orange, New Jersey, Klein holds a bachelor's degree in government and theology from Georgetown University.

Andrew Lautz works on policy and government affairs in Washington, DC. Before that, he spent almost four years working on research and communications teams for nationwide political and corporate campaigns. He also started a news blog on politics and policy in his home state of Connecticut that quickly reached tens of thousands of people. Andrew graduated from George Washington University with a BA in political communication and an MPS in political management. He is a native of Litchfield, Connecticut.

Jennifer Lees-Marshment is associate professor in the Faculty of Arts at the University of Auckland. She is a research-led but practice-oriented, cross-disciplinary academic working in the areas of political marketing, political management, and political leadership. She is the author/editor of fifteen books, a world expert in political marketing, and A-rated in the New Zealand research assessment.

Rosalyn Lemieux is a senior director of software engineering at Blackbaud Inc., the world's leading cloud software company powering social good, overseeing the Developer Platform and Blackbaud Labs. Previously, Roz was the CEO of Attentive.ly (a Blackbaud company) and founding partner at Fission Strategy (now DoBigThings.today), a creative agency that has helped hundreds of organizations "ignite social action for good" using the latest social, web, and mobile technology. She served as executive director of the New Organizing Institute (NOI), a training institute for tech-enabled grassroots organizers. Roz gained experience in large-scale grassroots organizing as an early member of the MoveOn.org team after getting her start in online advocacy in 1999, serving as the Feminist Majority Foundation's web team director. She has won awards for her work, including a Stevie Award for Women in Business, a Campaigns & Elections Innovator award, and the Women's Information Network "Young Women of Achievement" award. She has served on the boards of Turing School, National Priorities Project, and the Chattahoochee Hills Charter School Foundation, and was an adviser to LP2X, an Atlanta-based incubator for female-founded businesses.

Elisa Massimino is the Robert F. Drinan, S.J., Chair in Human Rights at Georgetown University Law Center and a senior fellow with the Carr Center for Human Rights Policy at Harvard's Kennedy School of Government. Massimino served for a decade as president and CEO of Human Rights First, one of the nation's leading human rights advocacy organizations. She has testified before Congress dozens of times on a wide range of human rights issues. The influential Washington newspaper *The Hill* has routinely named Massimino one of the most effective public advocates in the country. Before joining the legal profession, Massimino taught philosophy at several colleges and universities in Michigan.

Mark L. McPhail (PhD, University of Massachusetts, 1987) is professor of communication at Indiana University Northwest in Gary, Indiana. Dr. McPhail is the author of *Zen in the Art of Rhetoric: An Inquiry into Coherence*, and *The Rhetoric of Racism Revisited: Reparations or Separation?* His scholarship has been published in the *Quarterly Journal of Speech*, *Critical Studies in Mass Communication*, the *Howard Journal of Communications*, *Rhetoric and Public Affairs*, and *Rhetoric Review*.

Vincent Raynauld is associate professor in the Department of Communication Studies at Emerson College and affiliate professor in the Département de lettres et communication sociale at Université du Québec à Trois-Rivières. He is also serving as a research associate in the Groupe de Recherche en Communication Politique (GRCP) (Canada). His areas of research interest and publication include political communication, social media, research methods, e-politics, and political marketing.

Benjamin Voth has been an associate professor and director of debate at Southern Methodist University since 2008. He earned his doctorate in communication studies at the University of Kansas in 1994. Since that time he has coached more than a dozen national and international champions of speech and debate. His communication consultation work has been done for the United States Holocaust Memorial Museum, the George W. Bush Presidential Center unit for Human Freedom, the Calvin Coolidge Presidential Foundation (debate fellow), the government of Rwanda, and Bain Capital. He has published three books on the role that rhetoric, argumentation, and debate play in ethically reforming American and global politics. His books have won two national book awards, from the American Forensics Association (2015) and the Freedom Foundation (2018). His research and scholarship on American presidential debates is quoted by various major publications, such as the *Washington Post, NPR* affiliates, *USA Today, Rush Limbaugh*, and the *Dallas Morning News*. He has published more than one hundred edited essays, book chapters, and research articles over twenty-five years in political communication and ethics.

Kip F. Wainscott is an experienced lawyer and policy professional working on issues concerning democracy in the digital age. He is currently a senior adviser at Stanford University's Cyber Policy Center, where he is the director of program for the Global Digital Policy Incubator. Since 2017 he has also served as senior adviser and Silicon Valley representative for the National Democratic Institute for International Affairs. During the Obama administration, Kip served in the White House as senior director of cabinet affairs and senior adviser to the Domestic Policy Council and also was appointed senior counsel in the Office of Legal Policy at the Department of Justice. Prior to entering government, he practiced law in a leading elections and government ethics practice, serving as counsel to several members of Congress, national party committees, and numerous political and advocacy organizations. He was counsel and national delegate director for President Obama's 2012 reelection campaign and has held leadership roles in civic, political, and professional organizations. Kip is a contributing author to the American Bar Association's guide to ethics and lobbying laws and has spoken on the subject of ethics in politics at numerous venues in the United States and abroad. He lives in San Francisco, California.

Rachel Wallace has nearly a decade of experience as a speechwriter and communications adviser. She has helped US senators, diplomats, presidential campaigns, and nonprofits refine their messages and use effective communications strategies to reach key audiences. A proud graduate of the George Washington University's School of Media and Public Affairs, Rachel lives in Washington with her husband and their dog.